Bear!

BLACK

GRIZZLY

BROWN

POLAR

Bear!

By Clyde Ormond

THE STACKPOLE COMPANY
HARRISBURG, PENNSYLVANIA

To my grand-daughter
LaToni Ormond

JOE FOSS

The past accomplishments, activities and interests of Joe Foss are all the more amazing because he is only now entering that period in life we choose to call middle age. Currently he is the Commissioner of the American Football League, member of the Board of Directors of the Air Force Academy, officer of a firm which manufactures high-altitude research balloons, President of the National Society for Crippled Children and Adults, and National Defense Council of the American Legion.

After working his way through the University of South Dakota, where he was deeply involved in athletics, he shot down, as a U. S. Marine, 26 enemy planes, the first pilot to down that many since Eddie Rickenbacker of World War I fame. He was the recipient of the Congressional Medal of Honor and the Distinguished Flying Cross. He was selected as one of the ten most outstanding young men in the country. In 1954 he was elected Governor of South Dakota, then re-elected in 1956 in a state which under statute has a two-term maximum.

The hobbies of Joe Foss are flying, hunting and fishing, model airplanes and archery. The great complications in his whirlwind life are that there are not enough hours in the day and days in the year.

Foreword

I am probably the most unqualified guy in the world to write a Foreword to a book dealing with bear hunting. As of this writing, I have never looked twice at the same bear. When I have encountered one hunting, I have put as much distance as possible between myself and the bear in short order.

However, in view of the fact I know Clyde Ormond real well as a friend and a highly capable outdoorsman, it is with a great deal of enthusiasm that I set about this pleasure of kicking off a book that has long been needed.

While my personal experiences in pursuit of bear have been zero, my personal experiences with famous hunters all over the country who consider bear the apex of all hunting experiences have been numerous. I am confident the following pages will be one more exciting adventure to all of them. In fact, to every reader, whether he be a bear hunter or not. Once he puts down this dynamic book, he'll probably set about packing his gear for a bear hunt immediately.

Only Clyde Ormond would—and could—come up with a bear book of this magnitude, depth, and understanding. I may not know too much about bagging the bear, but personal experience has taught me how Clyde Ormond bags his material.

The first time I met him was in Jackson Hole country in 1955. Our outfitter, Old Slim Sanders, said, "I want you to meet your hunting partner. He's going to do a little story as you hunt."

I took one look at the dapper-looking little guy with a beady mustache, and thought we'd probably end up carrying this one back from the hunt along with the game. No chap who looked so neat and "dudey" could possibly qualify for membership in our club where guts and stamina were passwords.

We spent a pleasurable evening together, and this interesting personality really sold himself and cemented a friendship. However, the duds still fooled me, and the respect of one hunter to another was not yet born.

The next morning we lunged out for the head of Yellowstone, thirty-some miles down the trail by horse. Clyde appeared with a small, cocky-looking hat, as trim as ever. I figured he'd never quite finish the trip, even though he had a heavy pencil.

And Old Joe, who was in mighty good shape at the time, had the surprise of his life! I've never been accustomed to many hunters passing me on the mountainside, but in this instance Clyde Ormond not only kept pace, he outdid me. I chalked one up right then and there for a man who didn't merely pen words about a sport, but who participated like a pro.

He peered out from behind those glasses and never missed a thing in the great outdoors. Lugging a camera, which he was quick to use at a crucial moment, he made notes constantly. The stories resulting from that trek—as well as many others—have impressed sportsmen all over the country. As one who has watched this alert author participate, inquire, observe, and report, I know definitely what Clyde Ormond has to say about bears is not merely from recollection, but an honest report of facts which were accurately and dramatically collected by a sagacious sportsman turned author.

It came as no surprise to me to learn that Clyde journeyed to Alaska three times within eighteen months to get material for this book and spent one month in the Arctic, living with the Eskimos, to collect data on polar bears.

This book on bears is a culmination of thirty years of observation, hunting, studying, and photographing; and it is herewith wrapped up in delightful narrative form for our enjoyment and education.

It is a privilege and honor to preface such an inspiring story in a field where many might fear to tread. Knowing Clyde Ormond, I know he pioneered with enthusiasm on this book and has given us the greatest.

I invite you to turn the pages with me and acquaint yourself with the inscrutable bear and with big-game hunting at its best.

JOE FOSS

P. S. I've taken all this so seriously, by the time the book is published and in your hands, I will have returned from a polar bear hunt in Kotzebue, Alaska. So—as we used to say in combat—"I'm a veteran!"

(EDITOR'S NOTE: *The Alaskan bear hunt was so spectacular and successful that it received nation-wide notoriety.*)

Contents

Part One

1

BLACK BEAR

CHAPTER 1

Blackie as an Adolescent

The American black bear, *Eurarctos americanus*, has been called a variety of names ranging from "cute," "awkward," "clown," and "predator," to "pest," "vicious," "killer," "enemy," and "big-game."

These appellations, usually given on impulse, are, like other generalities, partly right and somewhat wrong. There is, however, sufficient justification to each moniker to be misleading; and certainly enough to add flavor to the over-all character of this interesting wild animal.

The whole truth about Blackie lies somewhere as a composite, and includes them all. Old *Eurarctos americanus* is a beast of many traits. The more one observes him, the more he is convinced that Blackie's true character is inter-related with his current age, and to the nature of his past experience.

In this, the situation is analogous to that of man. As a baby, a black bear may be cute. During adolescence, both are very apt to be awkward and uncertain. And if, with advancing years, each becomes surly and truculent, this, too, may be for the comparable reasons of poor teeth, body miseries, old wounds, painful encounters with antagonists, and loss of physical potency and vigor.

There is perhaps no better way of uncovering the true nature of Blackie than to observe intelligently all instances

2

possible of his field behavior, and then interpret such observation in terms of what is already known of his overall character.

A most revealing instance of what the black bear is like during his "boyhood" and puberty occurred to my friend Don DeHart, the Alaska outfitter.

This happened in Idaho's Selway Forest in 1934, during mid-summer, and just two days, incidentally, before that memorable, ravaging forest fire which completely gutted so much of that still primitive land known as the Primitive Area.

DeHart at that time was working for the Forest Service, mainly spotting smoke. The entire country was unusually hot, with earth and lower foliage parched and dry as a bone. At the time, Don was walking a game-trail in the Cub Creek region, the trail swinging into a big S-curve. He was far from any other humans—in fact, at that time, few men had ever seen the immediate area he was in.

As he went into the big curve, he spotted a young black bear headed his way, and along the same trail farther down. It looked to be a long-yearling or two-year-old.

In this region, innumerable patches of chaparral carpeted the lower hills, lying adjacent to, and over the trail. It so happened that the spot DeHart was in was partially covered with such foliage—probably helping to account for what happened.

DeHart is better than six feet tall, and built something like the running gears of a "shite-poke." He wore slim, levi riding-jeans, and upon spotting the bear, stopped short, spraddle-legged and hands on his hips. At the time he wore a Colt .22 Woodsman, but had no intention of using it. He just stood immobile, waiting to see what the young bear would do. Being an outdoorsman all his life, he had grown increasingly interested in the antics of game, and its overall unpredictability.

The young bear, unaware of any sign of danger, kept moseying along the trail. The intense day's heat had made

it logy and it swung along, looking neither to left nor right,
and with its nose nearly to the ground.

As usual with its species, this animal had been working
the high huckleberry patches over a broad and somewhat
circuitous route. The blue fruit at this season was just well

Cubs are playful and should be protected by law from any hunting.

under way; and while any of the many-acre patches provided a considerable quantity, no bear, black or grizzly,
seems ever full of fruit. The novice is perpetually amazed,
upon finding evidence, at how much of this mild diet a bear
can eat, and at the minimum of time it stays in him.

True to his species in another way, this bear also chose
to mosey along old game-trails. While his tough foot pads
could negotiate any terrain from rocks to brambles, Blackie
nevertheless always chose any available easier footing provided by the engineering of game, man, or horses.

Yard after yard, the bear came swaying along the dusty
trail, lessening the distance between them. Don remained
stock-still, largely to see just close the animal would, under
the optimum circumstances for not being discovered, come
before it learned of his presence.

By now he could see that the beast was lanky with youth,
shaggy of summer coat, slavering at the mouth from the un-

usual heat, and interested in nothing more pugnacious than
to find an additional berry-patch. It likely had never before
contacted a human being.

"By then," DeHart told me, "I could even see the expres-
sion on his face. He looked just like a confused sophomore
at some senior dance. Just like he didn't know what it was
all about, 'and besides, he was about half asleep with the
heat."

Amused, Don tried to figure out what the animal must be
thinking, if anything; how much longer it would take until
it discovered him; and, most important, what it would do
then.

DeHart had lived with wild game of many species all his
life. As he waited, he mused upon the beast's past and upon
what influence the months had had upon what the
youngster was doing now.

The bear had, of course, been born during a January
hibernation period. At birth, it would have been no larger
than a red tree squirrel, blind, and virtually hairless. During this birth, and in a way neither the layman nor obste-
trician could satisfactorily explain, the female bear had
slept through the whole natural process without knowing
about it.

While the mother had slept, the cub had nursed, grew
hair, reached maybe five pounds in weight, then emerged
from hibernation with her, likely in May. Together they'd
wandered far and wide. The sow had eaten grasses and
natural vegetable purgatives to start the "plug" from her
digestive system and to get her gastronomical functions
going again. The cub, during this, was starting its education. He'd learned to follow, to observe, and to mind
Mamma. When he didn't he got those short ears cuffed.

DeHart had watched numerous cubs at this stage—the
period of fun when they'd box, roll, and wrestle with their
twin; romp, and cavort like gamboling lambs. This was, of
course, the care-free period in a cub's life before its
character began to change with increased age, the altering

needs of its survival, experience with adversaries, and the later craze of reproduction.

This young Selway bear had lost most all the characteristics and appearance of this earlier, naive babyhood. It had subsequently, however, stayed constantly with the female, had depended entirely upon her, and lived without any inkling of the blunt and heartless awakening it was soon to get.

When, during hibernation, the next generation of cubs was born, the young black found a shocking and inexplicable change come over the mother. Upon emergence, she had turned savagely and without reason upon him. Repeatedly, and with vicious growls and bites, she'd chase him completely from her sight and presence. It was completely baffling to find that the one who'd nursed, guarded, and protected him, now turned on him like some enemy and would have nothing to do with him.

Old woodsmen who have witnessed the performance, have told me that often the sows will "—knock the livin' hell out of the youngsters. And the dumb-founded things will wander off a-bawlin' and lookin' back just like a hound pup that's lost his Ma."

Black bears are not alone in this driving off of the older generation of offspring, with all attention suddenly going over to the newest. Rocky Mountain goats do the same thing. Rose Peterson, at British Columbia's Muncho Lake, studied a family of goats all summer long with a spotting-scope from her cabin and witnessed the same phenomenon.

"The older kids, when the old nanny started in to butting them out of the family, would run off a little ways, then turn and look back in complete bewilderment. They'd bleat and try to come back and make up. But Mamma would have nothing to do with them. Finally, not being able to comprehend, they wandered off by themselves and I never saw the yearlings again. A week later, two tiny puffs of white showed up with the nanny goat; the two newest babies."

The young black bear which DeHart studied—now with a bit of apprehension since it was within mere feet—evidenced all the symptoms of a similar adolescent bewilderment. The mother bear, which had protected and fed him, and had tendered such obvious affection, abruptly had turned on him; knocked the stuffing out of him; kicked him out on his own. He was lonesome. He was confused. His belly was empty. All he knew was that he must wander continuously. And eat.

Cubs during the "fun" stage exhibit many curious and awkward characteristics of people during adolescence.

Here's how DeHart finished:

"By now, he was within ten feet of me, head down, paying no attention to anything except the dusty trail. His nose was nearly to the ground, but he didn't appear to be sniffing for anything. He still hadn't spotted or smelled me. I guess in the rocks and dirt my levis didn't show up much. Then, too, the sun was in his face.

"Up till then, I hadn't worried any. He hadn't looked big enough to do me any harm. But from ten feet on *in*, I got to worrying a little. At that distance he seemed to grow. I thought of jerking out the pistol and shooting over his head—scare the daylights out of him, maybe. But for some stubborn DeHart reason, I decided I'd see just how close he *would* come."

Here Don laughed uproariously at himself. "You know, if I'd waited, I think that scrawny feller would have walked right between my legs. Wouldn't it have been something if he'd discovered me *then?* Can't you just see me, riding a bear down a trail, hinder backwards, and can't git off?"

"What did you do?"

"Well, when he wasn't over thirty inches ahead of me, I couldn't take it any longer. I looked right down on him, kinda scared I guess by now, and yelled, 'Where the hell you think *you're* goin'?"

It's difficult to conceive of a situation wherein a wild bruin could be more abruptly or completely surprised. And, like man or other animals, a bruin is very apt to act, in such a moment, with pure instinct—an instinct revealing its true character.

Now, had this bear been but a "cute" harmless little cub (as many people regard all bears), it's likely that it would have jumped in surprise, stopped to ascertain the nature of the sound, and gawked at DeHart from a distance of feet.

Had it been, at the other extremity, a vicious killer, a foe, a human danger (as many other people regard all bears), it is probable that the beast would have swung first and investigated later.

But here again, in this most unusual encounter, Blackie tended to indicate an analogy to man. The young bear, still innocent of the basic dangers, and of man, reacted with typical confusion, and the instinct of the adolescent.

It took DeHart several minutes before he could complete the story. He laughed till he bawled, with tears literally streaming his cheeks at the memory.

Then— "You know that little guy must have been completely scared out of his wits. He didn't gather himself or nothin'. I don't think most of his feet were on the ground at the time. But just like an unsuspecting tom-cat you'd whack in the ribs with a spud, he switched ends completely, mid-air. One split second he was headed my way; then, in a blur you couldn't see, he was headed the other. He took off back down the trail, at least four jumps before his paws hit the ground, or he could get any traction. He just stood there, in the air, clawing for any footing, like a cat trying to take off on slick linoleum. When his feet finally did reach ground, he let out a *'Ooo-fff'* you could hear a half-mile.

"Later, I followed to see what he'd done. He'd stuck with the trail—the best footing for *fast*—for a good quarter-mile. His tracks were a full ten feet apart, and the last I ever saw of him he was picking them up and laying them down . . . all the way down the canyon.

"But this was the funniest part. While that bear was still in mid-air, swapping ends like he'd been jerked wrong-side-out, the scare I'd put into him was too much. He uncorked at thirty inches, and let go with a great stream of used huckleberries. Hell, I was plastered on one leg from my crotch clean to my ankles!"

CHAPTER 2

The Black Bear as an Adversary

How capable and determined is the black bear as an opponent of man and of other beasts?

As the black bear reaches adulthood, his overall surliness, his urge to live a hermit's existence, and his shortness of temper all grow. Adult males will have nothing to do with their offspring. Their desire to be with the females is limited to the urges of reproduction, after which they stay as far as possible from the company of the sows. And even the company of other males seems distasteful.

It is rare, except in instances of being at a kill, to find adult bears together, except in mating season. In a broad way, the adult black bear is, to a human's way of thinking, soured on life; out to look after no one's interests but his own; and ready to exercise his grumpiness and short temper on anything that gets in his way. Gregariousness is a foreign language to him.

Because of this preference to remain alone, his considerable size when fully grown, and his adequate fighting equipment, the black bear has long been considered as a worthy opponent, once into a fight. The fact of his unpredictable nature, plus the few authenticated instances where a black bear has attacked and killed a human without provocation, has added to this assumption. And, throughout the decades since the country's settlement, with man's dwindling contact and association with live bruins, legend, history, and half-truths have all added to the overall conviction that the black bear is a savage enemy of man.

Actually, the adult black bear is a coward. The smallest dog, in terrain where bruin has not been forced to a standstill, is apt to put him up a tree—this after an ignominious chase, grossly one-sided as to poundage.

In most any contact with man, the black bear may be depended upon to run. Either the sight, sound, or smell of a human is usually sufficient to make him depart the scene. His characteristic preference is to run, not put up a fight.

I have photographed big black bear in heavy berry-patch cover, where bruin would unknowingly meander up to within a matter of mere feet of where I stood, back to a pine, and ready to trip the shutter for an extreme close-up. One swipe at me with a paw would, before there was any time to duck or retreat, have put me out of commission. But at the first faint detection of movement, trace of scent, or

The author's first black bear and where he lit. An old one as shown by the yellow teeth and large white spot.

sound, bruin would invariably whirl and be off with nothing but undulating bushes showing for a hundred yards.

In British Columbia, old Pete Peterson, who has lived in the Muncho Lake area all his life among bears, and helped lay the pilot route for the Alaska Highway between Fort Nelson and Fort St. John, told me that repeatedly any sight of one of his sled dogs would cause any black bear to beat a retreat into the bush. Almost invariably, such a chase ended by bruin high-tailing it into cover so thick and impenetrable the dogs couldn't follow; and they'd come back later. The few times the dogs came *out* of the bush, as though the very devil was on their tails-between-legs, it meant but one thing. They'd run into a grizzly in there, not a black.

Despite the generality, there are times when a black bear will stand and fight even to the death. This is broadly true of any of nature's wilderness children.

The maternal instinct, despite the fact that sow bears will drive off their own yearlings forcibly, is pronounced in bears. Coming between a sow and cubs will often induce a fight. If the cub bawls with fright, a fight may be expected.

Old wounds, hunger, poor teeth, and similar aggravating factors all add to the adult black's orneriness; and under optimum conditions for a stand, rather than a retreat, such an enraged bear will fight.

Sudden surprise, especially at a kill or where the bear's food cache is endangered, will occasionally make a black bear stand his ground. I killed one such boar, old and with yellow teeth, which had found my partner's elk-kill. At a matter of mere yards, this bear reared up, curled his wicked snout back over his teeth, stood his ground and "whooshed" at me. The Forest ranger, in hearing of it, said, "He was trying to bluff you from what he considered *his* meat."

Such instances of an adult black's being willing to fight when he has a chance to run are rare. Percentage-wise, I'd say that in ninety cases in a hundred a black bear may be depended upon to "go the other way," in any normal contact with man.

It is the *other* instances which intrigue the outdoorsman, hunter, and even those who unexpectedly meet bruin in the woods. These rare, authentic cases where the bear "retreats forward" not only make this animal most interesting, but also lead the observing person to wonder just how correct his generalities are.

The most astounding instance of a black bear's choosing to fight by choice, and taking on, not a reasonable-size opponent, but his traditional enemy the grizzly in a fair fight to the death, occurred near Ishawooa Creek, in the Shoshone River country of western Wyoming. Actually, there were two black bears involved in this savage affray—the fact of their being together yet another evidence of the ultimate instability of any generalization.

The region at the headwaters of Ishawooa Creek is rugged, mountainous, high, and remote. The peaks, snow-covered in patches for most of the year, poke upward to 12,000 feet. Sheer bluffs both above and below timber line make it virtually inaccessible. It is indicative that even when Wild Bill Cody and Teddy Roosevelt hunted it, they had to ascend from a certain Camp Bob, up sheer cliffs via rope ladders anchored into the cliffs. They'd ascend, hunt the above-timber-line plateaus above, then climb back down, while Indian flunkeys lugged the meat of rams and elk, and the skins of grizzlies and blacks, down by hand, over these same rope ladders.

The region is one of the most primitive areas currently left in the whole United States, entirely unspoiled and almost inaccessible to the average man. I hunted the area in 1959, immediately recognizing it as grizzly country *per se*. Its grizzly potential is without doubt improved by the close proximity of Yellowstone Park, whose boundaries are shortly to the west.

In this rough, impenetrable region, prior to 1948, several outdoorsmen suddenly came upon the spoor of an enormous grizzly, at the lower periphery of the range. This occurred in early spring, with the melting snows, and when any grizzly's circuitous route after food is extended. Only three men ever saw the bear itself. But Les Bowman, a Cody, Wyoming outfitter, was one who saw his tracks.

"I measured his hind track—several of 'em," Bowman told me. "It ran between 13 and 14 inches with a steel tape. I'm convinced that that grizzly would weigh 1,000 pounds."

Over my own hunting years, I have repeatedly measured the spoor of grizzlies. My second grizzly, killed in British Columbia, had a hind track measuring exactly 11¼ inches, including claws. It weighed an estimated 400-500 pounds. I cannot doubt Bowman, but must say that any grizzly with a track of 13 inches is an exceptionally large one, as indeed events proved this one to be.

This grizzly came to be known as the "Scoria Creek grizzly" since most of the spoor was found where that creek trickles into the Ishawooa.

Except for amazement over the beast's size, not too much attention was paid to the Scoria Creek grizzly at first. But soon, stockmen in the lower valleys began having their cattle killed. The huge grizzly tracks accompanying each kill were observed, and studied with amazement. The quick conclusion was that no other grizzly could be responsible.

Stock depredations continued intermittently, but reached an intolerable climax. One rancher woke one morning to find seven of his pure-bred steers laid neatly out in a row, all their necks broken with a single swipe of a grizzly. That it was none other than Old Scoria there could be no doubt. As a final insult, nothing but the tongues of each steer had been neatly chewed out and eaten. No other portions of the carcasses were touched.

The ranchers immediately banded together, hired a professional bear hunter, and gave him free rein to do anything he pleased, but to get the Scoria Creek grizzly, regardless of time or cost.

It is indicative of this exceptional bear that the professional hunter failed completely, as did any subsequent effort to find, bait, trap, chase, or shoot the beast.

However, Les Bowman, the outfitter, became increasingly enraged and accepted the challenge. Les is, incidentally, one of the country's few outfitters with an annual success-ratio on bears, for his hunters, which is really exceptional. Les decided to go after the Scoria Creek grizzly, since it inhabited his own remote hunting country, and whose taking would help his professional reputation.

The method of taking grizzlies in that section is to bait them. This consists of killing a worthless or crippled horse, in an area normally frequented by bears, then wait till they find the carcass. As we'll touch upon later, this form of hunting, in that extended region and under the natural conditions which confront any hunter, is not at all unsporting. The chances are still ninety per cent in the bear's favor.

In 1948, Bowman put out his first bait. Once such a carcass is placed, the hunter never goes near it again. It is, rather, observed from a distance up to a mile, with high-power binoculars, and always with a skilled regard for canyon air currents, breezes, etc.

Even when the glasses show that a bear has begun to "work" the carcass, it is not approached. Experience has shown that the first time a grizzly finds a bait, he's nervous as a bride. The first trip old *Ursus horribilus* will eat but little, then warily leave. Similarly, his second trip he eats far less than he scouts the country, tests the breeze, and makes sure he's there alone.

The third trip, according to Bowman, "If he hasn't been scared by any evidences of the presence of humans, he'll come barreling in, swinging his great head from side to side, without hesitation, and like a true lord of the whole domain."

Grizzlies approach such a bait only at dusk, and perhaps are still near-by at daylight, adding to the difficulties of getting any kind of decent shot at long range, necessitated by the extreme wariness of the quarry.

The first bait indicated the pattern of Old Scoria for the

next several years. For a week, while it ripened, it wasn't touched. Then one night the rear end was clawed out of it. The next night at dusk, the big bear didn't show up. But in the next two nights, always after a patient watch till sheer darkness showed nothing, the entire carcass was gorged to nothing but bits of hide and bones—without Old Scoria ever showing himself. He simply came later, during the night.

This procedure went on with aggravating regularity for the next six years. With all the skill, experience, and know-how he could command, Bowman each spring set out a bait for the canny bruin. Each year the bait was eaten during the night, with never a sight of the big grizzly. Such "worthless-horse" baits cost an average of $100 each, and by 1954 Bowman had a considerable investment in Old Scoria, to say nothing of a desire to get him, which amounted to an obsession.

By 1954, Bowman's son-in-law had become extremely interested, and was helping in the plan to get the bear. This fellow, Jack Allen, lived in Oklahoma. Each spring he'd come out to the Bowman ranch on the Shoshone's South Fork, help Les set out a bait, and wait a week. But nothing fortunate happened. In his cunning way, Old Scoria would come in to the bait in some unanticipated manner, gobble it up with unbelievable rapidity, and leave the scene for another entire year. No matter where the bait was placed, no matter what added precautions were used, the net result was the same.

Bowman, by now, had resolved to get the bear if it was his last earthly act. So, regularly as the first thaws of spring came, he set out another $100 bait, with Jack assisting.

This year, tiring of the unproductive routine, Jack waited but a few days for Old Scoria to come in to the bait, then flew back home to Oklahoma, swearing that the old so-and-so had done it again.

Three days later, Les phoned him. "Old Scoria's working the bait. Get out here fast!"

Dropping all else, Jack, who was now almost as obsessed as Bowman, flew right back to Cody. The next evening at dusk, Jack, with a guide required by the State, was back up near the mouth of Yellow Creek. Tying the horses far back down the trail, out of sight and sound should they nicker, the two men cautiously worked up through the timber. Their objective was a natural "blind" consisting of nothing except a log jam of pines and cottonwood, piled into a "hog-pen" of timber by the spring runoff of Yellow Creek. From this log jam, it was but a short 200 yards to the bait—an easy shot for a good rifleman, with nothing unnatural or suspicious in the set-up.

On the way up, however, and knowing the uncanny nature of the great bear which had made fools of them, Jack got a hunch. By working up-creek a bit, they could reach a point where the bait would be visible at a distance of around 350 yards. Jack suggested they take a look, first, from this vantage point.

This they did. And once settled with the glasses in the new concealment, Allen and the guide made out two bears working the dead horse. Both were big blacks, oddly, not fighting over the stinking meat but simply gorging it.

"I sat there sweating blood," Jack told me. "I didn't want a mere black—I'd killed all the blacks I wanted. But Bowman had assured me that a grizzly had been working the kill—*the* grizzly we'd waited so long to get. And here were these two blacks, licking up that carcass pound by pound. Two nights and they'd clean it to where Old Scoria wouldn't touch it. I'd made two trips from Oklahoma, Les had wasted seven horses and as many years, and apparently there wasn't a damn thing we could do about it except watch."

So, with only the disappointment such a situation could induce, Jack and his guide watched another bait, and another fruitless year disappear, pound by pound. They watched till full dusk, almost too dark then to shoot even had they wanted.

But suddenly, both black bears jerked to full attention. In the high-power binoculars, Jack could see them actually stiffen their muscles. Their short ears pointed up into the timber, up-creek from the bait, and for a moment both bears stood immobile.

"I knew as sure as we lay there what had happened. The blacks had detected a grizzly coming in to the kill. I knew, without knowing why, that it must be Old Scoria."

Mesmerized by what he expected to be the sudden sight of the great bear which had eluded everyone for so many years, Jack admitted that he could do nothing but watch in heart-stopping fascination.

Suddenly from the fringe of the timber lumbered the grizzled form of a great bruin. Even in the fading light, his hulk was enormous to the point of being incredible. In characteristically shambling gait the big bear headed straight for the kill, head swaying, but unalarmed.

The grizzly had made only a few steps into the semi-clearing when he detected the presence of the blacks at "his" kill. At this he stiffened like a hot knife had been rammed through him. Immediately the silvertip reared to his full height, letting out a bawling roar that, according to Jack, shook the very earth.

With the blood-curdling roar but half done, the great beast dropped to all fours and bore down, like some animated bull-dozer, onto the two black intruders.

Here was a situation witnessed many times by mountain men. A case of a black bear's finding a grizzly kill, cache, or offal from a hunter's game-kill; and the silvertip's discovery of the lesser bear, and the awesome rage and fury with which the greater bruin drives the intruders off. Such a battle is to the death, if the grizzly can catch the smaller bear.

Duane Smith, a young settler and guide living at Mankomen Lake in southern Alaska, once told me of such an instance which he witnessed, and showed me where it took place, up the Slana River where it joins with the Dry Tok.

On either side of the river bars there, there are high mountains covered with blueberry bushes, Arctic birch, and alders. Duane pointed to the mountain to the east, fringing Gillette Pass.

"I was coming along here, just like we are now," Duane said. "In fact I was headed up towards the Pass, mainly to make a route across these bars where we might get some machinery up to some mining claims there, with a weasel, or a 4x4 army truck.

"All of a sudden, this big black bear came busting down the side of the mountain there, like all hell was after him. He hit the river bed here, and ran straight across—he wasn't two rods in front of me—paying no attention to me whatever. He was half-exhausted, looked like. His mouth was open and slobbering, and he grunted hard every time he hit the ground.

"I should have guessed what was wrong with him. But before I could think, or get to a rifle, here came this big silvertip out of the bush behind him. He acted, too, like I wasn't even there, but tore out across the gravel after the black—passed right in front of me! I can still see them piggy little eyes, and ears laid back.

"They must have been at it a full mile before they hit the river bars. And you see that mountain west there? It must be a mile to the top. Last I saw them, the grizzly was still after the black, and half-way up it. The blueberry bushes hid them out of sight by then. But my guess is that the grizzly finally caught up and killed the black."

This is the common reaction of grizzlies to blacks, though not always so pronounced or prolonged—especially when a cache kill is involved. The black bruin is mortally scared, and the silvertip chases him off.

Even in a sanctuary with bears which are conditioned to the presence of man, this generality is true. Times without number, visitors in Yellowstone Park have watched several black bears feeding at dusk at the ranger-guarded feeding grounds; seen them suddenly stiffen and become alert; watched them scatter; then saw the greater *ursus* come warily from the timber, to take over. His authority is unquestioned.

With the big Scoria grizzly, conditions were comparable. The blacks had fed on the dead horse to the point of near-satiety. They had detected the presence of the grizzly at sufficient distance to allow a grudging, semi-dignified retreat. The better-equipped, more "horrible" opponent had warned them both of his presence and intent. And now, in great bounds, the grizzly was backing his threat with savage action.

But as Jack and his guide watched, an incredulous thing took place. At the grizzly's first bounds, both blacks took off. But with ears laid flat, and snouts curled, they ran *for* the opponent, not from him!

Thereafter ensued a battle of such sound and fury as left Jack helpless to describe. The beasts met at the fringe of timber, tore into each other with tooth and claw, and all to roaring, enraged snarls, and bellows that shook the Ishawooa canyon air. It was savage, fast, and obviously to the death.

For a moment the two men hoped to witness a battle unmatched in nature, both in sheer brutality and a reversal of the accepted roles of the combatants. But even as the three bears met, tumbled, and sent bits of the earth flying, the course of the battle led back into the timber. Within the moment, all Jack and the guide could see was the movement of the timber above the fight.

The trees here are largely jack pines, with smaller, bushier junipers called "cedar-bush," and the smaller alders, nine-bark, and similar undergrowth. It is possible that the blacks, in their role of aggressor, had, upon contact, maneuvered the battle in that direction, instinctively knowing that if worst came, they could climb trees while the grizzly could not.

The day's light was now failing fast. Disappointed that they'd been cheated of the sight of a combat denied to most men, Jack and the guide nevertheless kept their eyes glued to their binoculars. And, as Jack told me recently, "it wasn't a bit hard to trace the fight by the tops of the jack pines above them." Periodically, a pine tree, with diameter of from four to six inches, would bend violently at the top, as some or all the bruins hit it. The terrifying sounds continued, and all tree movement appeared to be confined to an area of a half-acre, just off the bait clearing, and collaring the bluffs above.

How long the .fight continued, Jack hesitates to state. Engrossed as he was, all time seemed to stand still and await the outcome. It lasted possibly thirty minutes.

Then, suddenly, it was over. All sounds of fury ceased. Hastily glassing all surrounding country, to pick up any sight of a retreating foe, Jack saw another incredulous thing. Far up the bottom face of the blue cliffs, in an area closely approximating the Roosevelt-Cody rope-ladder bluffs, they saw the great, tired Scoria grizzly laboriously climbing.

These cliffs are hundreds of feet high, quite on the order of the time-cut banks of the Grand Canyon of the Colorado, and drop sheer off from the rolling, alpine plateau above. Here and there in the south face are the usual few crevices, tiny shelving ledges, and cracks where frost-loosened rock weathers and breaks, to fall to the valley floor as talus.

No man, so far as natives know, has ever been able to climb the face of these cliffs without rope ladders. In sheer unbelief the two men watched Old Scoria try to pull and pick his way up.

This, itself, was a spectacle of sheer magnificence. The great bear, obviously exhausted and weakened by the fight, would reach with a great claw, pull to lift his half-ton of weight vertically, slip and tumble back, then try again. In some spots, several attempts were necessary to gain a rod. Then, having gained but a few feet, he'd rest, slowly sway his great head while gazing back downward into the valley, then try again.

In such an interminable fashion, the big bruin made his

way half-way up the cliffs. Each pause, after he'd gained a tiny shelf, became longer. Finally, the beast made one more such place of temporary footing, lumbered over a puny ledge and seemed to lie down behind the small obstruction to rest.

Jack and the guide watched till they could see no longer. The great grizzly never did rise from this last place of rest. The two blacks never showed up again in the area.

Afterward, Jack went back to the area of the fight. He told me in sincerity, "That area for a whole half-acre had been torn literally clean of all brush, trees, and junipers. Every single jack pine was knocked over, for a space as big as Bowman's yard here. Every bush was torn out, and the ground was like it had been plowed and harrowed to a pulp. Hair, blood, and hunks of skin were scattered all over the place. You never saw such a mess. Never."

For days the men at the LB Ranch tried to figure some way to reach that final spot on the cliff's face, where the great grizzly had been last seen. But scaling the cliffs was physically impossible.

Neither the Scoria grizzly nor his spoor was ever seen again. All who knew anything about the matter were forced to conclude that the grizzly had never risen from that last spot, and that his bones still remain there.

They were forced also to the conclusion that the two blacks had completely licked the great silvertip in fair, if out-numbered, fight. The lesser blacks had, by force of numbers, for once reversed the conception that blacks *always* run from grizzlies. They had proven that, far from being harmless clowns of the woods, they were opponents of a high fighting order, capable of terrible physical damage. They had inadvertently, and luckily for themselves, caught one of Wyoming's greatest grizzlies during his old age, and most likely after his aging teeth had worn down to their least effectiveness.

Despite conjecture and supposition, one fact remained: Two blacks had defeated a mighty grizzly.

CHAPTER 3

Range and Distribution of Black Bear

The black bear enjoys a wider distribution in North America than most any other big-game species, although his ratio of numbers-to-acres is often spread mighty thin. The black's habitat includes a width of country from the Atlantic to the Pacific, and from central Mexico to virtually the Bering Strait, in a north-south direction.

This is a wide divergence of latitudes, climates, and food for any species to range, occupy, and adapt to differences of temperature and seasons.

Approximately three-fourths of Alaska has a black bear distribution. The two regions where no blacks are found are the frigid extreme northern portion bounding the Arctic Ocean, and a comparable western "end," including the island chain.

Similarly, about ninety per cent of Canada has a black bear population. This range is roughly coincident with the Canadian caribou range, and includes virtually all of the Dominion with the exception of the treeless tundra regions generally bounding the northern seacoast, and on either side of Hudson Bay.

The largest bear populations in the United States are found in Alaska; in another broad belt of country coincident with the Rocky Mountains, following this mountain system all the way southward into central Mexico; in a comparable wide belt of country on the Pacific Slope including the states of Washington, Oregon, California, and a western strip of Nevada; and in spot areas of the East and South. The greater bear regions in these two sections include the

Range of black bear in North America.

states of Maine, Michigan, Minnesota, New York, Pennsylvania, Virginia, West Virginia, Tennessee, and the Carolinas; and the Southern states of Mississippi, Louisiana, Arkansas, Alabama, and Florida.

The latest available census by the Fish & Wildlife Service lists 30 states as having black bear, outside natural sanctuaries.

Alaska, of course, leads. Of the remaining states within the same borders, Washington is next with an estimated 28,000 black bear. Other states with large numbers of this species are California, Colorado, Idaho, Maine, Michigan, Minnesota, Montana, New Mexico, North Carolina, Oregon, and Wyoming.

States having no known black bear outside of sanctuaries, in 1946, were Connecticut, Delaware, Illinois, Indiana, Iowa, Kansas, Kentucky, Massachusetts, Missouri, Nebraska, New Jersey, North Dakota, South Dakota, and Rhode Island.

In the years between 1946 and 1958, three states, Montana, Michigan, and New Jersey (with an estimated 18 black bear), have estimated increases in bear populations. Twenty other states list the bear population as the same as in 1946. And three states estimate fewer bears over this last decade.

In 1946, the total black bear population in the United States, plus Alaska, was 230,000. From the above estimates, it may therefore be assumed that Blackie is about holding his own as to numbers. This, despite the progressive increase in numbers of licensed hunters, and the mushrooming interest in the sport.

These figures, it must be remembered, are estimates. Too, it is far harder to estimate a bear population than a population of such a species as deer. For one thing, where deer will band together and often yard up on winter ranges, where they cannot move so freely because of snow, and where they may be easier seen and counted, the black bear is, at the time, concealed in hibernation.

More, the food of other species is usually more concentrated as to region and/or bulk than that of Blackie. A bruin is a great wanderer, primarily because his food supply is meager in comparison to the area over which it is spread. Blackie may be stripping off berries in one region today, and be fifteen miles away tomorrow, pulling rotten stumps apart in search of ants and grubs.

Because of his traveling widely in summer, and hibernating in winter, the black bear is hard to "pin down" for counting.

Another difficulty in getting any true census is the type
of cover the black bear inhabits. Unlike the greater grizzly,
which has been forced to the high, craggy, and remote
regions beyond the sounds and smells of humans and lesser
animals, the black bear is largely a woodland animal. He
loves thick timber, stays fairly close within it, and is consequently hard to see by man.

This is especially true in Canada and Alaska. The
Canadian "bush" and bushes-muskeg of Alaska are innately
hard to traverse by man. Foliage is thick, footing mushy.
A great percentage of the North country has not been seen
by man, except from the air. In the thick lush alders, wil-
low, Arctic birch, blueberry bushes, and similar foliage,
the black bear is hard to see, let alone count or estimate
as to numbers.

Spoor, too, is hard to estimate in terms of probable bears,
due to bruin's wandering habits—the tracks here today are
nearly as fresh as the tracks seen a dozen miles away by
tomorrow. And from the same bear.

The basic methods of estimating bears are (a) counting kills through checking stations, (b) interviews with

Our party on a spring trip into the Buffalo River country of Wyoming
to hunt and study the post-emergence habits of bears after hibernation.
Gear was hauled by toboggans. Teton Mountains in background.

hunters and ranchers, (c) general field observations, (d) information received from license stubs or cards returned by hunters, (e) ranchers' coupons, and (f) from post-season questionnaires returned by big-game hunters.

While such information does not provide an accurate game count, it does indicate general trends. It helps to show if any species is in the low or high of its cycle, or if it is generally increasing or decreasing.

No other game animal on the American scene has fired the imagination of man more than the bear—black or grizzly. The bear was found by the Pilgrims when they landed. As they colonized and built, bears raided their huts, stole their poultry, killed livestock. Continuous with the entire Westward movement, bruin lived on the tenuous, fluid line between settlement and wilderness, always content to steal and plunder the man-provided food which was easier to locate and take than food from his own foraging. By night bruin killed hogs, chickens, colts, and calves. By day he was hard to track down or find.

Encounters between bears and settlers were commonplace. Weapons those early days were skimpy or inadequate. People were clawed up, occasionally came out second best. Any loss represented economic hardship. Depredations by bears gradually gave bruin the reputation of killer and foe. That his potential fighting equipment was often better than man with his bare hands, knife, ax, or awkward firearms, was played up in importance in legend, in tradition, in re-told story.

Both literature and art of America have habitually played up bruin's role as pest, thief, predator, and awesome opponent of man. The constant incidence of bears, all during the Westward movement and recent settlement of the Far West, added fuel to legend, fact, half-truth, and tradition. Bears were bad, dangerous, a threat to settlement. This basic concept has constantly grown.

In my own youth I well remember how mischievous youngsters could handily be kept in line with the single

A pause, for rest, en route.

statement, "If you don't quit being mean, the bears'll get you." We *believed* it.

This form of romance continued after the majority of wild bears had been pushed by civilization to the remote regions. It continues today, exaggerated by re-telling and time until today's generation, having small contact with bruin, still retains a lop-sided conception. He's a dangerous adversary with the outcome of any encounter still romantically in doubt. That has been the past, and is the present status to many.

Because of this, there is likely no red-blooded hunter who does not, at some time, hope to kill a bear. It is the ultimate challenge to hunting. Even those sportsmen who must assume that their opportunity to hunt, contact, and shoot it out with a bear will never come, still love to play Injun and take their bear hunting vicariously through "bear" literature and art. And "bear stories."

There are roughly 20,000,000 licensed hunters in the United States today. Divide this number into a bear population of 230,000, and you come up with a fraction. It becomes obvious that every big-game hunter is not going to get that bearskin rug each autumn when he takes to the woods.

There are, however, sufficient bears so that any hunter who will spend the effort, time, and money will eventually get his bruin, if he'll stick with it. And on the basis of what any successful bear hunter will assure him, it will be worth it.

From the standpoint of pure mathematical odds, the best place to hunt a black bear is in Canada. This, simply because the Dominion has more black bears than any place else. Next comes Alaska, then the Pacific Coast area, next the Rocky Mountain states, then spot areas like Maine and other heavily bear-populated states.

Perhaps the first thing any hunter for bear should do is to learn the basic characteristics of his quarry. From this, in a bear area, the most productive hunting technique evolves.

To begin, a black bear is a species including many color phases and variations. A true "black" bear, *Eurarctos americanus,* may be pure black. He may also be cinnamon colored. He may be dark brown. He may have the characteristic white throat-patch, or he may not. He may have a predominantly tan face, or, with age, his face may become grizzly-colored in the way that an old dog's face tends to lighten.

More, a black female bear may have two cubs, one jet black, and one brown. Again, a brown-colored sow may give birth to twins of different color, or to two jet-black cubs.

One of the most pronounced color variations in the black bear is the blue-colored glacier bear of southwestern Alaska. It seems true with bear and with trout that often the species' coloration is affected by environment or region.

Twinning is common with black bear, as is single cubs. Three cubs at a single birth is more uncommon, though not too rare. Quadruplets are rare. And the most remarkable instance I've ever heard was reported by the National Wildlife Federation in 1958. A Pennsylvania black bear was observed to have *five* cubs. According to the bulletin, these cubs weighed seven or eight pounds, with the female bear weighing 150 pounds. It was not stated whether the weights of these cubs and the mother were estimated or actual.

Black bears breed in June, and, as mentioned, have their young in mid-winter. By spring emergence from hibernation, the cubs are large enough to follow the female, and

Examining grizzly tracks in the snow just after bruin's emergence from hibernation.

begin their training for a later and solitary existence.

Blackie is primarily a vegetarian. Food ranges from roots, berries, tree bark, grasses, and pine needles, to insects, the rodents, larger varmints when available, and carrion.

It has been the history of this animal that once a taste for meat is cultivated, the beast tends to become carnivorous; and if the opportunity exists, bruin then becomes a domestic-animal killer with an exaggerated, but real reputation. The black bear kills sheep, calves, small horses, and has an especial liking for penned hogs—possibly for the relative ease in dispatching them in such confinement.

Blackie kills by striking an animal about the neck, together with clawing at the throat. While the black bear doesn't have the great strength of the grizzly, nevertheless his power is amazing. An adult bear's skinned forearm looks quite like an over-developed man's arm, has muscles tough as whang leather, and runs six inches or more in diameter. A first look at such "peeled power" gives the viewer a new conception of the animal's strength; but he must also witness some of the results of a swipe with that same arm, to appreciate such power.

In 1941, I had occasion to witness an instance indicating just how strong a black bear is, under full steam coupled with anger.

My partner had killed a cow elk at sundown. Not having time to quarter and hang it, and make camp by dark, he dressed the animal, then located a pine tree nearby, which stood at the brink of an earth cut bank immediately above a tiny mountain creek. Tying the elk's neck solidly to this tree, he then rolled the carcass over the bank, until it hung suspended. Placing a stick spreader in the belly to have it cool, he came on into camp.

When the two of us returned to quarter and hang the meat, we found that a big black bear—his tracks were in the mud of the creek banks—had found the carcass during the night.

Parts of it were a mess. The entire brisket was eaten away,

as were portions of the hams. We estimated about twenty pounds of the hams. More, the whole carcass was not tied to the tree where my partner had left it, but instead, was in a heap down in the creek bottom, a full rod from where it had been left.

The amazing thing was this. The rope used in tying the carcass had been bought en route to the Selway and was new rope. It was of the size packers use for lash-ropes, for throwing a diamond-hitch over loaded pack mantas— one-half to five-eighths-inch diameter. This rope was broken in two between the cow's neck and the tree, at one of the knots.

To one familiar with bear habits, it was plain, if indeed it hadn't already been obvious from the readable tracks in the creek mud, what had happened. The big black bruin had eaten for a while, then decided either to pull the elk from the tree, or move it into a more favorable position for a cache. Seizing the carcass in his arms, he tugged. Finding it wouldn't give had enraged him, and he braced into the creek bottom and heaved. At one such mighty jerk, the carcass had broken free, and, as plainly showed by no intervening marks in the earth, this bear had literally *thrown* the carcass to where it had lit below.

The most amazing thing to me was breaking that new rope, a piece of which my partner had carried along for the express purpose of hanging game. There is an old formula for the breaking strength of rope which says that a rope's diameter, squared, times 7200 will give the breaking-strength of similar rope. It is true that the bruin *may* have weakened the rope by chewing. It was undoubtedly weakest at the knot, and *could* have been defective in some way. The interesting thing is that ½-inch squared, times 7200, equals 1800 pounds of breaking-strain!

We succeeded in killing this same bear later. It was a big boar, estimated at 400 pounds. I still have his skin in the form of a rug.

This brings up another controversial matter, the actual

weight of bears. Like deer, the size of bears varies with the region, the incidence of food, the quality of such food, the season, and—again as with deer—the probability of runting during early youth.

The average black bear will average somewhere between 200 and 500 pounds weight as an adult. In dimensions, such an adult will run roughly five feet long, by somewhat over two feet high. Tracks of such a bear will average about six inches for the hind foot (including the short claws), and five inches across for the front-foot pad.

I have measured innumerable tracks while hunting, both with the pocket tape carried to measure possible trophies, or with a stick, notched at either side of the spoor, carried to camp, and measured there. Any bear's spoor measuring more than that, was made by a very large bear. Any increase in the above five-by-plus-two-feet dimensions of a black bear as he stands on all fours and broadside, means a really big bear, since a small increase in inches, works in *all* directions. The five-foot length includes his neck and head, of course.

My friend, Merwyn Ransier, once killed an enormous black bear in Alaska, whose green hide squared nearly eight feet, as near as they could step it off. This trophy, like so many of the really exceptional ones, came by sheer luck.

Merwyn had hunted that day on the Coastal slopes, and had killed a nice billy goat. By the time he and his guide, Willie Kvasnikoff, had reached camp, they were dog-tired. At dusk they sat about the small fire, eating, resting, and letting the smoke drive off mosquitoes.

Suddenly, and certainly with a lack of caution unusual in so big a trophy, a big black bear came wandering into the small clearing. This beast spit in the face of another wild-game generality in that it paid no apparent attention to the fire at all. Rather it moseyed right up, batting furiously at the swarms of Alaska mosquitoes. Willie nodded, Merwyn reached out and grasped his rifle, and the great beast was dropped within the circle of fire light. "Not fifty feet away!" Merwyn told me, later.

Kvasnikoff estimated this bear's weight at nearly 800 pounds. I personally know Willie, and know him to be an honest man. If the beast did weigh that much, it certainly was in the record class.

There are several difficulties in arriving at the true weight of a wild bear. First, his shaggy coat makes him look deceptively large. An apparent 300-pounder, peeled down, may run 175 pounds, with the hide weighing no more than 25 additional pounds. Again, when the black's pelage is glossy, short, and in its prime, the overall bear at a distance does not give the appearance of weighing as much as the same bear in shaggy, scraggly summer coat.

The facilities and desire for weighing any adult wild bear are rather skimpy in the woods—there are no scales, and how do you let go?

Perhaps the biggest single factor in mis-estimating a bear's weight is the legendary and conditioned conclusion that he's "big and bad." Consequently, any wild bear seen, imagined, or actually shot, subsequently becomes a real whopper. Bears, of all our game species, have the greatest tendency to "grow" with each re-telling.

Upon emergence from hibernation, bears are enormously hungry. They feed first upon the tender grasses coming up after thaws and warming of the earth's south slopes. Dogtooth violets are among the first delicacies, when available, as are the under layers of bark from spruce trees. These first foods are cathartic in nature, and once again start the digestive system, so long dormant, to function. At first, emerging blacks won't touch fresh meat, but will hang around, evidently keeping it handy; and within ten days to two weeks, will then start to eat meat, once their systems are cleared out, and their stomachs stretched out a bit.

In 1953, a party of us made a hard trek into Wyoming's upper Buffalo River country, both to hunt bears and to study their hibernation-emergence pattern. During this extended stay—and after we'd tugged a complete camp and gear twenty miles or so over the snow on toboggans—the party killed several bears.

The stomachs of all bears taken, including a black, a brown, and a grizzly, averaged about the size of a man's doubled fists placed fingers together. All stomachs were partially filled with tender grass shoots, pine needles, and spruce bark. These animals had been out of hibernation from ten days to two weeks when we took them, with no evidence whatever of meat in any of the stomachs.

Partly to prove the point, the outfitter had killed a worthless horse in the area, and let it bloat to the point of actual stinking to see if the newly-emerged bruins would take meat. As an added incentive, one of the guides carried a jar of honey to the "ripe" horse, and burned it with a twig-fire upon the carcass.

The resulting smells of singed horse-hair, burnt honey, and putrid meat were something to sniff! The guide, experienced on bears, swore, "Any bruin within half a state, will be here in a couple of days. You just watch."

Several days later, the tracks of black bear in the snow around the animal showed they had, indeed, come. But the meat wasn't touched, at least during the length of our stay there. No doubt, once any bear in the area had conditioned himself on grasses, needles, and a tapering off on ants, grubs, etc., he'd later gorge himself on the ripe carcass.

On this jaunt I also photographed spruce trees, whose outer bark had been clawed off, and the inner bark sucked and eaten. Likely the spruce gum had the necessary "spring tonic" effect.

Too, we found one evidence of a big black's emergence from hibernation during a thaw in the snow, then a return to his den. Blacks generally emerge in all areas of a region within the space of a few days—as if they had an alarm clock set. But I was assured by veterans that during spring rain, or excessive thawing which allows moisture to wet a bear's den, he sometimes will emerge, then go back in if the weather gets clear and cold again, at least for a few days.

With the digestive system functioning full power again, Blackie starts his traveling in search of food. Within two to four weeks, the glossiness of his coat, which went into hibernation with him when he was lard-fat in the fall, starts to turn scraggly and worn. The annual spring itch comes full upon him, and he rubs against gummy spruce trees in the normal process of removing all the old winter hair, so a new crop can begin.

The summer's search for food is a constant process. The route broadly follows the "edge" regions of the melting snows downward from the high rocky den region. The summer diet is largely fruit, grubs, and ants ripped from rotten logs, rodents such as the western "chiseler" which he can dig from holes, any carrion previously caught in snowslides and saved for him in nature's deep-freeze, fish along the creek beds, and the offal left by game-kills, either nature's or man's.

The only interruption comes in June when the boar's urges of reproduction overcome his natural aversion to the company of his own kind, and he scours the country locating the sows. Once mated, each sex takes off on its own again, in the eternal pursuit of food.

The scrawny summer coat leaves by August, and by mid-September Blackie's coat is glossy again. From then till hibernation, usually late November, his biggest problem, save for enemies, is to eat enough to get sufficiently fat, so as to sleep out the deep winter with a big enough store of fat-energy.

Enemies of the black bear are mainly man, grizzlies within the same habitat, an occasional mountain lion, and the lowly porcupine. Black bears, like coyotes, will toy with the blundering porcupines, possibly for sport as much as for food. Once with a face and mouth full of the barbed, in-driving quills, each is then faced with misery, a festering mouth, eventual starvation and a horrible death.

If Blackie survives his enemies for another year, he finishes his fat-producing diet of the late fall with a gorging on the berries of mountain ash. These, filling his bowels as a last feed, assure him that he'll come out of hibernation able to un-plug . . . and the cycle is completed.

An understanding of the life cycle of the black bear in no way detracts from his appeal as a game animal. Instead, such a knowledge adds to the desire of the red-blooded sportsman, by increasing his chances to eventually bag one.

My friend Henry is a good example of the average hunter's deep-seated yen to kill a bear.

Henry is middle-aged, has lived here in Idaho's marvelous hunting country all his life, and has pursued the sport of big-game hunting annually and intensely. He has killed innumerable elk, deer, antelope—the works. The one animal which he has wanted the longest, and which has most successfully eluded him, is a bear. All his life, Henry has wanted to "bust a bruin." "If I could just get one bear," he told me years ago, "I'd then be satisfied. I'd almost be willing to give up hunting."

But it seems that wherever Henry hunted in the hills, any bear wasn't. He found plenty of sign. He was with other hunters who, while being separated only short distances, ran into the bruin instead of Henry. But he never gave up, and annually hunted such choice bear country as Montana's Bitter Roots, Idaho's Selway and Salmon River country, and western Wyoming.

Henry's desire for a bear increased still further some ten years ago when he acquired a timber lot in the beautiful Island Park country adjacent to Yellowstone, and built himself a beautiful summer home. This rustic edifice was of peeled and varnished pine logs, magnificent of design and execution with numerous guest rooms, kitchen, bath, and great living room with log rafters, huge fireplace, hardwood floors, and mounted trophies all over the walls—a sportsman's dream home in the woods.

"All it lacks," Henry said, while hosting me there, "is that danged bear, which *some* day I'm still going to get. See, I've left a place for his hide, there by the fireplace."

A few years after that, I was hunting the Salmon River Of No Return, with Henry when one day he did get his chance. He simply missed a good chance at a dandy black bear, because he wanted the trophy so badly he got buck fever. He literally shed tears that night, in camp.

But anyway, as the years rolled on, and after he'd given up on bruins, Henry did *finally* get his bear.

Like any proud owner, he had a rug made up, and installed the trophy in his summer home.

One autumn, a year or so back, his wife suggested that the trophies all needed cleaning and airing out. So Henry, still unbelievably proud of his black bear rug, took it down from the wall, out into the yard, and shook the dust from it. In order to give it a good airing, he then laid it over his sawhorse, on which he'd logged up wood for the fireplace, and with the feet draped down somewhat naturally on each side. The wooden sawhorse was but a few feet from the living room window. Like on a front lawn, in town.

As he worked about the front yard, he heard a car come easily down the dirt road past his property. It is all wooded country there, with the North Fork of the Snake River just a few rods in front of the house. Henry was used to anglers passing that way, but the thing he forgot was that the hunting season for elk was currently open in that area.

Before he could imagine what was happening, the car squealed to a stop. Five or six red-clad hunters piled out of it, dragging rifles, and with blood in their eager eyes.

Bang! Bang! . . . *Bang!* . . .

With Henry there in plain view, as was his big summer home, and only a few yards from the invaders, he stood and watched the bear he'd hunted so long to find, and prized so highly, "killed" at least a dozen times more with bullets poured into the inoffensive hide, draped over the sawhorse!

CHAPTER 4

How To Hunt Black Bear

The best overall way to hunt black bear is in conjunction with the hunting of another species.

This is true for several basic reasons. First, the habitat of the black bear coincides with that of other big-game species such as deer, elk, caribou, and moose. With the more alpine species of mountain goats and sheep, bear may be hunted both in the lower country as the hunter ascends towards the cliff country from base camp in the wooded regions below; and on his way down.

Because of the black bear's wanderings, and his habits of working one region for but a few days, then moving to another, it is hard to predict with any degree of certainty just where he ought to, or may, be. To hunt him as a species, *per se,* is discouraging. But to hunt him with another species doubles the enjoyment of the hunt; and more to the point, is often more productive of bears than to hunt him alone.

My neighbor Lawrence, and his partner Eldon, are good examples of the advantage in hunting bear along with other game.

The two had been hunting chiefly for elk in Idaho's Selway country, near Gardiner Creek. There are some nice bucks also in that area, and while after the bigger wapiti, Eldon killed a deer, dressed it out, and went back to camp.

A day or so later, after it had thoroughly cooled out, he took one of the horses they'd trucked in, and headed back down the canyon to pack it in.

That area is good black bear country, and indeed, they'd seen lots of sign—pad marks in the dusty trails and piles of fresh berry dung. As he left, Eldon picked up his rifle. "I'll take this along. A bear just might have been eating on that deer, and if so, I'll get myself a rug."

When he'd left, Lawrence picked up his own rifle, and struck off down the ridge paralleling the canyon.

Briefly, when Eldon reached the deer, he found that a big black bear *had* been eating on the carcass. The sounds of himself and the approaching horse had frightened bruin off. And, as such lucky things often occur, the big bear loped to safety up the adjacent ridge. However, it just happened that Lawrence was headed down that same ridge. He simply upped his rifle at short range, and bagged the rug Eldon had expected to get.

Or again, consider what happened to two youngsters up Kelly Canyon, just twelve miles from where I sit.

Four years ago, these two were hunting deer in the aspen-pine canyon bordering the dry-farm lands. There are some wonderful mule deer bucks in there—something in the calcium-limestone formation there which goes into their food, producing the largest antlers of most anywhere in the state.

At dusk they came back down the dirt canyon road, happy that their hunt for deer had been successful, and slowly herding their ancient jalopy along.

Suddenly, across the narrow road, calmly walked a huge black bear. He had no fear of the car, moseyed slowly across and into a semi-opening between the adjacent pines. Here was a chance at a bear which neither young hunter would likely ever get again. A big, desirable trophy, within mere rods, and simply asking for it. All that was necessary was for one to stop the car, while the other stepped from the car, and shot the beast.

Bear are often hunted as incidental game. Here a bear hide comes in along with the elk trophy.

Do you know what they did?

Far from greeting the unexpected opportunity with fervor and gusto, these two youngsters were typically filled with the stories of the legendary badness of all bear. Hastily rolling up the windows of the car, they ducked their heads as though a bear-human collision were in the making, poured on the gas, and screeched down the canyon, leaving the astounded bruin to gawk, and likely blinded with dust.

In telling of the affair later to my neighbor Jim, one of them said with great remaining excitement, "Shoot 'im? Not on your life. We only had .30-06's and that bear was bigger'n a piano. No wounded bear climbin' into a car with *us!*"

I could cite numerous instances. My son Ted's first black was shot while he was really after elk, with no thought of getting a bear—though black bear were legally in season. Too, my son-in-law John killed his first black bear while also hunting wapiti. My own first two black bears were killed, one on an elk hunt, the other while I was after deer.

Part of the sensible reason for hunting a bear while after other game is economic. Today's game is being pushed farther and farther back into the remaining wilderness country. Hunts into the real game country today are costly; and many hunters, especially the younger hunters, must save up for such a hunt, sometimes for years for a single hunt. If on such a trip the hunter gets the main species he is after, fine. If he incidentally bags his bruin, it is a bonus.

A more basic reason for combining species is the fact that often the successful bagging of some other species lays the groundwork for getting a bear, when sheer hunting would fail. This is due to bruin's liking for carrion and the offal left from game-kills.

The smart hunter, after taking an elk, deer, moose, or caribou will then carefully hunt the "ripening" offal for the remainder of his hunt. Hunting such left-overs is an art in itself.

First, and before leaving the sight of the game-kill, the wise hunter will study the surrounding area for possible cover behind which he may later approach the scene undetected. Big game must, of course, be killed where it is found. Often this isn't in the best position for a later, unobserved approach. However, with the exception of the purely plains animals such as antelope, there will either be some form of foliage which may be utilized or the terrain itself may be manipulated (because of its unevenness of surface) to advantage.

Consideration should be given to possible breezes, which would warn a bear of the hunter's approach—and this in regards to different times of day. Briefly, warming air goes upward, cooling air descends. Since the two most productive times, both for bruin's approach to the kill and the hunter's stalk, are at dusk and daylight, air currents have a definite bearing on the outcome. Broadly speaking, the warming air of morning will move up a canyon, or ridge, or any rise in the terrain's elevation. Similarly, cooling air will move downward at evening.

Consequently, *two* routes by which the hunter can later

"stalk" the offal must be outlined, depending upon whether he hunts at daylight or dusk.

In 1958, I had this identical situation in Alaska. I'd killed an exceptional Barren Ground caribou on Sheep Creek, three miles from camp. There was considerable bear spoor in the whole area, only this time it was grizzly spoor, making the whole affair more interesting. I'd shot the caribou in the fringing spruce trees, as he crossed from one drainage to another from the high, bare plateaus above. However, the animal had, after the lung shot, made it out into a tiny open pocket before collapsing.

The only route by which I could subsequently approach the remaining offal at dusk, was to circle it far and wide, and come to a certain small rise, covered with blueberry bushes and at 175 yards distance to the north. However, due to prevailing morning breezes in that basin, the only morning route to the kill which would not carry man scent was from the opposing direction to the south. There, the only place from which one could peer over and see the remains of the caribou in the tiny pocket, was from sixty

Some of the best remaining bear country can only be reached via pack-string.

yards, with sparse concealment. This distance, when confronting a grizzly which may be startled, or consider his cache molested, is interesting indeed!

Briefly, I hunted that kill for the remaining days of the hunt. The offal became riper and riper. Magpies worked it, cackling its presence to the whole basin. But no bear ever came until we had to leave Sheep Creek, for moose country up the Slana River. However, the day we had to break camp and leave, the fresh tracks of two grizzlies—likely a sow and full-grown cub—were in the creek-bed sand not a hundred yards from camp. They'd headed in a straight line from the country up toward Tanada Glacier, and I have no doubt at all, headed directly for the caribou kill whose presence the prevailing winds had disclosed to them. They likely cleaned it up, after we left.

Bears, both blacks and grizzlies, have the keenest of noses. They can, with the vagaries of even the mildest breeze, detect carrion at unbelievable distances—literally miles.

More, the presence of such offal is more easily disclosed to them by an odd brotherhood of the wilds. The sequence is simple. Once a game-kill is made, a pair of camp robbers is certain to appear, if in wilderness game country. Where these semi-tame, dusky little scavengers come from baffles man. And they habitually travel in pairs. But before the animal is dressed, these birds will be there. Leave the carcass a few rods, and they are flying with bits of fat, meat, or insides up into adjacent trees to store or eat it.

The ubiquitous and canny magpies, common to all game country, will spot the flight of these camp robbers, whiskey jacks, or larger blue jays which act similarly. The magpie comes in, scavenges, and cackles his presence to the hills.

Coyotes hear this, come within twenty-four hours, and wail their eerie cries as they circle the offal, waiting another twenty-four hours for the man scent to die. Any bruin within the region, either currently or traveling through, hears all this and heads for the remains. The one

difference between bruin and the coyotes is that he sometimes comes without regard for any man scent, and starts
gorging.

In hunting the offal of game-kills for bear, the cardinal
rule is to approach the spot entirely undetected, and *never*
molest such offal by approaching closer than reasonable
rifle range, until bruin does come. It's a big temptation to
bust the occasional coyote that feeds on the innards, and
often cleans them all up, while waiting for a possible bear;
or to walk up close and take a good look at the increasing
damage from such smaller scavengers. This is unwise. It's
best never to approach the offal, but do all looking with
binoculars from a place of concealment.

Such a spot, incidentally, should not be made into a
comfortable or more suitable "blind." It should simply be
some place of unobstrusive, natural concealment which
won't spook any kind of predator.

It is interesting in this connection to observe the relationship existing between these several species of predators
and scavengers while actually working the remains of a
game-kill. Bears and coyotes usually won't be alarmed or
spooked until a magpie cackles a warning. So the wise
hunter considers this pinto predator with great care, in any
hunting of a carcass or offal.

There are productive ways of hunting a black bear as
an individual species. The success of this procedure depends upon the incidence or number of bruins in an area,
and a knowledge of the bear's basic habits.

With spring emergence from hibernation, the bear's first
diet consists of tender grass shoots, dog-tooth violets, and
similar conditioners. These, with spring thaws, follow the
first warming of the earth; and the areas are the south
slopes of mountainous country.

The accompanying mud of these thawing areas will dis-
close both any bear's presence and working of the vegetable
shoots, and how recent it has been. A careful hunting, via
stalking and woods hunting, of such places may produce

a spring bear, in the two to four weeks while his pelt is still glossy and prime after hibernation.

Too, at the latter portion of this period, many a mountainous area will have its first showing of rodents such as ground squirrels, rock chucks, and gophers. When Blackie's diet tapers onto meat, he digs for these, naturally, in the areas of greatest concentration.

Rodent colonies, in spring, are also good places to hunt.

During the summer months, and until the berry crops of the wilds come on, is a poor time to hunt bear. This largely because at that time of year, bruin has a shaggy coat, usually rubbed bare of hair in spots, and entirely unsuitable for a trophy. Killing a bear at this season is sheer waste, and many states set the legal bear season to eliminate this.

Early fall, after September first, is a good time to hunt bear. The pelage is glossy and full again, and at that season bruin may be hunted in conjunction with the remaining berry crop.

The black bear likes fruit. He'll eat most every variety of wild berry the hills produce, but his preference is for those highly edible to man—huckleberries, elderberries, blueberries, wild raspberries, and serviceberries.

Those areas of greatest berry productivity will attract the most bears. The high huckleberry patches of such states as Idaho and Wyoming are certain, during August, to show the spoor of any black bear in the area. The bears mosey through the patches of thickest fruit, stripping off leaves and berries with their mouths, always headed on for more. Even after the first frosts, bruin stays on picking off the last of the remaining crop.

Similarly, in British Columbia in the Liard River region, I have hunted black bears in thick, profuse patches of wild raspberries, where it was literally impossible to walk without stepping into piles of fresh bear dung, full of berry seeds. Entire acre-sized patches had been completely "worked" for days on end, until the fruit crop was stripped.

Old abandoned orchards are likewise worked in early fall, especially for apples. A black bear, working apple trees, is most destructive. I've seen such old orchards completely ruined in the space of a few nights, where some bear has climbed, broken off all the big branches with his weight, and gathered from below the fruit he couldn't reach while up the tree.

Patience is the greatest virtue when hunting bear in berry or fruit country. The best technique is to get to some high vantage point where considerable country may be scrutinized, then stay there and continuously glass the whole region for signs of game. Except for short cat naps during the day, any bear is constantly on the move when foraging. He's most apt to be spotted while the hunter is still, not on the move himself.

Blackie is like man, when changing from one drainage to another. While a black bear, especially when pursued, can climb and negotiate with speed any type of rugged terrain—even into places where man simply can't get—his natural preference is to take the easy route. Black bear love trails, both game- and man- or horse-made. They will often wander for a half-mile or more along such a trail rather than walk in the more difficult footing on either side. The hunter glassing any berry country for bruin should, naturally, include all trails in the area.

There is a direct relationship between the extent of a wild berry crop, the elevation at which bears may be found, and the way black bears may best be hunted.

In years of a good berry crop, black bears will stay high within the periphery of their range. The berry diet is complemented by the grubs and ants available in rotten logs at the same elevations; and with ample food, bears, like other game, prefer to stay high where it is cool and away from summer flies and mosquitoes.

During seasons of few berries, the same bears will be found lower where they must forage around creek beds, dig roots, and scavenge the countryside for carrion, what

A glance at these three bear skulls will indicate why the sloping head of a bear makes a brain shot, head on, almost impossible. The big black on the left was shot at a distance of two rods, just under the left eye, with a factory load from a .30-30 rifle. The bullet didn't penetrate the skull but disintegrated just under the hide.

domestic stock they can steal from outlying ranches, and the refuse left at outdoor camps.

The years of worst depredation done by pest bears are invariably those years of poor wild berry crops. During these lean years, it's wiser to hunt the lower areas where bear sign has been seen, damage has been done, and bears are known to be raiding.

As an example, my friend Hilmer George bagged his first black bear, in a year of no berries, right at his own summer home in Island Park. The beast began to come with regularity to Hilmer's refuse barrel. Hilmer simply waited night after night with patience; sneaked outside when bruin began rattling the cans; and one moonlight night got lucky and bagged the beast.

Again, our hunting party once barely got into bed at the end-of-the-road campground, when a big black bear jumped onto the car trailer shortly after dark, grabbed a slab of bacon and some dried beans, and made off before we could get up. Shortly after midnight, the same prowling beast crawled upon a sturdy camp table which some other hunters had used several rods beyond, started licking up the remains of a pie they'd had for supper—and one of the lucky fellows simply turned over in his sleeping bag and shot the animal.

Three years afterward, my hunting partner similarly sat up for several nights in the cook shack of a summer forest camp, watching the garbage pile through a window. Bruin eventually came, as his tracks earlier indicated he had been doing, and my partner shot him shortly after dusk.

Once a black bear becomes a camp pest, there is no way of discouraging him so long as the camp lasts without killing him. He'll return so long as there is anything, garbage or food, to plunder. This is especially true in the lean years of no berries.

A person has to witness the destructiveness of a pest bear to believe it. The pattern of his actions seems broadly similar in each case. First, he'll cautiously circle the camp to learn if he's alone. With this preliminary done, bruin then literally "breaks and enters." If it's a tent, he'll open or tear his way through the canvas. If it's a closed building, he'll try all doors and windows. If they're locked or battened, he'll bite at every corner, batten, jutting edge of timber, or place where his strong teeth can take hold—then start ripping things off. Eventually, unless strongly secured, camp buildings are some way entered.

Once inside, a pet habit of the black bear seems to be the raking of everything loose onto the floor. With a scything motion, he'll swipe dishes off a table; knock over a camp stove; up-end chairs, tables, any available cupboards. He takes a fiendish delight in flattening any stovepipe with his paws, as though it had been hammered shut.

All the while, his keen nose is working. Foodstuff not in cans is quickly gorged, stirred, likely piled up in the center of the room or tent. All canned goods are individually bitten into, the contents of fruit, milk, vegetables, and soup cans all sucked. What juices he can't get in this fashion drip all over everything else, where later he'll lick and paw at it. This is especially aggravating to the camp owner, later, if such dripping occurs on sleeping bags and prized personal gear.

Don L. Smith, who's boated the famed River Of No Return all his life, once had such a pest bear work over his high camp up near Bargamin Creek. This was a high elk camp, which couldn't be tended between hunting parties which floated down river that far, hunted in the high country, and had to be taken back out.

Between two hunting parties, the black bear found the tents and supplies. Afterward, Don took to the policy of storing, during his absence, every available item in steel oil drums, and wiring them shut. But this was learned the hard way, and was like locking the barn after the horse had been stolen.

Briefly, the big bruin stirred everything, punched all cans with his teeth, piled all remnants into the big tent's center, pulled a smaller canvas tent upon the heap and slept at least one night, or day, on it.

"Worse," Don told me, "he didn't have the gumption to even go outside to crap. He'd made his pile right on top of the big mess. When I got the next party in, I was stuck for eats till we could get back down with the horses to the river. We had some fresh meat we'd packed in, but nothing to fry it in. All the shortening in that camp had been mostly eaten, then the rest scraped into the pile in the middle of the tent."

"What did you do?"

"Hell, what would *you* have done? I dug around in the dung and mess till I found some of the shortening, which didn't look *too* bad—" Don finished, laughing uproariously. "I never did let the dudes know."

Such a loss can often be laughed off, since it is relatively rare; and when it does occur in regions where supplies can be replenished. It is a far different matter in the bush country of Canada for the trappers and other woodsmen there. Black bears in any of their overnight camps on a trapping or prospecting route, often spell an irreparable loss. Supplies laboriously lugged in during summer months, and depended upon at each cache on the circuitous route, can't be replenished. They are assumed to be there upon arrival. Often their loss could be tragic.

Consequently, black bears there are regarded as pests, and shot on sight around any cache. For the visiting hunter, this is vital hunting information and the areas of any known cache are fine places to glass from a distance for signs of bruin's appearance.

My friend, J. B. Yoder, had an enlightening experience a year ago with a black bear, indicating both the methods of such a marauder and his tenacity.

Yoder owns some cabin property on Moose Creek, just on the Idaho side of Yellowstone. Last spring he wanted to begin on his summer cabin. As is customary, his plan was first to set up a semi-permanent, boarded-up wall tent in which to store tools and materials while working on the peeled-log cabin. Such a tent would serve as overnight quarters, also, for fishing trips in the area.

In early June, J. B. and his wife Opal, with the station wagon loaded with building materials, went up to the cabin site. My wife and I went with them, to set up the tent.

In a short day's work, we had the 12x14-foot tent set up, boarded to a height of three feet all around, the screen door installed against mosquitoes, and a table cabinet built all along one side. With the tools and other materials (including one sealed box of non-perishable groceries) stored, and stove set up, the quarters looked ship-shape and highly livable. J. B.'s intention was to come up each available weekend, do some trout fishing on the Snake's North Fork, and build some more on the cabin—the clearing for which was already done.

As we lolled about in the finished tent, Yoder remarked, "Yes, it looks pretty good. Now if some *bear* doesn't get in here."

"Any around this spring?"

"Bud, the neighbor up the creek, has seen signs of one or two. One big bastard."

At the time, I was facing that portion of the tent end between the wall and screen door—a section of bare canvas just above the three feet of boarding. "You know, J. B., if a bear *does* come, you know where he'll come in?"

"Through the door?"

"Nope. He'll just walk up to this tent, to that section of canvas there, and with one swipe he'll rip it down and walk right in."

"Why won't he break through the door, instead?"

"Bears don't think that way—if at all."

"Why do you say that?"

"Well, in British Columbia once, our outfitter, Dal Dalziel, had flown a canoe and tent in for us to Rainbow Lake, on the pontoon of his plane. He'd set up the tent, so it'd be ready when we showed up. There, of course, the bears were all grizzlies. Dal knew if he tied the tent shut, any bear would rip it to pieces to get inside."

"Anything inside?" Yoder asked.

"Not a thing. But that doesn't matter, it seems. Anyway, Dal tied the flaps open. The tent set in the full open, and he didn't leave a single thing around except the canoe, which he ditched in the bush. But before we flew in, a few days later, the tracks in the dirt around the lake showed that a big grizzly had come wandering up. He's spotted the tent and naturally headed for it. There was all the room in the world around it, but his course had made him come up from the tent's rear. Instead of passing to the side, and going around to look in, he'd simply raised a paw, made one great ripping swipe at the tent's back, walked right on through—and *without even stopping!*"

Yoder laughed at the notion, obviously didn't believe the story, and we forgot about it.

The next week, he and Opal went back. They found perhaps the most accurate prediction I've ever made had come true. A 300-pound black bear, whose big spoor Bud had seen in the area, had simply walked up to and *through* the tent between the door and the wall. In the identical spot I'd half-jokingly predicted he would.

The whole inside was a typical mess. Tools, stove, lantern, boxes, cabinet—the whole works were strewn from hell to breakfast. The box of groceries, which looked entirely bear-proof, had been broken open, and the cans typically sucked. The big bear had then walked casually out of the tent, but in another area where there was no opening! Each rip was two yards long, in the heavy canvas.

Besides the loss and inconvenience, Yoder was maddened by the sheer manner in which that bruin had worked the outfit over. The next week he was back there, not only to repair the damage, but to kill that bear if at all possible.

That night he and Opal slept in the rear of the station wagon. In order to make room for the sleeping bags, he set all the gear just outside the wagon. This included a big beverage-type cooler, in which they had ice and the weekend groceries.

Along past midnight, Yoder thought he heard something outside. Hearing nothing further, he again slept till daybreak. This time his sleep was more rudely shattered, by the banging sound of something metal being overturned and slapped around, just outside the car.

He came fully awake just in time to see a huge black bruin making off with sundry packages of weiners, bacon, and other bear goodies from the overturned cooler. Yoder also had time to grab his .30-06, barge from the wagon, catch sight of bruin just inside the timber, and shoot him. "Right in the bacon," he said with grim satisfaction.

His repaired tent remained intact for the rest of the summer.

Other methods of hunting bear include baiting, mentioned previously, and coursing the animals with bear dogs specially trained on that species.

Some states legislate against bear baiting, claiming it

is too unsporting. The way it is practiced in Wyoming is not, in my opinion, any more unsporting that to dangle bait in front of a trout's nose. As we'll detail later in the section on grizzlies, baiting a bear with a dead horse involves too many variables, is too costly to become widely used, and it still gives the bear a decidedly top-heavy advantage in never being taken.

Baiting for blacks isn't widely done because of the expense of the bait. Only those well-heeled sportsmen who can afford expensive bear hunts are willing to pay the freight, where only a black bear is involved. It is another matter when the possibility of bagging the more prized grizzly is the incentive.

Coursing bear with dogs is not practiced in the West, Canada, or Alaska to any appreciable extent. Hunting with dogs is reserved for the heavily-foliaged country of the Southern swamp-lands, the brushy country of the Ozarks, and similar terrain where the foot hunter without the aid of dogs to locate the quarry would be farther ahead to stay home.

A reason why more dogs aren't used in other types of country is the expense of buying and breeding suitable types for the purpose; and the high cost of supporting such packs for twelve months of the year, for use only a few days.

Only a few experienced dog men cater to bear hunters on a commercial basis. These fellows advertise their services in the outdoor journals, and the hunter who wants to take on a bear hunt with the aid of dogs may easily contact them from current ads.

Other than that, there is, of course, the occasional outdoors person—rancher, hunter, or dog lover—who owns a pooch that will run bear. Occasionally, such a man will haul his dog into known bear country, and try for a bruin. I know one outfitter who hauled two such dogs into Idaho's Sawtooth Mountains annually for this purpose. But all I could see that they accomplished was to bark and bay at the moon while other hunters tried to sleep.

The hunting or killing of cub bears is now outlawed in most hunting regions, and should be. The black bear has, over a long period of years, been grudgingly elevated from the status of sheer killer and pest to the new role of big game. There are not now enough black bears to go around for all hunters, and the brutal killing of cubs while in the "innocent" stage so far as hunting for any sport is concerned, would soon eradicate the bulk of our remaining bear population.

Incidentally, in this slow evolvement of bruin from killer to sporting game, one of the biggest drawbacks has been the evil reputation which stockmen, especially sheepmen, have given him. It is true that Blackie likes mutton. It is equally true that he loves carrion. Often he has been caught cleaning the landscape of such carrion in nature's simple plan for cleansing the earth, and accused of killing the animal in the first place.

A final way, often, of getting a black bear, in good bear

Because of a bear's shaggy hair, the vital area is often hard to locate. This condition is augmented when he is running.

country, is to contact a stockman or sheepherder. Such an individual will know of the presence of any bears within the region, and is usually most cooperative with anyone who intends to kill one of his habitual enemies.

Much has been said and written about the edibility of bear meat. Like any other animal, bruin is a product of what he eats, and the edibility of his flesh depends to a large extent upon his diet, age, and condition. Another factor was disclosed to me by my taxidermist, Frank Keefer. "You ever noticed," he asked, "that a bear in hibernation has a stinky odor? A bear in the wilds doesn't. I know because I've mounted dozens of 'em—park bear they had to kill, and the kind you guys bring in."

Most hunters and other outdoorsmen won't eat a grizzly. A knowledge of his diet, and his preference for carrion turns their stomachs. On the other hand, the flesh of a young black bear, whose diet has been predominantly berries, is mightly fine if prepared right. The trick is to pare off all fat, then fry or broil the steaks for a longer time than you would prime pork—which it resembles. I know several men who have eaten bear steak unwittingly, and have pronounced it most excellent. I've grazed on an occasional bear steak myself. But I always like to know from what bear it came, first. And the season of the year, and area in which the beast was killed.

The fat of a bear is greatly prized by mountain men, as lard. After being rendered, it is pure white, odorless, and exceedingly fine of texture. Old Frank Horrace, a rugged mountain man who homesteaded a ranch far down the Selway River in that day when all supplies had to be mule packed for sixty trail miles, once told me: "We just feel lost here any winter we don't git a bear for lard. You can't beat it for cooking."

A hilarious incident involving Frank's older crippled brother Bill occurred one fall, which indicates this. The fellow to whom it occurred is a friend of mine, but I'm sure that, after all these years, he won't mind my mentioning it.

This fellow had killed his game and was back at the Horrace ranch, waiting the others of his party to fill up and come out. Being an excellent cook himself, and with a growing case of impatience and cabin fever, he began to ride old Bill about the grub. Not too much, but just enough to get Bill's canny mind to working. Previously, this same hunter had fried a couple of bear steaks for me and Joe Novachek. After cooking the steaks, he'd turned his own steak down. "By gadfrey, you and Joe can gulp down that dog food if you want. But I can't go it!" The steaks were excellent.

So Bill, to please the grumbling fellow, spent all afternoon one day baking him a pie.

This tickled the fellow all over. He about-faced and raved about the excellent pastry, and Bill's great consideration for cooking up something entirely delectable. "Now *that's* a man's food," he complimented Bill. "Something fit to be *eaten.*"

At this point he remembered frying the bear steaks, and made the mistake of mentioning it. "Just think, Bill, You and me can set here and eat pie that rivals a chef's or a bakery's. And Joe and Clyde actually liking bear steaks. Ha-ha-ha!"

In his dry way, old Bill never cracked a smile. He asked, casually, "Where do you think I got the lard that made that flaky piecrust you liked so well?"

The fellow began turning green around the gills. "Wh— where?"

"That was bear lard." Old Bill could not resist finishing. "And where do you think Frank and me got the meat that went into that mincemeat?"

At this point, the poor man hastily unswallowed everything Bill had served him.

CHAPTER 5

Arrows, Pistols, and Slugs for Bear

No phase of American big-game hunting is blossoming with greater rapidity than the sport of archery hunting. The bow-and-arrow clan seem to have discovered the real answer to man's secret yearning to "play Injun;" and to have re-instilled into game hunting that elusive romance which has partly died during these last decades of dwindling game populations, increasing hunters, and sporting firearms developed to the point of long-range deadliness.

My friend Joe Foss, recent Governor of South Dakota and currently appointed as Commissioner of the new American Football League, is a good example of how a bow and arrow can boost the enthusiasm of a hunter overnight.

Foss has always hunted big game, loved it, and is an accomplished rifleman. Indeed, it was while on a big-game hunt for elk in Wyoming a couple of years ago that he told me about the archery incident.

A close friend of his, who manufactures a nationally-known line of archery equipment, knew of Joe's love of the high-powered rifle. But likely aware of what might take place, the bow maker simply gave the Governor a complete outfit, asking only that he give it a trial.

"That's the only reason I gave it a second thought," Governor Joe told me. "Just to please him. Fact was, I thought it was just kid's stuff. But the more I played with the dang thing, the more it intrigued me. So one day I took it into the Black Hills after deer. You know what?"

"What?"

"Hell, I went nuts over the thing. Not only that but Duke" (Colonel Duke Corning, head of South Dakota's Air National Guard, and Joe's hunting partner) "got the notion and started bow and arrow hunting. Now, the whole gang back home are nuts over it. They hunt deer and even took to hunting antelope with arrows. Our bunch practically forgot their rifles back there."

A similar thing abruptly took place in our locality a year ago. Rigby, Idaho, our little town, is situated in the Upper Snake River Valley, where the river debouches from the canyon and mountains on the high Wyoming-Idaho border. It is hunting country of the first order, most any direction. I have always maintained that within a matter of two gallons of gas from where I now sit, I can be in good hunting areas for deer, elk, moose, bear, antelope, and varmints from yodel dogs (coyotes) to rock chucks. With a car.

Quite naturally, hunting is *the* sport in the fall, and roughly one hundred and ten per cent of the population hereabouts annually hunt at least deer and elk.

Despite this, and the fact that everyone possesses guns, there is no organized pistol club; and the rifle club has a hard time, and always has, barely staying alive. You can count on the fingers of one hand all the local boys who do anything seriously about rifle shooting, other than to sight in, then whang away each autumn at game.

But about a year ago, a handful of bow enthusiasts organized themselves into a county-wide archery club. Currently, they have over fifty eager members in this small community, and these include the most rabid gun bugs. More, this wild-eyed bunch hastily acquired their own range—a sizable strip of cottonwood land along the river —set up target butts at the various ranges, cleared land, put up guest facilities, and held weekly meets all this summer.

These meets included competition shoots between themselves and regional clubs, with nice trophies (bought by the club itself) for each event. The shoots included standard bull's-eye targets, and also life-size game targets—all scored according to vital areas in each animal species.

These local eager beavers have an individual and a collective pride about it all not found in the rifle shooters. They sport a float in local parades, buy uniforms, approved Robin Hood tunics and hats for formal shooting, and stalk their game utilizing camouflaged clothes bought from army surplus, and like the Marines used in the late war. In short, they're all pepped up, do things strictly according to Hoyle, and, instead of having to promote enthusiasm, they find everyone boiling over with it.

On the other hand, seasoned riflemen in this same region barely do more than squint through Old Betsy, take a couple of practice shots, and are ready to take to the hills. Often, instead of the natty garb of the bowman, such fellows look like something the cat dragged in, while they hunt.

Having only been organized a year, this small club has had but one fall to hunt big game. However, they hunt jack rabbits, cotton-tails, ground squirrels, and rock chucks in off seasons with blunts; and predator birds with their regular hunting bows, and "flu-flu" arrows.

It is a significant comparison that last fall, while practically everyone lugged home a deer or elk, rifle-shot, and no one paid any attention, yet when Earl Hansen, president of the local bowmen, bagged his three-point buck with an arrow, he got considerable newspaper publicity. His picture in the paper, with the trusty bow and buck, started the red corpuscles flowing anew in all the he-men hereabouts; and everyone wanted to drop all work, head for the tall timber, and "play Injun" some more.

A similar thing happened to my friend Cliff Jensen, who

is just starting with the long bow, and belongs to another regional archery club. Cliff, too, got his deer last fall with an arrow. He also got interviews on the local TV station, similar newspaper publicity, and a lot of envy. His feat was the talk of the town.

Cliff drove twenty miles just to show me the mug picture of him-and-deer which he'd killed with the broadhead, and tell me about it. Previously, he'd hunted with a rifle all his life, and I've shot kegs of powder with him, through sniping rifles, at western chucks. Only last year did he get "bow-fever."

"In all my years of hunting," he beamed, "I've yet to get such a thrill. Even the long, patient stalking of that deer was a bigger thrill than with a rifle. With a gun, I'd not had to get so close. And, if he took off, I'd have plastered him anyway. But with this bow-and-arrow business I took all afternoon to get close enough. One movement, one sniff of me, one wrong action or bit of noise and *phooey!* But when I did get to forty yards or so, and let the arrow fly—brother, you don't know what a thrill, to see a hit!"

This is typical archer reaction. Tap any bowman and you find a person enthused with his sport. Become familiar with most any archery club, and you discover a group of eager beavers.

An incidental thrill to archery is that it appeals to the ladies. The wives of many confirmed bowmen are sold on the sport. In the case of Cliff Jensen, mentioned above, both his wife and his teen-aged daughter are able archers, and hunt with him.

Most archers bring more than enthusiasm and their club dues to the sport. Realizing the range limitations of their weapon for game hunting, they set earnestly about developing a personal skill as nearly as possible up to the outside capacity of their tool, the bow. Many ranges approximate the distances at which they'll later try for game. Many have stations in simulated big-game cover. Many clubs impose obstruction handicaps—fine conditioners for later shots at game.

But perhaps most important, archers *practice*. Many a rifle game hunter, unfortunately, doesn't. He assumes that, "If the gun's dead on, I'll hit 'im all right."

Basic archery equipment for hunting is the bow, hunting arrows, quiver, finger and wrist-guards, and whatever drab or camouflaging clothing the archer chooses, to help him stalk closely enough.

For many decades, the standard woods for bows were osage, yew, lemonwood, and Japanese bamboo. In America, the two most popular bow shapes have been a modified form of the English long bow, or the semi-long bow; and recurved bows, following the pattern of the early Turkish bows.

In the past decade, a step forward has been made in bow materials. Today, laminated and spun-glass bows are increasingly popular, not only for ease and uniformity of construction, but also for the near-perfection of their cast. An extremely popular bow today is a glass-bamboo laminated bow. Another is one built with a maple core, laminated with glass and/or bamboo.

The weight (pull in pounds) varies considerably, and must suit the bowman's physical strength and purpose. Broadly speaking, target bows have lightest weight. Hunting bows have medium weight. Bows meant specially for extreme distances, in competition shooting have greatest weight.

As regards archery, the hunting regulations vary with the different states and provinces, and are subject to continual changing. Some states set a limitation on the bow's weight, below which one may not be used for hunting. The minimum runs usually about 50 pounds. It is interesting to note in this connection that today's 40-pound hunting bows are so much improved that they often shoot with a greater cast than the 50-pound bows of five to ten years ago.

Hunting arrows, for big game, must be broadheads in most states having archery limitations, and a minimum of at least one inch in width. A good proportion for the hunting broadhead is a length at least three times the head's width. Broadheads are regularly filed razor-sharp, before being used in hunting.

Standard arrows for six-foot bows run approximately 28 inches in length, and are proportionately shortened to fit the dimensions of smaller bows. Most hunting arrows are straight of shaft, and feathered to a length slightly exceeding the length of the broadhead.

Archers hunting big game usually wear some form of drab clothing which won't advertise their presence to game. The green-mottled coveralls used in the Pacific during World War II have proven fine. Many bowmen use plain drab-colored clothes, which simulate the coloration of the foliage in which they expect to hunt, and various kinds of camouflage suits for hunting use are now commercially available.

Some archers complement the clothing with a similarly-colored bow sock, to eliminate sun glare on a highly-polished bow. I know of at least one hunter who, as a final touch, sprinkles himself with a liquid pine-scent before taking to the woods. This scent, he says, was developed and used by a wildlife photographer, who swore it killed body odor and allowed him to approach game far more closely than otherwise.

At first glance it would seem that archers using drab, nearly invisible clothing would be subject to a high hunting-casualty rate. This is quite contrary to facts. The American Rifleman, in its 1957-58 survey of all types of hunting accidents, and involving 36 states and two Canadian provinces, and 3240 separate hunting-accident reports, found this: Shotguns accounted for 59% of all hunting accidents, rifles were responsible for 36%, handguns 4%, and bow and arrows only 1%!

That's an enviable safety record.

Such a low accident rate is due largely to the fact that archers *must* approach game closely to get a decent shot. This proximity induces extreme hunting care, intense observation, and exceptional object identification—all before the arrow is released. Such care and caution reduce accidents in any field.

Black bear are medium-sized big game. And since their habitat often coincides with the ranges of deer, bears are often hunted with the same weapons. And, with the growing popularity of archery, it is but natural that the black bear is going to be hunted with broadheads.

How adequate is the bow and arrow for bears?

To answer this, consideration must be given both to the weapon itself, and to the user.

Broadly speaking, today's modern high-powered bullet kills by nerve and tissue destruction, by a secondary hy-

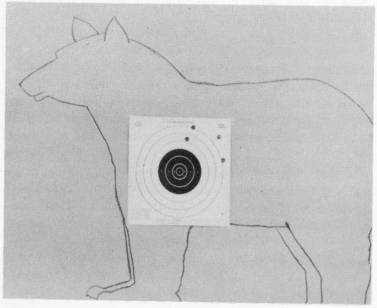

Typical bow-and-arrow group of four releases, at 40 yards, on life-size black bear target.

draulic destruction (often forcing bones and tissue through other tissue and skin), and by shock.

A razor-sharp broadhead arrow, on the other hand, imparts little knock-down power, little shock, and relatively very little tissue destruction. An arrow-shot beast, unless hit in the unlikely areas of the brain and spinal cord, is going to die largely of hemorrhage. This is at best a slow and painful death. If the shaft entirely pierces and traverses the body cavity, few large blood vessels are severed. If the broadhead stays within the body after the shot, and is within the heart-lungs area, then additional cutting of blood vessels is done through the beast's action as it races away wounded. This often speeds up the bleeding-out, dying process.

A deer, lung-shot with an arrow, will usually run from fifty to a hundred yards before piling up. Poorer arrow placement will prolong both the time and this distance, before the weakened animal drops. I know of one spike mule deer buck, shot through the lungs, which ran seventy paced yards. A larger buck, in which the arrow hit just ahead of the flank, penetrated the lungs, went out through the opposite shoulder, and never was found in heavy brush—this one made it sixty yards and lay down. Earl Hansen, mentioned before, killed an elk with his bow and arrow. The wapiti (roughly three times as large as a muley) took two arrows, one broadside, the other after it had lain down and was closely approached.

A black bear is intrinsically a more difficult woods-target than a deer or elk. First, a bear is a woods-animal, wanders mostly in relatively thick foliage, and, with a normal height of just over two feet, is more apt to be partially concealed by ground foliage than the higher-legged animals. Most any foliage will deflect an arrow to the extent of either a miss, or a slanting shot into an undesirable body area. A peculiarity of an arrow in flight is its tendency to "yaw." Often even after the head has successfully missed intervening branches or foliage, the feathered shaft will, because of yaw, hit at the arrow's tail end, causing the shaft to glance off at an oblique angle.

Another deceiving thing about bear is the heavy coat of hair they wear over the vital areas. This flowing crop of hair, especially in a moving bear, makes the under-lying vital areas often "look where they ain't." Again, a slow-moving, or standing bear, often is a rooting, sniffing, or eating bear. In this position, he's bunched up in a length-wise dimension, making the placement of any arrow into the vitals difficult in such a heads-down posture. Lastly, a black bear, fat in the fall against approaching hiberna-tion, is tough to penetrate with an arrow. The arrow head must go through a tough hide, matted hair, a thick layer of pulpy fat, and still get into, or through, the heart-lungs area.

From all these factors, a conclusion is not hard to reach. Any hunter owes any game he pursues a swift and certain death. He further owes it to the game, regardless of the hunting difficulty or scarcity of opportunities to shoot, to eternally refrain from shooting unless and until he's reason-ably sure of a clean kill.

These ethics should be adopted by *any* hunter regardless of how he hunts, where, what species, or with what weapon. With such a sporting code, and a full realization of the individual's own limitations, the actual weapon becomes a secondary consideration. In instances where an arrow will surely kill, it becomes ethical to use one. In instances where to shoot would be only to wound, and the hunter is aware of it, then he is ethically unfitted to be in the woods, if he chances it.

Getting back to this fellow Hansen, I can offer a con-crete example of just what is meant. Earl has hunted big game for five years now—for four years before forming the local archery club. In those five years he has meticulously turned down *all* shots at game through foliage where the outcome was probable, and at any range over fifty yards— which he considers the "safe" usable range for big game, for the average archer. Last year, he turned down a shot at a bull elk at 20 yards, along Canyon Creek in eastern Idaho, because the bull happened to be standing in brush too heavy for certain arrow penetration.

In the five years, Hansen has had just four chances, within the self-imposed range of 50 yards, in the open, at game. In those four optimum opportunities, he has released just five arrows, and killed all four head of game. The elk, as mentioned, required a finisher.

How accurate must an archer be, to do this?

Last July I asked Hansen to shoot me a group of four released arrows, at a target set up at the measured forty-yard range. After "tuning up," Earl placed the four arrows in a group measuring exactly 6 inches. The group center lay at one o'clock above the 6-inch bull's-eye, a distance of just 5 inches.

The same afternoon I shot a 5-shot group with a .38 Special Smith & Wesson revolver, offhand, and at the same range of 40 yards. This group clusters around the bull and measures 7½ inches.

Hansen is an average bowman. I'm just a run-of-the-mill revolver shot. The accuracy factor as between a bow and a pistol would appear to be broadly comparable. And, considering the square of vital area on a black bear, the "boiler-room," to be roughly twelve inches each way, such accuracy would place both the bow and the revolver as adequate up to an outside range of fifty yards, so far as the probability of a certain hit is concerned.

This brings up the increasingly controversial question of the suitability of a revolver for game shooting. This discussion will be limited to the use of a handgun on bears.

Until recently, the use of a revolver or pistol on any kind of big game has been increasingly frowned upon. Over the years of field experience it has been collectively found that the average run-of-the-mill hunter couldn't hit the broad side of a country back-house with a handgun; and that the net result, those rare times he did, was little more than game crippling.

Because of these facts, plus the necessary game-conservation restrictions brought on by a dwindling game supply matched against a mushrooming army of hunters, the use of a revolver on game was legislated against in many areas. In other states, the trend was in that direction. Despite the occasional publicized report of a big game animal being taken with the sixgun, the whole procedure was regarded largely as a stunt. This was increasingly true since in these instances a rifle was often handy, by another hunter, to "back up" the revolver man if he missed.

Personally, I love the revolver and any handgun as much as the next man. It is an appealing, romantic piece of equipment that will never cease to intrigue the red-blooded. But like others, I was convinced that it had no real place in the big-game hunting fields, other than as a substitute.

Five revolver shots at 40 yards, on life-size black bear target.

The recent development of two higher-powered revolvers, whose cartridges approach the ballistics of high-powered rifles, has altered the thinking of many shooters. It has partially stopped the trend to prohibit the handgun from *any* kind of game shooting—at least to the extent that currently at least one state allows the use of a handgun on deer—and it has added a burst of new fuel to the handgun-game controversy.

These two new high-powered revolvers are, of course, the .357 Magnum and the newer, more powerful .44 Magnum. This last cartridge is, with the exception of a few experimental hand-cannons, the "most powerful revolver cartridge."

Let's see what each will do, both practically and in theory.

The .357 Magnum cartridge, in a 6-inch barrel, will send a 158-grain bullet at a muzzle velocity of 1450 foot-seconds, with a muzzle energy of 690 foot-pounds.

The more potent .44 Magnum will shoot a 240-grain bullet at 1570 foot-seconds muzzle velocity, with a muzzle energy of 1314 foot-pounds.

Energy-wise, this makes the .357 Magnum cartridge almost identical with the old Winchester .25-20 rifle cartridge. And, as to energy, the .44 Magnum revolver cartridge is just under the energy of the Winchester .25-35 rifle cartridge, shooting the 117-grain bullet.

In our consideration here of the use of a cartridge on black bear, the question immediately arises, "Is the .25-20, or the .25-35 rifle adequate for black bear?"

Like the question, "Have you stopped beating your wife?," this is difficult to answer with a simple yes or no. Here are some additional factors, not seen on the ballistics tables.

To begin, the above figures are *muzzle* energies and velocities—not necessarily out where the game is. Revolver game is, *per se*, short-range game, or always should be. Under comparable hunting conditions, the hunter is habitually apt to try shots at longer range with the rifle, simply because he has a far better accuracy factor with it. The rifle has a longer sighting radius. The user has a three-point anchorage upon it—hand on forearm, hand on grip, and shoulder on the butt—not a single point of hold at the grip.

Under this condition, the punch of the revolver bullet is apt to be more, simply because it has more remaining oomph where it connects with the game. This, because of a very short range.

Again, both the .357 Magnum and the .44 Magnum have far greater bullet diameters than puny rifle cartridges like the .25-20 or the .25-35. And, other factors being equal, the larger a bullet's diameter, the greater its shocking power and tissue destruction.

Also, the handgun has a handiness factor. It is usually faster for a good revolver man to draw a handgun from a holster and aim, than to get a rifle from its scabbard and aim. Or even from its carrying position over a shoulder, on a sling, while foot hunting. This, too, tends to utilize the cartridge's power before it has lost so much.

Lastly, the handgun has five or six cartridges for instant use as against ordinarily fewer in the rifle (if it's bolt action).

On the opposite side of the fence, the handgun has many shortcomings. It has a short barrel, necessitating a brief sighting radius. It has, in typical cowboy-western off-hand position, but one point of suspension. Because of its relatively low velocity, the revolver bullet has a high trajectory arc. Because of its exaggerated diameter-to-length bullets in such large calibers, the initial velocities rapidly fall off, once out of the barrel.

But perhaps the biggest drawback to the revolver's use on game lies in the shooter himself. Briefly, it takes a whale of a lot more practice with a handgun to attain, and retain the ability to shoot accurately, than it does with a rifle. I know many rifle hunters who can lay off an entire year, then still lay their first shot well into the target the first time they fire, the next fall. This is especially true if they utilize some good field-shooting position such as sitting or prone.

Conversely, the man who lays off a whole year with a revolver simply loses much of his muscular co-ordination. It's axiomatic that to be a good pistol shot, one must practice continuously. The average hunter, who practices occasionally with a handgun, and who can regularly shoot five shots off-hand into a nine-inch ring at forty yards, is a pretty fair handgun shot. That's a one-to-three ratio of accuracy as compared to what a good rifleman can do, off-hand.

There are ways of stepping up this accuracy factor. First, the handgun man who wants to do accurate shooting informally, or at possible game, should forget the off-hand position whenever possible. A position with the master hand holding the grip, and the other hand gripping either the opposite wrist, or wrapped around the fingers, is far steadier. Too, it takes no longer to assume.

An even steadier game or field-shooting position is this same two-handed grip, but while sitting and with the elbows tightly held inside the upraised knees. Again, by holding the gun over a branch, against a tree bole, or upon any solid object (always with some form of cushioning between, such as a cap, coat-sleeve, or the hand—otherwise the gun will shoot away from the solid object), a far steadier aim can easily be achieved.

As a sample of this, I was recently testing a Ruger Single-Six pistol, with the new .22 Winchester Magnum Rimfire cartridge. To ascertain the accuracy-potential at 100 yards, I used the bench rest. The pistol was held in the padded, foam-rubber notch just under the front sight, with both hands firmly holding the grip, and placed upon a wool-padded "bean-bag," with elbows solidly upon the table.

One five-shot group ran just 5½ inches, center-to-center of the bullet holes. That's exceptional for my eyesight and rather mediocre ability with a handgun. It does indicate that the handgun is far more accurate than the skill of any shooter.

The growing clan of pistol shooters present valid arguments for the use of their pet weapon on game. Most serious revolvers shooters admit the limitations of the handgun on game. But they point out, with basic common sense, that an adequate revolver is as accurate as the bow and arrow; that death of an animal by a bullet is far more humane than hemorrhage death by a broadhead; and that if the same degree of caution, stalking skill, shooting ability, practice, and sportsmanship which the archers use is applied, the results will be comparable or greater.

This is true. The real danger in advocating the use of any pistol on game is that through lack of skill, imagination, or poor judgment, a lot of hunters would surely misuse such a weapon. They'd try 100-yard shots at game, and farther. They'd assume (from today's TV and literature conditioning) that to start throwing lead would make up for a lack of personal skill; and they'd surely kill their game through the law of averages. More, they wouldn't practice the amount necessary to acquire any degree of accuracy; and because of the necessary severity of recoil of such handguns as the .357 and the .44 Magnums, they'd drop to even less adequate cartridges.

In answer to all this, the handgunners who today are clamoring for its legal use on game come right back with the nearly unanswerable question: "Why permit archery on game, then? The handicaps and sportsmanship involved are largely the same identical thing."

To prove the point and strengthen their position, the handgun clan are going to extreme lengths to make the short gun more effective on game. Some are removing the short barrels from the larger handguns and replacing them with 12-inch and longer barrels—this, to increase sighting radius, weight (for steadiness), and to gain more velocity.

Others equip the .357 and the .44 Magnums with scopes,

for a better sight picture, more accurate sighting-in, and an added safety factor as regards object identification. Even muzzle brakes are being installed, to cut down recoil.

With such tuned-up versions of Sam Colt's gun, an occasional head of really big big-game is being taken in areas permitting the handgun's use. Several head of elk have now been killed with different .44 Magnums in Idaho. There is one recorded instance of an Alaska Brown bear being killed with a worked-over .44 Magnum. This revolver sported a 12-inch barrel, sighting rib, muzzle brake, and a lanyard attached to the grip and held against the shoulder *a la* rifle sling.

It is interesting in this instance, as in similar encounters, that a really high-powered rifle (in the above case a .300 H&H Magnum) was used and *recommended* as a "backing-up" weapon.

Those who oppose the handgun's use on game say, with considerable point, "So long as *any* weapon must depend upon another weapon to get it out of a jam, then it is not adequate for the job at hand."

There are many occasions when a heavy revolver would seem the ideal weapon for that occasional black bear. Packers, outfitters. guides, ranchers, and other outdoorsmen such as wildlife photographers who must limit weight and yet have an emergency weapon, all find a heavy-caliber revolver mighty useful. A black bear, often as not, will be found just around that bend in the trail, or invading the camp when the owner returns. Indeed, Les Bowman once shot such a pest black bear after he'd opened the tent-flap at his Cut Coulee camp, and met the beast *inside!*

An adequate pistol in such cases, and at such short range, will fill the bill if the owner can shoot it well. It carries easier than a rifle, and many a Westerner who spends much time in the mountains would feel as naked without his six-shooter as without his levi breeches.

The question of a handgun's use on any game all boils down, basically, to the sporting ethics of the man using it. If a hunter loves the handgun, practices enough to become proficient, realizes the short gun's limitations and *abides* by them—limiting himself to an outside range of sixty or seventy yards even with the .357 or .44 Magnum, and religiously turns down all chancy shots and everything beyond this self-imposed limit—then the .357 and .44 Magnums would prove more reliable on black bear than even an adequate rifle in the hands of a greenhorn, bang-bang type of hunter.

One thing may alter the revolver-game controversy to a great extent in the near future. That's the constant experimentation in the hope of making the handgun even more powerful.

As this is being written, two Utah handgunners have just come up with an experimental, hand-made revolver which is more powerful than the factory .44 Magnum. They call this the .454 Magnum. Their early efforts were concentrated on the Single-Action Colt .45, and consisted of two basic changes—a new barrel, and a cylinder drilled for only five cartridges instead of the six. This was to withstand the added pressures.

Briefly, the finished .454 Magnum revolver has a built-in recoil compensator, weighs but two ounces more than a standard .44 Magnum, but will drive a 230-grain bullet at over 2,000 feet per second!

If and when handguns of that potential become popular and available—along with shooters who can really shoot them—then the revolver-game picture is bound to change.

This brings us to those states which currently prohibit the use of either a revolver or a rifle on deer. In these states the hunter must use a shotgun. And since the "incidental" black bear is just as apt to be run into on a deer hunt as on a bear hunt, this brings up the shotgun's efficiency on black bear, with buckshot and/or rifled shotgun slugs.

Briefly, I do not consider buckshot loads either sporting or adequate for black bear under the hunting conditions which such an animal is apt to be shot.

To begin, let's see just how formidable the standard 12-gauge shotgun is, with the heaviest loadings of Number 0 and Number 00 buckshot.

The pellets of Number 0 buckshot measure .32-caliber. They weigh 48 grains each, with twelve pellets to the load. Assuming a muzzle velocity of 1200 foot-seconds, this gives each pellet a muzzle energy of just under 160 foot-pounds energy. Due to the round shape, velocity falls off faster than with a bullet having greater length and sectional density. Energy, too, falls off correspondingly.

The initial energy of one such pellet is approximately that of a .32-caliber automatic pistol cartridge.

The puny .32 auto pistol would hardly be classed as a "bear gun." One old-timer of my acquaintance summed it up pretty well, as he regarded the .32 pistol a greenhorn hunter carried in the Island Park country as, "an emergency gun, if my rifle fails or jams and I meet a bear."

"Son," the grizzled oldster said, "if you was to meet a bear with that squirt gun, you might jist as well have it loaded with a bucket of swill. If you was to shoot the sonofabitch with that thing, and he ever found *out* about it, he'd sure git mighty mad!"

Even the larger-size buckshot are relatively inadequate. In the standard 12-gauge loading, there are nine Number 00 pellets. Each weighs 54 grains, and is of .33 caliber. Assuming the above velocity, each grain has but 175 foot-pounds of energy at the muzzle. This is comparable to the power of the .38 Smith & Wesson revolver cartridge, not the .38 Special.

"But if you hit a black bear with a lot of 'em," the novice asks, "wouldn't that be enough?"

Let's see.

Recently I've been testing a lot of such loads, for both accuracy and penetration. This testing has been done both on life-size game targets, and on squares of heavy cardboard measuring 18 x 18 inches.

These sheets represent the vital area, or "boiler-room"—

from withers to belly line, and from brisket to rear of rib-cage—on mule deer and similar game. This vital area is far smaller on black bear, once the shaggy hide is peeled off. Ranges varied, but most of the groups were fired at 40 measured yards.

Sample targets are indicative:

Number 1 was shot with a 12-gauge Browning automatic shotgun, at 40 yards, full choke, and using #0 Buckshot. Of the 12 pellets, four hit the 18-inch target. Two pellets hit within 2 inches of each other, the others measure 8 and 13 inches apart. Penetration was ¾-inch into the heart wood of the red-pine planking of the back-stop.

Number 2 target was fired at 40 yards, using a 12-gauge, Winchester Magnum Duck Gun, full choke. The load was #0 Buckshot, 12 pellets to the load. Four of these also hit the 18-inch size of paper. The two closest together measured 1½ inches apart. The greatest dispersion was 15 inches. Penetration was ¾-inch.

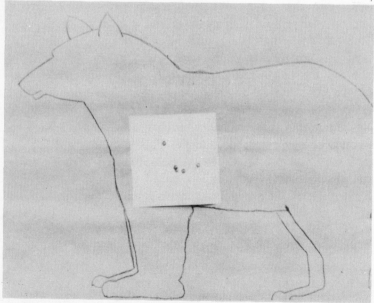

Average group of rifled slugs from 20-gauge, full-choke barrel, at 50 yards, on life-size target.

Target Number 3 was shot with the Browning auto, 12-gauge, full choke, at 40 yards, using #00 Buckshot, nine pellets per load. Two of the nine pellets hit the 18-inch paper, with a dispersion of just 6 inches. Penetration was 1½ inches in heart wood, and the pellet which struck the outer "sap" wood went all the way through the 2-inch pine planking.

Target Number 4 was shot using the 12-gauge Duck Gun, full choke, at 40 yards, and using #00 Buckshot, nine pellets per load. Four of these struck the 18-inch square of target. The two closest together measured 3 inches apart, with the greatest shot dispersion 14 inches. It was interesting to note that penetration here was identical with target Number 3.

Shotgun borings are individualistic and, as in violin making, one never knows during manufacture the results he'll get. Certain borings and chokes of shotguns will handle buckshot far better than others. However, the above results are average for numerous rounds fired, and are generally about what average shotguns of the same gauge will do with buckshot.

It has long been assumed that the cartridge ideal for deer will also be suitable for black bear. My experience has been that a better cartridge for black bear is one just a "notch" above the power considered sufficient for deer—this for reasons hinging upon hunting conditions and which we'll get to later.

But even on the basis above, these experiments convince me that buckshot, even for that occasional chance at Blackie, should never be considered. Buckshot loads are crippling loads. For deer they should never be used at ranges over forty yards, and not then if a substitute load can be used. For black bear such a load is unethical. Buckshot pellets have not the penetration, the energy, or the expansion to kill cleanly on bear.

There *is*, however, a shotgun load which is a nag of a different hue—a real killer up to the short range of 100 yards, and for which it is intended. That's the modern rifled shotgun slug.

The early shotgun slugs were nothing more than round lead balls. I have on the desk before me some of these, purchased nearly thirty years ago. They are called Peters No. 12 Target.

The spherical lead balls in these loads weigh just a strong ounce each. The ball is set between two open-ended hair-felt wads, with just sufficient aperture in each wad to make the ball seat solidly. No data is given on the powder charge, but these early "slugs" are loaded into low-base paper shells. The lead ball will rattle loosely all the way up the barrels of both my Browning auto 12-gauge, and my Model 12 Winchester pump; and slips easily into the bore from the full-choke muzzle of each.

Because of the solid nature of the ball, with no provisions made for swaging, or "giving" in any way, this looseness was necessary. Otherwise, the barrel of a tight full-choke would have been split, or the choke shot out—a mental hazard to those who used these first shotgun solids.

This type of slug would not give better than around 10-inch accuracy at fifty yards, and represented a truly "emergency" load, emergency here meaning the shooter could get nothing else.

Today's shotgun slugs are not balls, but rifled missiles. The forward end of the lead slug carries the most of the mass. The rear portion is hollow, allowing it to sail head-on in flight quite like an arrow. In all modern slugs, some provision is made for spinning the projectile though being fired from a smooth, unrifled bore. Generally, this is accomplished by rifling the rear portion of the slug itself with wide spiral grooves.

Upon being fired, the rear portion of the lead "shell" swages to fit the individual tube, sealing off gases and achieving a considerable velocity for so large a missile. At the same time, friction from this swaged and rifled slug causes the missile to turn in the barrel, and later in the air, inducing a remarkable accuracy. They will work in any degree of choke without any possibility of shooting it out. Since these modern slugs are loaded to maximum, only shotguns in good shape, and *not* of Damascus twist, should be used.

A look at the paper ballistics will convince anyone of their innate potency. Here are Winchester's figures for their Super-X Rifled Slugs:

Gauge	Range	Velocity	Energy
12	0	1600	2480
12	25 yards	1370	1825
12	50 yards	1185	1365
12	100 yards	960	895
16	0	1600	2170
16	25 yards	1400	1665
16	50 yards	1235	1300
16	100 yards	1010	870
20	0	1600	1560
20	25 yards	1360	1125
20	50 yards	1165	830
20	100 yards	940	535
410	0	1630	650
410	50 yards	1185	270
410	100 yards	890	155

In these loads, the 12-gauge slug weighs 437 grains. The 16-gauge slug weighs 382 grains. The 20-gauge slug weighs 273 grains. And the 410-gauge slug weighs but 87 grains.

The ballistics for Remington Rifled Slugs are comparable.

As to wallop, a quick look at these figures will show that the 12-gauge slug at the muzzle has approximately the energy of the .300 Savage, the .30-40 Krag, or the 7x57 Mauser rifle. And while it is true that velocity falls off fast with such a blunt shape of missile, it's equally true that, other factors being equal, the larger diameter will make up, at reasonable range, for this in killing power.

As to the use of rifled slugs on black bear, it may safely be said that at all ranges up to 100 yards, the 12-gauge, the 16-gauge, and the 20-gauge slugs may be considered adequate. The puny 410-gauge slug should never be used on any kind of big game, in my estimation. The energy of this slug at 100 yards is just about the exact amount of "soup" a .22 rim-fire cartridge has at the muzzle.

In an effort to learn both the accuracy and penetration of these modern slugs, I made some extensive tests this past summer. Two guns were used, a Model 24 Winchester 20-gauge double-barrel, and a Winchester Model 12 Duck Gun chambered for the 3-inch magnum shells, but used with the standard 2¾-inch-length slug shells.

Both were standard factory guns, with no sights other than the front bead on the Model 12, and the low matted rib between the barrels, and the end bead, on the double.

For accuracy tests, a bench rest was used at ranges of 40, 50, and 100 yards. Here are some typical results:

#1 Target. 20-gauge, full-choke barrel, 40 yards, 5 shots, 3½ inches center to center.

#2 Target. 20-gauge, 5 shots, 50 yards, full-choke barrel, 5⅜ inches.

#3 Target. 20-gauge, 5 shots, 100 yards, full-choke, 6 inches, center to center. The interesting thing here was that the apparent drop in elevation, as between 50 and 100 yards, was only a bit over 2 inches, as nearly as could be told with such crude sights.

#4 Target. 20-gauge, 4 shots, 40 yards, modified-choke barrel, 2¼-inch group, center to center. Two of the four slugs cut the same hole! I quit at 4 shots on this target, not wishing to spoil such a tight group with a flyer.

Briefly, 5-shot groups using either gun, and either barrel of the double, ran around 5 inches per fifty yards, with a similar angle of dispersion for other ranges.

It is interesting to note that both Remington and Ithaca, in order to take advantage of such intrinsic accuracy in a shotgun, have now marketed shotgun barrels especially for the use of rifled slugs. The hunter can buy either the separate barrel and install it on his gun, or get the entire gun with integral barrel. These barrels have open sights on them, similar to those on a rifle. And, of course, with sighting arrangements like that, the above accuracy can be improved upon.

As an example, Ithaca claims 9-inch accuracy at 100 yards, and regular 2-inch groups at 40 yards with their new slug shotgun. Remington's gun will likely match this performance.

The tests for wallop and penetration were equally revealing.

First, both gauges were tested on the heart wood of red pine planking, seasoned several years until tough and dry. At 40 yards both sizes of slugs hummed through this 2-inch thickness, tearing out sizable craters on exit. The rib cage, or shoulder of a black bear would have been less tough, and destruction would have been terrific inside, in the light of this.

Next, 1-inch-thick red pine boards, partially seasoned, were stacked tightly together against the back-stop, and fired into. Slugs from the 20-gauge at 40 yards penetrated an average of five boards. The holes in these boards increased in diameter as the slug expanded. In the first board, the hole was slug sized. In the fifth board, the holes varied from the size of a quarter dollar to that of a fifty-cent piece.

Mushrooming was consistent in all cases, with no part of the slug shed. The 20-gauge slugs expanded to an average of .75 caliber.

The 12-gauge slugs similarly penetrated an average of five of these tough one-inch boards. The channel, or "wound" left by the larger slug was noticeably bigger. The 12-gauge slugs expanded to an average size of .875 inches, or .87 caliber.

The final test was a tough one for any missile. From a local lumber yard, I sorted out the tough butt stock of red pine trees, which had been sawed into blocks measuring 4 inches thick. I chose only straight-grained wood, not conducive to splitting. These blocks were center shot, from a solid sitting position. The "smack," as the slugs tore into these, could be heard a half-mile.

Briefly, the 20-gauge slugs penetrated an average of 2½ inches. The 12-gauge slugs penetrated just an inch more, 3½ inches. In all cases the 12-gauge slugs tended to cause more wood-fiber pulping, splitting, and overall destruction.

I ended these tests with the definite feeling that the rifled shotgun slug, in any gauge from 20-gauge to 12-gauge, is a powerful knock-down "bullet," when limited to its intended range of 100 yards and under. I'd have no hesitancy in using it for black bear in those areas restricted to the use of a shotgun on big game. A few such loads, carried while bird-hunting and when bear are legally in season, may easily mean the difference between a bear rug, and a bare floor.

Regardless of the sporting method by which Blackie is taken, he's always a challenge. I know of one instance, even, where the greatest thrill, and the most intensive danger occurred *after* the lucky hunter had bagged his bruin.

This was years ago, on the North Fork of the Buffalo River in western Wyoming. An old mountain man had hunted for his supply of black-bear lard all fall without success. However, knowing the uncertain nature of any type of bear hunting, and that church is never over until you finish the singing, this hardy fellow kept at it. At the time he actually had his chance, there was six inches of snow on the ground, the weather was cold as the left nostril of a hound dog, and all bears were about to go into hibernation.

As was the custom of many a mountain man, this fellow hadn't shaved all summer. His beard, at the time, was long as a polygamist's clothesline, and possibly even offered him some insulation against the now bitter weather.

This character was hunting near the Enos Lake section at the time he killed his bear. It happened just at dusk, with only a few minutes of light left. He'd tracked bruin to the edge of the lake.

Kindling a fire for warmth, he began dressing and peeling his shortening supply. At this season, bruin was fat as butter. I once skinned a black bear I'd killed in Idaho at a similar season; and when the knife was lifted, the bear oil would literally drip off the blade, just like thin motor oil.

This man's bear was similarly fat. As he'd hastily skin and cut, he'd wipe his cold hands free of oil, on his beard— probably it being the warmest, most absorbent thing handy.

Anyway at one stage of the process, he leaned over too close to the fire. As might have been expected, the fat on his beard caught fire, and took off quite like coal-oil.

So did he. With a yell that would have woke Jim Bridger, he dropped the knife, raced to the cliff, and dove over into the icy water of Enos Lake!

CHAPTER 6

Hunting Blackie With Dogs

As the status of the bear changed from pest to that of sporting quarry, so has the overall sportsmanship involved in hunting him been gradually elevated. Today there are methods considered highly ethical by the lay sportsman, and some which are viewed with prejudice among certain groups.

One way of hunting bear which remains criticized is the hunting of this species with dogs. As with anything else, often those who criticize the most are those who know least about the practice.

Hunting bear with dogs is based on bruin's fundamental dislike of the sight, sound, or smell of any dog. Size, so long as bruin has an escape route open, has little to do with it; and in most any normal contact with a dog, a bear may be expected to run.

One instance illustrates this.

A lady school teacher friend of ours once took her tiny terrier to Yellowstone Park. Restrictions at the time necessitated her keeping the dog on leash, and in that early day camping out was the practice of most tourists.

As the lady and her husband ate supper at a rustic table, a great black bear moseyed out of the timber, casually heading their way. The big bruin was, no doubt, conditioned to tourists, and his current intent was the food on that table.

When bruin had approached within a matter of feet, his moist nose twitching and his hulk becoming too noticeable, the man, with great courage said, "If there's anything he wants here, he's entirely welcome." Grabbing the hand of his wife, he left for anywhere else, and with great alacrity.

The tiny dog, at the other end of the leash, had been lying at his mistress' feet, engaged in the pastime of gulping any tid-bit she handed down.

By the time man and wife had departed, the puny urbanized little dog saw, or smelled, the bear. With a peppery yap, which, to a bear must sound as grating as it does to some humans, the toy dog went after the great bruin. In his first rush, he jerked the leash loose from the lady's hand, and the battle was on.

"Oh, my poor darling Bosco," the lady wailed, "he'll be et up by that big savage brute! *Do* something!"

The husband stopped, paralyzed by the indecision as to which was the greater evil, to be eaten himself or to have Bosco consumed.

However, the situation abruptly solved itself, as others, more used to wild bears, might have anticipated. At Bosco's rasping yap, and first optimistic rush, the three-hundred-pound bruin switched ends and took off for the tall timber, ingloriously.

To the delight of several spectators, and the husband who followed gingerly, the small dog was found a few rods beyond, at the foot of a pine tree. The bear was perched fifteen feet up, hanging on for dear life, and scared half out of his wits.

Hunting bear with dogs today is not practiced to capitalize on bruin's fear of a canine, but, rather, to take advantage of the fact in order to give the hunter a sporting chance for a shot. In short, this form of hunting is done in areas of thick brush, swamp land, broken rough country where the hunter's chances at finding or flushing out a bear are next to nil; and where the use of dogs brings his advantage up to something of a sporting level. Specifically, dogs are used on bear in the South, the Southwest, the Tellico Plains and Great Smoky Mountains of Tennessee, and similar regions.

As with any other hunting, certain breeds of dogs have proven best. In past years, such dogs as the Black-and-Tan coonhound, bloodhound, and Airedale have been used successfully. One dog man I know insists on one-eighth part bloodhound in his dogs, for cold trails, and "some" Airedale for this breed's fearlessness in a fight. Other dog owners like mixtures of several breeds, in an effort to bring out certain characteristics necessary to the chase. Often a dog of most democratic ancestry proves to be one of the best dogs in a pack.

But, as with other forms of specialized hunting, one breed is rapidly gaining the lead for use on bear. That's the Plott hound.

Briefly, this hound was brought from Germany back in the middle of the eighteenth century by a man named Jonathan Plott. These dogs had been bred for courage, strength, and stamina in a long chase. The breed was originally thought to have been used in leopard hunting.

Plott settled in North Carolina, and discovered that his hounds were almost ideal for hunting the black bears in that region and the adjacent Great Smokies. The fellow was a canny breeder and kept his secrets of developing the strain to himself. One basic procedure with Plott hounds, down through the years, has been to destroy those dogs of any litter which didn't measure up to the original high standard—not sell them for "overhead," and cause the strain to be eventually diluted. Claims are that the original strain of Plott hounds has never been allowed to cross with other breeds.

The Plott hound is a big fellow, heavy of head, pleasant of disposition, and most intelligent. More, so far as bear-hunting is concerned, he is almost indefatigable on the chase, and courageous in a fight.

My outfitter friend, Glen Rice of Whitebird, Idaho, has a Plott hound which is a good example of the breed. This dog weighs nearly sixty pounds, is a beautiful, slick, dark brown animal, and is three years old. On a recent field trip into strange country, Glen said to the dog as we approached the cabin, "You can't come in. This place here on the grass is yours." Thereafter, any time we wanted to find the dog, we simply went to the spot where his owner had told him to be, and the hound was there.

"Intelligent and obedient," I offered. "Isn't he?"

"Yes and no," Rice answered. "He's fine except when it comes to deer. I use him on cougar, and he knows better than to chase deer. But here's how he works it. I'll be going along a trail, with him following at my heels. Maybe ten times in good deer country. Then, one time, I'll happen to look back and he ain't there. He's stood temptation as long as he can, then, quiet as a mouse, he'd start falling behind me. The minute I was out of sight he'd take off like a bat out of hell on a deer track.

"When he'd come back, he knew he was in for a walloping with the rolled newspaper. He'd lay down and beller like a baby, but just as if he was saying, 'I can't help it, boss. So lay it on'."

In the Great Smokies and Cherokee National Forest of Tennessee, where the Plott hound has made his reputation, he is used on both bear and wild boars. There, the bears are hunted in conjunction with boars, just as bears are hunted in the West in conjunction with elk, deer, and moose.

Parties of hunters are made up in advance, and are usually placed on stands or run-ways. Packs of dogs run from five to ten, and are turned loose after the hunters are situated. When a trail is struck, the course of the quarry is marked from the baying of the dogs; and, of course, the object of the hunter is to intercept the beast fleeing ahead of the dogs. Often in the Tellico Plains area, the hunter doesn't know whether he's going to see a wild boar or a bear. Often on a single hunt, both species are taken.

My friend, John Phillips, tells of one hunt with a noted outfitter of that region, which is a fine illustration of what the hunter might expect.

"It was rough country, where we hunted," John told me. "All choked up with a heavy growth of mountain laurel and rhododendron. It was too heavy foliage for horses, and all of us either walked, or were placed on stands.

"I wanted a bear mainly, but also was interested in boars. The dogs our outfitter used were Plotts, a couple of Blue Ticks, and some Airedales. They looked gaunt and hungry as hell to me, but the outfitter said they always kept bear dogs hungry so they'd hunt. And did I find this out!

"Anyway, I got separated a little from the others, on the side of a ridge where there was a small opening. So I laid down my lunch and stood around, waiting for the sound of the hounds running something.

"Suddenly, I heard them bellering like they were hot on the tail of something, and coming my way. Sure enough, in a few minutes, out of the laurel and rhododendron busted a boar on a dead run. They hadn't cornered him yet, and he was sure getting out of there.

"I cut loose with the rifle and was lucky. I rolled him over, and had myself my first wild boar! Then you know what happened?"

"What?"

"Well, it seems that those hungry hounds thought the fun had just begun. Then ran up to that hog, before I could even get there, and started chawin' on him. Not killing him, mind you, but *eating* him. Before I could get them beat off, they had his testicles chewed off, and tail, and was eating on his flanks.

"I had to kick and knock hell out of them to get them off, and so's there'd be any hog left for *me*. And then, before I knew what was going on, two of them lank, lean, and hungry bastards had snuck over and licked up all my lunch!"

Blackie will either sit down or climb a tree when faced with the realization that there is no other escape from trailing dogs.

One of the biggest difficulties in training dogs for use on bear is breaking them of the desire, or habit, of chasing deer. It is aggravating, to say the least, to have a party hunting in good bear country; to have the standers all keyed up to the excitement and course of the chase; then discover that the hounds are pursuing venison instead of rugs.

This single fact has been responsible for making the use of dogs on any game illegal, in many areas.

The rifles and ammunition used in this form of sport differ a bit from the rifles needed in more open-country shooting. In general, the rifle-and-cartridge should be one which is handy to use, quick in action, and capable of considerable knock-down power at close ranges. Shots at coursed bear usually are close, and "on the fly." Any time for assuming a prone position, tightening a sling, and precision shooting "fine and fur off" simply doesn't exist. It's quick off-hand shooting, and usually one shot is all the lucky hunter gets as the bear runs by.

For these reasons lever-action, slide-action, and even automatic rifles, where permitted, are popular. Cartridges having the close-range power of the .358 Winchester, the .300 Savage, the .348 Winchester, and the venerable .35 Remington are suitable.

The only logical way for the hunter to arrange for a bear hunt using dogs is to contact an outfitter in the region he wishes to hunt who has a pack of trained bear dogs, and arrange in advance for a hunt. Such men, in the areas where hunting with dogs is permitted and popular usually advertise in the outdoor journals, and may be contacted. Often, too, a hunting partner or acquaintance from a distant and good bear-hunting region will know of such a guide, or outfitter. State game departments often make suggestions.

Maybe even such a hunt might come your way unexpectedly and from sheer luck, as did a lion hunt for me last fall.

While deer hunting in Wyoming with a stranger, I offered him the chance at a 35-inch muley buck, which both of us wanted. After the fellow had killed the prize—incidentally, the best he'd ever taken in a lifetime of hunting—he beamed all over, like a kid with a new red wagon. On the way back in to camp, he suddenly said, "You know, I own 800 acres of good lion country in Utah and a pack of good lion dogs. Any time it's convenient for you, just write or wire me. You and I are going lion hunting."

As touched upon at the beginning, bear hunting with dogs is still a practiced sport despite a degree of prejudice. Many outfitters are helping overcome this by not allowing their hunters to shoot any bear brought to bay with dogs —only permitting shots at bruin while on the run.

Like any other form of game hunting, the sportsmanship involved, in the final analysis, lies in the innate sporting ethics of the hunter.

Part Two

GRIZZLY BEAR

CHAPTER 7

The Unpredictable Bear

No big-game species on the American continent has been subject to more controversy than the grizzly bear—*Ursus horribilus*, or the "horrible bear."

Reams have been written, volumes spoken, and innumerable camp fires burned far into the night in either attacks upon, or defense of the characteristics of this great bruin. Opinion throughout the years has been divided; and the gist of each controversy invariably hinges on, or gets back to, the question of whether or not a grizzly will attack a human being. And for those who agree that he will, then the equally important question, so far as the hunter and outdoorsman is concerned, *when?*

Not too long ago, one noted outdoors "authority" stated in a national outdoor journal that he could "—chase any big-game animal in North America from the scene with a buggy whip."

Those few unfortunate souls who have actually been chewed upon by a maddened grizzly bear, and lived, would seem to have an air-tight rebuttal. Indeed, only a decade ago, I thought with some wonder, and considerable haste, of that noted man and his buggy whip, as a huge British Columbia grizzly came bounding, head on, out of the Arctic birch at us, ears flattened to his head, little pig-like eyes glittering, and a mouthful of yellow teeth quite like my both hands when arched into a claw shape. This, at a matter of mere yards, and my guide with a fine high-powered rifle with which he was mighty adept, but which at the moment was five miles back at camp.

Of course, we'd angered this grizzly by "surrounding" him in the short bushes at a basin head, from which he couldn't escape without being seen. A measured hour and twenty minutes of this, and this aggravation only, and his trigger temper could stand it no longer. In sudden, twelve-foot bounds, he burst from the bush, retreating violently forward. Of course, the outcome might have been somewhat less exciting if I had only my buggy whip, not a .300 H.&H. Magnum.

The more I traverse grizzly country, meet these grizzled bruins at any range or under any circumstances, and the more intensely I study and observe them, the less positive I am as to their probable reasoning, or exactly what each individual bear might, or might not do, under any given circumstance.

As a result, I have come to the conclusion that the best indication of what any grizzly might do, had best be based upon the things his species has collectively done in the past. This observation should include not only the more or less "standard" probabilities, but must, to present a true and overall picture, cover those highly unusual, virtually un-believable actions and reactions of this great beast, which have for so long kept the stamp of certainty from being put upon his characteristics and behavior.

An example of the most extremely unusual grizzly be-havior I've run into in thirty years among America's big game was shown in a grizzly encounter involving Harry Boyden, currently of Slana, Alaska.

Lee Hancock, Anchorage, an Alaska outfitter, mentioned this encounter in 1958, while I was in the Copper River district doing research on grizzlies. "If you really want a grizzly yarn, something that will make your guts stand on end, get old Harry Boyden to tell you his bear story. In fifteen years, Harry has only told it twice. Both times they laughed at him and called him a liar. Now, old Harry's a truthful man, but sensitive as hell. So he refuses to talk about it any more."

Briefly, I got Harry to re-tell it to me that same fall,

Harry Boyden, still alive today and no worse for his unusual grizzly encounter poses with his pet Alaska dog.

somewhat by discreet prying, but largely through our mutual interest in bears.

Harry Boyden was born in England, November 13, 1884, and was christened Henry Boyden. Where the Harry came from, no one is certain. He came to Alaska in 1906 and has remained in the general Nebesna-McCarthy-Chisana (pronounced Shu-Shanna) region ever since.

Some of Harry's doings have made the headlines. As a guide during Alaska's real sour dough era, he outfitted such noted sportsmen as Samuel Webb of the Boone & Crockett Club; and Wiley Post, for brown bear on Kodiak Island, before Post's untimely death up that way with Will Rogers. Again, Harry is mentioned in G. O. Young's book, *Yukon Trophies Won And Lost,* being referred to as the "English Gentleman." Young devotes considerable space in his book to Boyden, largely because of a single incident, which Harry shrugs off even today as being but routine. Briefly, Harry Boyden helped the Young party to cross the Russell Glacier of Alaska's divide country, by the simple expedient of chopping hoof holes for the horses in the ice, so the animals wouldn't skid off into eternity with their loads. This chore took seven hours—all on the polished ice-face of a glacier steeper than what forest officials call the "angle of repose."

Boyden's real significance still lies buried, largely, in the history of the land. In Alaska he is known with awe and respect as the "King of the dog-mushers." This appellation came because of Harry's real contribution to the country during its rugged and formative years. Briefly, he freighted commercially, via dog team and pack-horse, over that impossible link in the early transportation system—the "backbone" glacial spine between Chisana and McCarthy.

Boyden's recent years have been spent in a small cabin on the Nebesna River, near the old Nebesna mine. Intermittently, and as the rigors of the still near-wilderness land dictates, he attends to such things as serving as midwife to an Indian woman who hadn't eaten for two days, tramped for the same period in winter snow, and fell in child-birth on Harry's cabin step. "She'd of died right there, if I 'adn't of been home," he assured me, simply.

I met Harry in August, 1957, in Duffy's Store at Slana. He came up, introduced himself, and wondered aloud if I wasn't "—the young feller who writes those ar-tickles."

From his first words, I marked him down as one whose very survival with the land had depended upon a complete and continuing honesty, both in his observations and his association with people. What I later learned of Harry's life and exploits, from local inhabitants, reaffirmed this conviction. I am certain that every word Harry subsequently told me about his special grizzly encounter was the unvarnished truth. I was staying with Don DeHart at the time.

Harry, himself, provided the opening, only a few days after Hancock had mentioned it. He had come over for the prosaic purpose of bringing Marge DeHart, Don's wife, an Alaska cabbage for dinner. Seeing me taking notes in the den, he came over and sat down.

"Well, you must now 'ave considerable material in the little black book?"

"I've uncovered some amazing things, in the limited time."

"Int'resting creatures, bears."

"In all your own years in the bush, Harry, you must have had some amazing experiences. Probably would make this research seem awfully tame."

Harry likely sensed my earnestness and open-mindedness about the subject. "Yes, you might say I 'ave."

Before I knew it, he was off. For an hour, I had the good sense to shut up entirely, except for a prompting question here and there. Here's what Harry Boyden told me.

By 1943, Boyden's dog-mushing and commercial freighting days had tapered off, and his annual winter trap-line was a main source of income. Periodically along this line, as is common practice in the North country, he had small trapper's huts, each complete with a cache of supplies previously hauled in and stored for winter use. One such cabin was located on the Chitna River.

A neighbor, meaning anyone within a radius of a hundred miles, told Harry he'd lost a horse near this cabin, but across the Chitna River. Horses that far north are most valuable, but have to forage for food in the bush. Ordinarily horses will choose river bars and remain there, freer from black flies, gnats, and mosquitoes, during the summer. But occasionally one will swim a river and leave an area, becoming hopelessly lost until in snow, when it can be tracked.

This neighbor told Harry, "He's somewhere across the river from your cabin. You know the country. If you can find him and will get him, he's yours." In that country a good, bush-wise horse is worth $500.

So on November 14, the day after his birthday, Harry got a friend, Joe Malloy, to go with him up the Chitna for the horse. By now the snow was deep, the river low; and, since the distance was many miles, they went light. Both men walked, leading one rather old horse packed with all their supplies. It might take a couple of weeks or more to find the horse.

At this late season, most grizzly bear in the area had already hibernated in the higher rocky country. For this reason, plus the necessity of going light, neither considered it vital to lug a rifle along.

Towards dusk on the day they reached the cabin, the old pack-horse fagged out. It was necessary to give him long, periodic rests before he could walk at all. Finding that the horse couldn't keep up, Harry suggested, "Joe, you stay and bring him along, slow-like. I'll go on ahead, get a fire going, and thaw out a bit of meat for supper."

A slab of Dall sheep ribs was stored in the cache. Harry took a small cruiser-type ax off the pack-horse, and carried it along, largely to use if necessary in prying the cache door open.

The going was tough, and it was nearly dark by the time he'd reached the cabin clearing.

This small log cabin was located on a tiny area of flat ground, itself set upon a small rise in elevation. This fact is most important, not only to an understanding of what happened later; but it also prevented Boyden from seeing the cabin surroundings, at mere rods, until he'd climbed this small rise.

As he came up and almost onto the cabin, he suddenly

saw a hulking dark object, hunched and busy over something, a few yards from the cabin itself.

"At first I thought, 'Old 'orse, we won't 'ave to travel very
far to find you. And you already a grazin'.' Then I saw it
wasn't a horse, but an hawfully big bear. He was a chewin'
on an old mattress I'd tossed out of the cabin. Rat-spoiled,
y' know. He was tearin' it all to pieces."

"How big?" I interrupted.

"The average grizzly for that region is maybe 500 pounds.
An eight-foot bear (meaning each dimension of a squared
hide), for that country is big. Hawfully big. I estimated
that bear at 800 pounds."

Boyden's years of association with the big bruins had
taught him many things considered to be standard to
grizzly behavior. For one, let a grizzly scent a man, or see
him at considerable distance, and the bruin is apt to spook
away being, innately, one of the most wary of beasts. But
to startle one, or annoy one with sudden shouting, whistling,
or violent movement at reasonably close range, is, conversely, apt to induce a charge.

Harry was far enough away, he figured, to risk hollering.
So he yelled, calling the beast things bearing on its ancestry,
and brandished the small ax.

"I expected 'im to beat it. At least after 'e'd got my smell
and satisfied 'is curiosity. But 'e didn't. 'E dropped the
mattress and came, deliberate like, right up at me."

Natives in British Columbia and Alaska have assured me
that occasionally an unmaddened grizzly will do this. Also,
if one has the guts to stand his ground, and *look* unper-
turbed, that the beast will usually stop at twenty feet or
so, sniff and chomp until the vile man scent is too much,
then whoof off, hackles up, into the timber. However, these
old-timers do mark off a mental distance of approximately
fifteen feet; and if bruin steps across that invisible line,
they kill him. Under fifteen feet is *too* close.

Boyden banked on the above trait. But the unusually
large grizzly didn't pause. It came full upon him, its intent

obviously belligerent. At this awesome point, a quick decision had to be made. Boyden, in his years in the bush, never learned how to run much from anything. Besides, it's useless to try running from a grizzly. The apparently lumbering beasts can cover ground in the ratio of four yards to man's one. More, any show of fear is a quick way to induce a charge. Such a beast must be brow beaten, if at all possible.

Not wishing fully to anger the animal, Harry nevertheless swung his small ax, hoping somehow to scare, or to slap the beast with just sufficient force to let it know he didn't intend to give ground. But the animal, with a speed the inexperienced cannot envision, met the tool with a slap, knocking the puny weapon two rods beyond and into the snow.

The bear was now virtually in his face, snout curled back, intent obvious. In desperation, Harry drew upon his knowledge of the noise factor, as regards grizzlies. At some distance, noise usually would turn one. Quite close, noise would annoy and startle one dangerously. But at mere *inches*, a rifle blast would often make one hesitate.

Screaming to the top of his lungs, Boyden yelled full into the bear's face. At the same time he jerked off his heavy woolen cap, and began beating the beast around the eyes with it.

Two things are significant here. First, Harry didn't try to run, though he did inch slowly backward, with the thin hope of maybe reaching the flung ax. But while he flailed a tattoo upon the animal's eyes, hoping at least to keep it blinded, he nevertheless scrutinized the animal sufficiently to remember that, " 'E 'ad four long scars, diagonal on 'is face. Like another grizzly 'ad tried 'ard to rake off 'is scalp." Only a fearless, observing man would recall this.

Secondly, upon finding that the cap's effect was but temporary, and no real deterrent to the bear's intention, he didn't drop, but *replaced* the cap on his head. Then, with no weapon but voice and hand, he started beating the animal full in the face with doubled fists. He kept yelling. He refused to give ground.

At this point (in Harry's two previous tellings), both his two lone listeners had suddenly quit believing him. One of them, and a veteran woodsman at that, told him blandly, "Harry, you ain't got one scratch on your hide. There's not a single rip in your clothes. And I know for sure you don't

An unusually large grizzly bear killed in Alaska by Harry Boyden prior to his near-fatal encounter.

own boxing gloves. Therefore, you're a liar." The reaction of his second listener was comparable.

What happened at this point becomes the crux of the story, and is beyond the comprehension of most any man.

Knowing that his life now was but a matter of mere seconds, Boyden nevertheless stood his ground and beat the bear furiously in the face with his bare hands. He told me that, afterward, both his fists and arms were black and blue from the elbows down. His hands were swollen into small hams. For two weeks afterward he couldn't speak above a whisper, because of the intensity of his yelling.

Each second, he expected the beast to bat him into eternity. Many a lesser grizzly has broken the neck of a two-year-old Hereford steer with but a single swipe of its powerful fore-paw. And once into combat, a grizzly fears nothing.

But for moments, nothing fatal happened. Several aspects are beyond credulity. For one, never once did the silvertip rear upon its hind legs—a favored position for paw swinging. It curled back its wicked snout, exposing "'andfuls" of yellow teeth. It snarled, roared till Boyden's ears rang, snapping with a slobbering mouth at his face, and making a sound which Harry demonstrated by rounding his mouth and coughing, "Ho! Ho! Ho!"

Most unbelievable, especially at such short range, was the fact that none of its slapping at him landed either on his face or his body. Neither was his flesh torn nor his clothes ripped!

I've watched Yellowstone Park black bears reach out a paw and grab a sack of candy out of some astounded visitor's hand (after he'd fed the "tame" bears in violation of the rules), in a single motion so swift the eye couldn't follow. Again, last fall I watched a three-year-old black bear in captivity at Burwash, Yukon Territory, reach between iron bars at arm's length and take a candy bar from a man, literally grabbing it between his hand and his open mouth as he was eating it; and all before he realized what was happening.

A grizzly's movement is as fast, or faster; and far quicker than the most rapid boxing of any pugilist.

Why that big grizzly didn't knock Boyden over, killing him with one blow, remains the paramount incredulity in that grizzly encounter. Why, or how, he survived those moments of sheer contact Harry doesn't know today.

There may be one of three partial explanations. One, the great over-size bear *meant* to miss him. Secondly, it is possible that its initial slap at the ax may have cut its paw and the memory remained painful. Lastly, and perhaps less taxing to the credulity of men knowing grizzlies, the immediate terrain *may* have been temporarily unsuited for the bear's best footing. Boyden's actual contact, remember, had come just at the lip of the small, snowy rise in elevation. The bear was positioned above him, and to rise, uphill, might have put it in an awkward slapping position. And above Boyden.

Amazed at still being alive, Harry continued slowly backing toward the ax, all the time beating at his foe like a boxer back pedaling. By now he was down the slope of the rise. Suddenly his moccasin caught in a clump of dry wood, and he fell full backward into the snow.

"I figured 'ere it was all over," Harry said. "But as I keeled over, my cap flew off. For some reason, that bear stopped to bite at it. And as I tried for my feet, my 'and came up with this hunk of cottonwood I'd tripped over." He measured three feet, with his hands.

Regaining his feet, Boyden began furiously poking at the animal with the hunk of wood, as if it were some clumsy fencing tool. Oddly, while the grizzly hadn't batted *him*, it now began to slap the wood, still snarling and coughing.

"I wasn't dead yet," Harry said. "No use givin' up till I was done in. Then I got this idea."

Harry's idea was the sudden, desperation remembrance of the string of horse-bells dangling against the cabin wall.

He'd hauled in these old horse-bells for a similar purpose, while stocking the cache in early fall. Summer grizzlies had the habit of coming in bunches up the Chitna, for the late-fall salmon run. The sound of horse-bells carries far, and has the implication of horses and men about. The periodic ringing of these old bells served to keep the bears away from the cabin while he was there.

Circling slowly, he inched back to the cabin where he grabbed the bells—all the time poking the beast off him with the wood chunk. But even at the sudden clanging of the bells in its face, the big grizzly did no more than to retreat a few yards back into the clearing.

Here, manifested afresh, was another of the strangest paradoxes known to grizzly behavior. This monstrous animal was nearly twice the hulk of others of its own species. It now stood its ground, facing an ear-racking noise which had previously sent many a lesser grizzly racing, half-scared out of its wits. Yet for all this bear's size, power, and apparent bravery, it hadn't killed Boyden as he'd pummeled its face with his bare fists!

At this most opportune moment, luck played a part. Hearing the sounds of yelling, Malloy had urged the weary horse forward. He came to the clearing, himself hollering, "Harry? What in hell ails you? You after a wolverine?"

"A bear! Give me a 'and!"

As he broke into the open, Malloy saw. Dropping the lead rope, he got into the fuss. Picking up the flung ax, he helped Harry beat at the animal. Even at the sight of the horse, and the threatening of two men, the bear refused to make off, but kept roaring and slapping at them.

"Work 'im round back of the cabin," Harry suggested.

Slowly, they inched to the cabin again, to where a larger ax stood against the rear wall. Trading the chunk of wood for the better tool, Harry and Malloy continued beating until they'd driven the beast back, a few rods, to the clearing's edge.

When they saw that the breather was an actuality, one broke for the horse and the other for the cabin door.

The big bruin had, previous to the men's arrival, tried to enter the cabin. There were claw marks by the door hasp, and the panes of the small window had been broken out— this aperture having been purposely made too small for a grizzly's entrance. Having gone into the timber, the animal made no immediate move to attack again. Quickly, in the few minutes of remaining daylight, the men made preparation for an all-night vigil. Malloy tied the old pack horse full against the broken window. Boyden got his breath, and built a fire in the sheet-iron stove. As further "bear-scare," they hung a dishtowel over the broken panes, and hung the lit, coal-oil lantern just inside, to burn all night.

Trapper caches in the bush are built upon three or four spruces growing handily together. The trees are sawed off at an even height, twelve to fifteen feet off the ground, and a platform built upon their stumps. A solid hut-like cache is built upon this platform. Mature grizzlies can't climb, at least that high; and the cache's legs are safeguarded against molestation by black-bears and wolverines by nailing gasoline-can tin around them. The cache is reached via a pole ladder, itself thrown back into the bush after use.

While Malloy guarded with the ax, Boyden climbed the cache and got the ram ribs. Once inside the low cabin, they felt secure, at least temporarily.

Harry thawed the ribs and made supper. It's an unwritten law of the woods that the cook does no dishes. "Malloy was one of them hurry-up fellers. Good woodsman, but fidgety like. 'E couldn't wait till supper was over till he 'ad to get at the dishes. No reason the bear should 'ave made *him* nervous."

At this unexpected point, both men abruptly understood that their encounter wasn't over. Dish pan in hand, Malloy pulled open the in-swinging door, to heave out the dish water. There was no room. The big bear stood crosswise on the step, effectively closing the door opening to Malloy's waist. As the door swung open, the beast turned and inched forward into the frame, meaning to enter the cabin.

Joe dropped the dish water, yelling at Harry. Upon entering the hut previously, they'd taken both axes inside. In one jump, each seized an ax, one man taking either side of the door. The first thought was to chop into the skull of the grizzly, as he entered the cabin. His position, as he entered, would at long last be favorable.

"Before he padded all the way in," Harry told me, "I was struck with the notion that such a bear, complete with two men swingin' haxes, and in a ten-foot cabin, might be somethin' worse of a fuss. Then, too, I was on the door side. And while lookin' at its two-inch thickness, you might say I got another idea. The door was whip-sawed plankin', you understand. I just kicked the door shut in the bear's face, after which Malloy and I pushed him on out and slammed the latch."

It may be indicative of the two men to say that at this point, Harry went to bed on the bunk, and, as he said, "slept most soundly till mornin'." Malloy sat up, tending the fire all night.

By daybreak, they were at breakfast. With the meal done, Malloy again gingerly opened the cabin door to learn the whereabouts of the grizzly. Once again, "quite like a reception committee," the bear stood on the step, ready to enter.

This, for Malloy (perhaps aggravated after an all night's vigil) was too much. Perhaps, too, he had gained confidence from Boyden's indestructibility. At any rate, instead of again slamming the plank door in the bruin's face, Joe jerked it open. Seizing chunks of split wood, which lay stacked behind the stove, he began a rapid and systematic pelting of the bear, full in the face, with the firewood.

"Pretty fair shot, Malloy was," Harry recalled. "Hit 'im seven times of the nine sticks he got off."

At this, the grizzly retreated a few rods back into the edge of the bush. With the temporary breather, the men took stock. Neither the dish towel nor the lantern had been molested at the window all night. More unusual, the old pack horse had actually remained at his post just outside the broken pane, all night. He likely drew comfort from the presence of the men, just inside the cabin, or the closer lantern. Again, he may have been petrified with fear. For, as Malloy and Boyden looked outside, they saw that the big grizzly had bedded down all night in the snow, just a paced forty feet from the cabin door!

With the current reprieve from the bear's attack, they decided swiftly. All thought of staying to find the other horse was abandoned—they'd be lucky to escape with their lives.

Quickly getting the ancient pack horse, they moved gingerly into the clearing, and then away into the bush. Only then did they try to find a reasonable explanation, as to why the bear had been so intent upon pushing its way into the cabin. They remembered that the unused portion of the sheep ribs had been laid on the woodpile by the stove.

What remains of canned goods after a grizzly has found a cache. These cans were photographed by author after a raid on a Sheep Creek, Alaska, cache.

The remains of any game kill, such as that left when bringing in a trophy head, should be carefully watched for a grizzly.

"Simple, once we 'ad time to think on it," Harry told me. "He smelled the slab and wanted a bit of it. That's why 'e waited on the cabin step."

Had Harry's yarn been fictitious instead of stark truth, there would have been, no doubt, some breath-taking climax. In some dramatic fashion, the great grizzly might have been lost, except to legend and history, as a super-natural individual of its species, always manifesting the contrary characteristics of being able at one cuff to dispatch any mortal man, yet for once refusing to use such powers; or some legendary beast bearing a charmed life, which no man could take.

Among wilderness children, however, the end is usually more prosaic and tragic.

This great silvertip lived two more years. The second spring after Boyden's encounter, there was indisputable evidence in the Chitna River country of some monster bear invading two more similar trapper's cabins. The beast had churned the contents of each into an irreparable mess.

In one of these small overnight huts, the grizzly had tooth-punctured a gallon can of motor oil, likely stored for outboard motor or truck use; and had drunk the contents. This oil had become active while the animal still tore at the cabin. It had obviously produced a prodigious belly-ache and subsequent diarrhea. Bear dung was splattered all over the cabin's contents, with globs of it still hanging from the low ceiling—a fact which escapes reasonable explanation.

At the second hut, the owner came into view while the big bruin was still engaged in looting the contents. This trapper had a rifle. He shot the beast, knowing nothing of Boyden's encounter, or that it was the same bear.

Later, Boyden got to hear of it—how the monstrous beast had been estimated conservatively at twice the size of any ordinary grizzly. And more, that it had four deep scars running diagonally down its face, as though some lesser beast, long ago, had tried to rake off its scalp.

Thus ended, in undramatic fashion, the life of an unusual beast which, itself, had come to grips with an unusual man.

CHAPTER 8

Range, Distribution, and Basic Habits of the Grizzly

Like the lordly wapiti, or elk, the grizzly bear was once primarily a plains animal. He roamed the foothills and low timbered regions of western North America in an overall area reaching from Mexico City on the south, to the Arctic Circle on the north. Although the grizzly's history may be traced back as far as the Pleistocene Age, no evidence can be found that he ever inhabited the eastern half of this continent.

As with the elk, civilization drove the grizzly farther and farther back until today, his range, broadly speaking, is in the most remote, rugged, and primitive areas left. Canada and Alaska have the greatest grizzly populations, with but a relatively small number yet remaining in Montana, Wyoming, and Idaho. Of these three western states, Montana has the most, with Idaho the fewest. In 1946, the census listed Montana as having 770 grizzlies, Wyoming nearly 500, with most of the remaining estimated 1400 bears in Idaho.

The 1957 census of the Fish & Wildlife Service shows Montana having 626 grizzlies, Idaho 50, and Wyoming as "less." This means that only approximate 1200 grizzlies remain today in these three states.

The grizzly's cycle is roughly comparable to the life cycle of the black bear.

As a plains animal, the grizzly didn't go into hibernation until winter set in, or December. Due to his being driven by civilization to a higher, colder habitat, this has been slightly modified. Grizzlies now hibernate usually by No-

Range of grizzly bear in North America.

vember, and emerge by April. We found on the Wyoming study mentioned earlier that snow depth and severity of spring weather affect this somewhat.

The cubs are born, as with blacks, during hibernation, and approximate the size of tree squirrels. Twinning is most common, with occasional triplets and quadruplets being observed.

June is the mating month of the grizzly. Mating occurs in alternate years. The female grizzly guards her offspring with a greater ferocity than does a black bear; and if a grizzly can be said to possess one inalterable characteristic, it is that of defending her cubs to the death, and fighting *every* time her cubs are endangered or apparently threatened.

There are several basic and distinguishing characteristics of the grizzly. His name, and his nickname "silvertip," come from the fact that in every grizzly regardless of overall coloration, there will be found these badger-colored guard hairs along the spine.

As to color, grizzlies range from nearly pure black to cinnamon brown, to almost cream color, to an overall badger hue, and often with combinations of these colors. I killed one Wyoming grizzly which was nearly yellow on the back and sides, with this light color gradually tapering into dark brown on the legs, darkening into sheer black at the feet, and tipped with polished ivory-colored claws.

The grizzly I took in Alaska in 1958 had a salt-and-pepper colored pelt, which closely resembled the color of a dark timber wolf. Again, the largest grizzly I ever killed is nearly pure brown all over, with the exception of darker brown paws. All, however, have the same silver-tipped guard hairs along the spine.

Another distinguishing mark of the grizzly is the hump at his withers. This is more pronounced in older bears, and at a distance, broadside, gives the grizzly the general big-shouldered appearance of a bison or old male mountain goat.

Again, most grizzlies have broader skulls than black bears, giving their snouts a short, stubby appearance. Grizzlies also have more of a tendency to look "dish-faced" than do blacks.

When moving, or traveling, the grizzly has a peculiar swaying of the head, slowly from side to side, which the black bear doesn't have. This characteristic may be for the purpose of catching the vagaries of even the faintest breeze as he moves, and which a moist, moving nose can pick up. It may also assist him greatly with his vision. The grizzly has relatively good eyesight straight ahead, but poor vision sideways due to close-set eyes. The characteristic oscillating motion of the head undoubtedly improves this.

A final difference between the grizzly and the black is in size. A black bear may average 250-300 pounds. The average grizzly will run from 400 to 500. Exceptional grizzlies will weigh up to a half-ton and over.

The spoor of a grizzly is a fair indication of his size. Front pad marks of adult grizzlies will measure from 6½ inches on up. Hind tracks, including the claw marks, will run from 11 inches on up to 14 inches. One hears many tales of grizzly tracks measuring up to 18 inches in length. Most of these yarns are "enlarged" with each re-telling, and are often taken from grizzly spoor in snow where later melting will enlarge the original imprint in every direction.

Upon emergence from hibernation, the grizzly's main intent is to obtain food. It takes considerable poundage and variety to keep a grizzly going; and since, like the black bear, a grizzly is usually a solitary character, he chooses a broad, remote area for his wanderings which includes a variety of elevations and kinds of food. These range from the lowlands and south slopes, where he'll find tender spring grasses; to the creekbeds of spawning salmon where he finds his summer diet of fish; to the high blueberry patches where he goes for fruit; to available lake shores where game and carrion may be found; and, with September, to the high alpine areas just under snowline where he fattens on whistling marmots for approaching hibernation.

Such a range may spread to fifteen or twenty miles. It is covered as to season, in a loosely-circuitous route, and may be considered an individual bear's private domain. This is especially true of the old boars.

As personal property, the boundaries are marked by the bear each spring. Periodically along the periphery of the range, a grizzly will establish "rubbing trees." These, in most grizzly country, are the larger spruce trees. He'll stand for moments, upright and with back against the tree, rubbing back and forth. The thick spruce gum helps to remove itch and loose hair from his long-unused hide, and the marks and wounds left in the tree bole henceforth become his private brand. To finish the job of identifying his range, the bear will then reach as far up the bole as possible with his fore-paws and rip long scratches in the bark. These will last until the following spring, and plainly say, "Keep Off The Grass!" to all lesser beasts.

The first spring food of grizzlies is tender grass shoots, supplemented later with green pine needles and the cambian layer of spruce bark. These stretch the stomach, and are cathartic in nature, helping to unplug the digestive tract which has lain dormant for five to six months.

Next on the menu are the grubs and ants available after the first thaws. Along Prochniak Creek in British Columbia I have seen whole patches of low grassland literally "plowed" by spring grizzlies in search of grubs. Every inch of half-acre patches would be rooted up, as though overturned with a shovel. And rotten logs containing ants and big, white wood worms are customarily ripped to shreds, in a grizzly's search even for tidbits.

When the stomach is again stretched, the grizzly will once more take meat. Evidence shows that the grizzly is more carnivorous than a black, and will begin on meat sooner than his smaller cousin.

Such meat consists of what live game the bear can catch and kill, plus the carcasses of game caught in avalanches, died of disease, starvation, or old age, or winter-weakened and lost to the preying of wolves and coyotes.

With the salmon runs of summer on, the grizzly will scour the creek spawning grounds so long as a single fish remains. He loves the red Sockeye, or "hump-back" salmon and can easily take him even in sizable water.

John C. Belcher, California millionaire and sportsman who hunts for nothing except record specimens, showed me a certain knoll overlooking southern Alaska's Granite Creek where he'd sat the year before and counted 17 separate grizzly bear—all at one time, and working the salmon run.

With the summer fishing over, the grizzly turns to berries,

mainly the Far North's blueberries. This delicious fruit grows on short thick bushes, one berry in a place but many on a single stem. The berry resembles a huckleberry except being dark blue instead of purple, and is usually larger. Individual berries get as large as a small thumb nail, are especially sweet after the first September frost, and grow in great abundance.

Both in Canada and Alaska, blueberry patches will average anywhere from a square rod, up to ten acres or more in extent.

Jake Butler, Indian guide in Alaska, once told our outfitter when he'd asked if we hunted grizzlies that day, "Yep, we hunt grizzly. All day we set down. I glass country with binoculars, Clyde eat blueberries."

Grizzlies love this fruit, and will stay with the high patches until heavy frosts and falling berries ruin the crop. As with black bears, the incidence of berries often tells the hunter at what elevation he'll find his grizzly. In years of a prodigious fruit crop, such as 1958 in the Wrangell's, the very abundance of berries proves a handicap. Once the first shots of a hunting season are fired, the canny grizzlies of the region know what it means; and they'll head for, and stay in, the most remote areas, living on the abundant berries far away from any evidences of man's use of the country, until the annual danger is over. Many an old grizzly lives to the age of 20 or 25 years. The old boars which are so trophy-worthy, also have learned much connected with the sounds of an ax, horse, or rifle report, and the smell of wood smoke. And, like a Chink pheasant, shot in the rump with a charge of sixes on opening day, they become mighty scarce thereafter.

Mixed with this diet is the occasional animal kill which the grizzly makes, plus gorging on carrion left by hunters and wolf-killed moose. Also are the wild-pea vines he digs from glacial streambeds.

The last basic food before hibernation again is a fattening on the grizzled whistling marmots common to the North

High rugged plateau country like this is grizzly environment of the
first order.

Country. These rodents burrow and den up in the high
rocky areas above timberline and just under the snowline
remaining from the previous winter. The grizzly, now sleek
and fat from his fall diet, methodically digs out these little
animals and devours them. In size they will average maybe
five or six pounds, and look quite like our western rock
chuck except being badger colored instead of brown.

Mud-fat from these, the grizzly takes on a last filling of
vegetation, to keep his digestive track from collapsing during the "long sleep," and again goes into his rocky den for
winter, completing the cycle.

The basic traits of a grizzly are his size and great strength,
his courage and fear of nothing, his hair-triggered temper,
and his awesome ferocity and rage when aroused. Couple
all these to an incredible tenacity of life when mortally
wounded, and a fundamental policy of fighting literally to
the death once into a fight, and the result is an opponent
of the first order.

To set down in black and white just what any grizzly will
do under any circumstance is a job for the rank amateur.

As hinted before, the more one observes these interesting and awe-inspiring beasts, the less certain are his conclusions. Those who know the grizzly best are those who conclude that a grizzly *may* do one thing under certain conditions a majority of the time; but are willing to concede that the exceptional time he *won't* do it is just as probable, with the results far more exciting.

Let's consider first the grizzly's known, basic trait of wariness.

In the majority of instances, a grizzly wants only to be left alone. He's retreated from civilization. He lives in the remotest areas left. In most every instance with normal contact with man, he'll spook from the sight, smell, or known presence of a human being. Hunters know this—that the faintest breeze carrying man scent, or the faintest noise during a last portion of a careful stalk, will usually send the quarry away without even a sight of it. As mentioned in an earlier chapter, when baiting for a grizzly with a dead horse, the hunter must use every conceivable precaution never to allow his presence at a bait, or a hint of man's association with it to reach a grizzly, or he'll never show up. And even after he's begun working such a bait, the smart hunter always stays away until the third or fourth feeding, for the very same reason.

The evidences of a grizzly's innate wariness are all about, in good grizzly country. Many a time I've walked dusty trails in Canada or Alaska, and upon returning, have found where a big grizzly had wandered along for a hundred yards or so, right over the fresh boot prints. Invariably the spoor would indicate that he'd detected my presence as I returned, and had bounded off a few rods into surrounding bush, undoubtedly to watch unseen as I passed.

Three different mornings on B. C.'s Prochniak Creek, I found where a great bruin had come regularly to within a hundred yards of where the pack horses stood tied to trees about camp. The circling tracks and steaming, gallon-sized piles of blueberry dung told with amazing clarity just what the beast was considering. Yet we never, in a week, got a sight of that particular bear. And we hunted him hard and continuously.

Again, while hunting Stone rams with Tom Mould, out-fitter from Fort Nelson, British Columbia, we once spooked a grizzly from above timber line at a basin head. The beast, at our scent, raced in great bounds down into the bush surrounding the melting glacier edge and creek beginnings, to become concealed from our sight.

As we stood full in the open, at just over a hundred yards, Tom, who'd lived with the unpredictable beasts for a quarter century said with conviction, "He'll try to get away unseen if at all possible. But if he finds he can't, he'll come out fighting."

It was easy from our position in the full open above that great grizzly to read his thinking clearly. At first, nothing showed or moved in the bush below us. Then, periodically, the animal became increasingly nervous and angered. The short Arctic birch would wiggle first here, then ten feet away. These "wiggles" became closer together until, as Tom asked, "Are you ready with that rifle?", the grizzly burst forth from the bush right at us! Mad as a wet hen!

In hunting a grizzly, it's exasperating to witness his ex-ceptional cunning in the matter of trying to elude man, once the bruin gets the faintest suspicion that man is near.

However, this generality isn't a fast rule, as many a person has abruptly discovered.

Consider what happened to Bart Bowlby's wife, at their homestead near Alaska's Kenny Lake.

Bart was away at the time, and Elaine, his wife, had a six-months-old baby. As she moved about outside, chopping wood and bringing it inside, she suddenly saw two grizzlies mosey into the clearing. Two silvertips together was a mild surprise to her, but not so surprising as the fact that they'd come up within sight of her after the noise of the ax.

From the looks of the animals at just over 100 yards, together with Bart's measurement of the larger track afterward, Elaine estimated the smaller beast as a seven-footer, with the larger one close to nine feet. Incidentally, grizzlies are estimated and measured in that region by their "squared" hides. That is, a bear's hide is spread flat, measured across the fore-paws and again from snout to tail, then both measurements added and divided by two. The result may be a seven-foot bear, an eight-foot bear, etc.

Too, a bear's probable size is estimated quite accurately by adding one inch to the width of his front paw. A grizzly with a 6-inch front pad would therefore be a seven-footer.

When the grizzlies made no attempt to leave, as Elaine carried the wood inside, she began to get frightened. Such a fear, for the rugged people who homestead such areas, doesn't prevent their doing something about a situation, however. Dropping the wood inside, Mrs. Bowlby came outside, jacking the cartridge into Bart's .348 Winchester.

This spunky little lady (she weighs about ninety pounds) had killed such game as moose, and even one black bear which they'd had made into a rug. But the sight, and apparent intention of the two bruins made her hesitate. In an effort to scare them off, she fired two shots just over the head of the larger beast.

"Why didn't you shoot at him?" I asked her.

"Well, the baby was just inside. I didn't want to just wound a bear that size, so I'd have to leave the baby and follow to finish him off."

"What did they do when you shot?"

"The first time, nothing. But the second time, the smaller grizzly took off and went loping out of sight into the timber. But that big devil! He just stood still there, looking me right in the eye. He was plumb into the clearing by then, and for a minute I thought he'd come on into the cabin. I ran back inside and shut the door. But for a while I thought he'd come up and bust right in . . . Maybe you don't think I was relieved when he sauntered off into the brush."

As another example that exceptions often prove a rule,

old Pete Peterson told me that during his lifetime with grizzlies in the Muncho Lake area of British Columbia, he had repeatedly run into a grizzly at short range, usually when walking a moose trail through the muskeg and bush. Instead of fleeing at his presence, as they ordinarily will do if a hunter is after one, many of them would head right for him.

"They would chomp and whoosh, quite like an angry boar," Pete would say. "Their neck hair would come up, ears flatten, and they'd make a great fuss. Had I moved, or acted frightened, no doubt they'd have taken me, righto. But when I didn't give ground, they would slow down, maybe stop completely at two or three rods from me. Most of them chomped and whooshed off into the bush after their curiosity and mad had died down a bit. But I would always mark off a distance of maybe fifteen feet or so, in the trail. The ones which came beyond that came *too* close."

"What did you do?"

"I shot them."

Or again as a sample of a grizzly's wariness, one elusive bruin we'd hunted all fall in Wyoming, without getting sight of him, came at midnight one night, and gorged himself on a dead horse, just behind the horse corral—a matter of yards from where we all slept!

As another instance of a grizzly's wariness, consider what happened to a "lucky" hunter near Wyoming's Flagg Ranch some years back.

This man had killed a small elk, and had it draped across the back of his coupe, en route home. Not being able to make it in a single day, he'd rented a small cabin, pulled the car up just outside the window, and went to bed. There were no dogs in the neighborhood, or anything else to bother the meat. So, rather than unload the heavy carcass, he left it tied securely on the car. In case anything did molest it, he would surely hear any noise just a matter of feet away.

When he woke at sunup, the entire elk was gone. The

tracks around the car left no doubt—a big grizzly had sneaked up, ripped the carcass free, unheard, and had carried it off.

The amazing thing was not only that the canny beast had braved all man smells and done the job undetected— they never did find any trace of the elk! The spoor became obliterated a short distance away in the pines, and despite a thorough search, no one could find where, or how far, the bruin had moved that elk carcass.

Furious not alone at the loss of his elk, but also at the cleverness of the theft, the hunter hurried to Jackson Hole, and bought the "innards" of a beef, from the local slaughter-house. This he took back and carefully planted near the cabin, hoping that the grizzly would return. But after several days of around-the-clock watching, and not a sign of the canny animal, the hunter got disgusted both with himself and the smell of the ripening offal, and "high-tailed" it for home.

In these instances, as indeed in innumerable similar grizzly contacts, there is a common pattern. In cases where a silvertip, especially a canny, man-experienced old beast, seems to disregard all caution on certain occasions, the element of food is usually involved. Second only to a sow grizzly's ferocious battling against a threat to her cubs, is the grizzly's defense of food. This food may be either his or belong to anyone, or anything else.

Hunters' game kills, carrion, the kill of wolves—anything a grizzly finds he immediately appropriates. Meat that he can't gorge at once is either pulled and carried to better concealment and cached, or mounded up on the spot with sticks and mud. Thereafter, the big bruin will remain, either upon the mound, at the side of it, or nearby until the bones are picked.

The distances at which a grizzly can find meat or carrion are unbelievable to the novice. The riper the carrion, the easier it is to find, and apparently he likes it. An old guide once told me that on one occasion he'd back-tracked a big grizzly that had come in to a crippled horse which had been destroyed and left for a week, for a distance of nearly three miles. "His big tracks showed that he'd come straight as a beeline," the man assured me.

Not only carrion but fresh blood will be smelled by the grizzly's keen nose, and gone immediately to—sometimes with embarrassing rapidity.

Consider the West Coast hunter some years ago, who'd just killed a prize caribou bull in the Yukon. At the time he was hunting with a partner and a guide. With the bull down and pictures taken, the happy hunter and his partner (being old woodsmen themselves) began the butchering. The guide, probably to locate any other game in the region, was, at the moment, a hundred yards away glassing the country.

As is common to caribou habitat and hunting, the bull had been dropped on a small plateau, overlooking several small slash-gulleys.

Suddenly, the guide began hollering and waving his arms frantically. The hunters, bewildered at his antics, stood up from their disemboweling chore and stared in amazement. The fellow who'd killed the caribou did, however, have presence of mind enough to pick up his rifle. In this instance, he would immediately thereafter have traded such presence of mind for absence of body.

Briefly, the guide from his better position to see the region below, had abruptly seen a big boar grizzly headed straight for the caribou, and in long loping bounds. The silvertip had, of course, smelled the fresh blood from a short distance, and was on his way to appropriate it. This, despite assorted man smells and the recent shooting.

From the hunters' position, they could not see the bear. But suddenly, up the sharp decline of the small plateau came Mr. Grizzly. When he came into view, he was just a matter of yards from the astounded men—ears flat, snout curled, and bounding straight for them.

It takes nerve in a situation like that. People who survive do their shooting first, and their getting scared afterward. The lucky hunter upped the rifle and dropped the grizzly. Ten seconds more and that bear would have been in there, batting men all over the place.

"Dal" Dalziel, who lives at Watson Lake in the Yukon, has lived with the great beasts all his life. He's killed scores of them, has had several close squeaks, and has a high regard for the fury of a grizzly. "As to ferocity," he once assured me, after we'd all got our limit on grizzlies in his own hunting country, "you simply cannot over-rate a grizzly. He's tops as an adversary, old man."

Stench in wilderness country usually means carrion. So does the presence of several predator birds like magpies, ravens, and whiskey jacks. Carrion, similarly, means that a grizzly is likely on the carrion or working it.

It's a cardinal rule in any bear country to approach any carrion smell, or areas where birds are congregated, with extreme caution.

Another long-standing "fact" of grizzly behavior is that he can't climb trees after becoming an adult. Because of the stiffening of his wrists and shape of the long fore-claws, the full-grown bear cannot pull his considerable poundage aloft.

But here again, generality must occasionally give way to the exception.

In Don DeHart's Sheep Creek camp, in Alaska's Wrangell Mountains, DeHart annually leaves some of the heavier gear over winter. This is necessary because of no trails in, and all camp supplies must be hauled in either by pack horse for thirty miles, or via caterpillar-tractor and trailer—an outfit, incidentally, which makes its own road as it travels.

To prevent the ravages of grizzlies in that area, all gear is hoisted up onto a high, typical northern cache mentioned before. Such a cache consists largely of a platform set on four sawed-off tree boles, which have grown conveniently together. The boles are cut off at twelve- to fifteen-foot

height, joists of timber are set across, and a base, or platform of green spruce poles, averaging five inches in
diameter, is made quite like a floor. Such trappers' caches
are completed by erecting a small hut over this platform.

Don's cache, however, consisted largely of a pile of gear,
and a covering of heavy neoprene plastic tied down over
the entire cache. To further the safety of the gear from
bears, all upright tree-bole supports are cut free of boughs,
and a covering of tin nailed around each support. The tin
in this case was simply five-gallon gasoline cans split open
and nailed down.

This particular year, DeHart left not only the stoves, saw,
axes, camp dishes, and similar imperishables, but also
several wooden boxes filled with canned food. A new 12x14-
foot wall tent was placed on top, under the waterproof
covering. Then everything was lashed down.

When DeHart returned the following summer, to set up
hunting camp, the cache was a shambles. Briefly, a large
grizzly had found the cache, as was to be expected. He had
gotten to it, which wasn't.

Every can had been sorted from the boxes, tooth-punctured, and the contents sucked. All dishes were flattened
shut, likely between the beast's two fore-paws. Even the
gasoline-can tins around the tree boles had been bitten
through, though the bear hadn't succeeded in ripping them
off the trees.

Such items as the stove, saw, lanterns, ax, and boxes had
all been battered around and scattered here and there. The
new wall tent was not found for some time. When it was
accidently located, by a wrangler after horses, it was a full
quarter-mile from the camp site. It had been dragged there,
ripped to shreds, and apparently used at least for one night,
as a bed by the grizzly.

In all, DeHart lost $700 worth of gear to that single raid.
The tracks beneath, the tooth marks on cans and tin, and
marks left on the tree boles, all indicated a grizzly of
superior size.

I photographed that cache in 1957, together with some of the evidence of damage. A picture of some of the tooth-marked cans is included in this book.

The point is, a huge grizzly, which couldn't climb, *did*. I have no plausible explanation, other than the fact that the four supports were reasonably close together; and on one bole, there was a six-inch length of a chopped-off branch. The platform is an estimated 15 feet off the earth, and reached by man only with a pole ladder. This is thrown away after the cache is used, and descent made.

The only logical conclusion I could reach was that in *some* fashion, that grizzly had climbed the full height, possibly by bracing himself (for an assist) between the boles much as a mountain climber ascends up a small crevice, or "gut." He may have been able to help lift himself, by hanging onto the short length of limb butt.

Once at the platform, the beast had not been able to lift himself up over the flat edge. He had solved this problem by biting through enough of the bottom poles of the flat platform to cause it to give way and let the gear tumble down.

DeHart uses that same cache still. No change has been made except to lop off the lone limb stump. No grizzly has succeeded in raiding it since. And the exact procedure by which the one bear did climb it, remains a mystery.

To return to that basic short temper and innate fury with which a female grizzly greets any semblance of danger to her offspring, I know of no better example than one which occurred in Wyoming in 1958.

Les Bowman, the outfitter, and his guide Roy Glasgow were scouting rams for a hunting party then in camp. For Rocky Mountain rams, one must go high, both to scout for them and to hunt. Since the hunter "lard-hinders" couldn't make the initial climb, Les and Roy had left them behind, and had, at the time, worked their way to the head of Yellow Creek. This is in the Shoshone River drainage, west of Cody. Their hope was simply to locate game.

In order to cover more ground, the men split, each to glass one rim of the canyon, in that craggy region.

Bowman came in that evening, but Glasgow didn't show up until late enough to worry the camp. When finally he did come in, his hand was roughly bandaged with a blood-stained cloth. Les noticed, too, that his tough, whang-leather chaps were cut in several places.

"What happened to you?" Les asked. "Horse buck you off, like some tenderfoot dude?"

Glasgow wasn't amused. In fact, he still looked white. "How," he asked, "would you like to have your own hand down a grizzly's throat?"

Glasgow then told what happened soon after they'd separated. He had gone to the rim rock, at the basin's apex, on the opposite side. Tying his saddle horse to some low shrubs back out of sight, Roy then crept cautiously up nearly to the brink. He knew rams have eyesight eight times keener than man, and he wanted to make certain that any sheep along the opposite shelving ledges saw neither him nor the horse.

The foliage here was sparse. It consisted largely of low, scraggly juniper bush, reaching to half the height of a man. Cautiously seating himself, so as to loosen no rocks to give away his presence, Glasgow began glassing for rams.

"Suddenly," he told us that night, "the whole binoculars blacked out. I couldn't figure what the hell was wrong with 'em. But I put them down to figure it out, and *then* I saw! A yearling grizzly cub had heard or smelt me, from just on the other side of that juniper. He stood there, eight feet away, and lookin' me smack in the eye!"

"What did you do?" Bowman asked.

"I let out a yell, hoping to scare him off, and waved the binoculars at him. But instead of runnin', the little bastard let out a bawl. Then, before I could even think, all hell broke loose!"

As near as Glasgow could piece it together, the mother bear had been asleep along with the cub and also just a few feet beyond him. Due to the care he'd used in approaching the brink, neither had heard him until the cub had smelled him and rose before the glasses. Now, in one swish of cedar boughs, and a bawling roar that curdled his blood, the sow bear sprang for him.

Instinctively, Glasgow swung his arm, still holding the Bushnell binoculars, to fend her off somewhat. The simple act saved his life. The beast grabbed his hand in her open mouth and clamped down. The force of her teeth drove through the metal frame of the glasses, and punctured his hand with each tooth. However the instrument did keep the fangs from coming together.

In sheer terror, Glasgow began fighting at her with his hands, and trying to roll away.

The surface of the immediate terrain could either be a mighty big help, or his entire undoing. The brink sloped off sharply for 30 feet in a kind of inclined "step." The next step broke off far more sharply into a sheer pitch for perhaps fifty feet more, then dropped over vertical walls all the way down to the canyon bottom. Hoping someway to dodge the awesome fangs and claws before his face, Glasgow chose injury and almost certain death by gravity, to the grizzly.

Failing in the first attempt to bite his hand, the bear spit out the binoculars and grabbed at his body. This time she connected, seizing him full by the hips, since he was now prone.

Again he was saved, this time by the heavy chaps he wore (all Wyoming cowboys are born with chaps and boots). They were of tough horsehide, and of the "gunbarrel" type, easier to walk in than the flappy bat-wing models. The grizzly's teeth sank full into the leather, again miraculously hitting his pocket cigarette lighter which he carried in the chaps pocket. All five teeth cut through the chaps, but as the bear bit down, the force was slowed by the metal lighter and the tough levis beneath. This bite "slipped" off Glasgow's hip without cutting into it, incidentally leaving the whole thigh black and blue for weeks.

In a blur of motion, he saw the bear with a mouthful of chaps, whose buckles had ripped off his leg as she pulled. In a flash of decision, Glasgow decided in favor of gravity. Over and over he tumbled down the upper face of the cliff. The sow followed him down, roaring in rage and fury and grabbing at his catapulting form.

At the bottom of the first step, they were still together. Then over and over he went onto the steeper incline. One thought kept ringing in his brain. "If I went to the bottom of *that* one, I was a goner. There wasn't a damn thing I could grab onto—nothin'. All I could do was try to stop rolling over, and spread eagle."

Holding both arms and legs stiff, he ended the tumbling with a steep belly-slide down the face of the mountain. Friction finally slowed him.

Here again, luck played a vital part. As they hit the steeper descent, the sow was torn loose from him. And at this moment, the cub started racing up, away from the cliff. Possibly the smell, or sudden sight of the saddle horse caused it additional consternation. It let out another frightened bellow. The sow, herself now confronted with death by gravity, turned her head towards the bawling cub.

"For *some* reason," Glasgow finished, "that dirty old sonofabitch chose the cub instead of me. She headed for it, and lucky for me, kept goin'."

Glasgow wasn't out of the proverbial woods yet. He figured even if he could get enough traction on the cliff to ascend on all fours, that the bears would spook his horse sufficiently to make it "high-tail" it for camp. In his condition, he likely couldn't have walked and the tragedy would have been completed.

"But I guess my rabbit's foot worked all the way that day," he said, still amazed. "They went right past the horse, payin' him no never mind. All he done was snort. But he stayed anchored."

This, to veteran outdoorsmen who have lived with the great unpredictable beasts, is typical though amazing grizzly behavior.

The more controversial point is, will a grizzly attack, unprovoked? And, will it "hunt" a man down with intent to kill?

Some answer yes to both questions. Some are equally vehement in saying no. Here again the most enlightening answer would seem to come from instances of what the grizzly has done in each case.

What happened a few years ago to an Alaska prospector along the Slana River would seem to illustrate the first question.

This was an elderly fellow who, at the time, had a small log cabin set back in the woods some distance from the Glenn Highway which follows the river there. In order to reach the cabin, the old fellow had to leave his jeep and hike some distance into the spruce. This he did, staying overnight with his partner.

The next morning, he started back for the jeep.

Midway of the few hundred yards, he was abruptly startled into virtual paralysis by the roar of a grizzly, *behind* him!

This man carried no rifle. Neither did he have any kind of food with him which the bruin could smell. Neither were there any cubs about, nor any sign of bear as he'd traversed the trail. Turning, he saw the big silvertip bearing down on him. There could be no doubt that the animal had waited, concealed and silent, until he'd passed, then it had charged him from the rear.

In telling of it, this unfortunate fellow said everything that happened left him dazed and uncertain from that point. All he remembered with clarity was that it was a huge boar—being close enough that he could see its genitals.

Before the enraged beast left him, it had broken his arm, bit his face, bit holes in both his hips and back, and in an effort to crush his head, had bitten off the whole top of his scalp. This left him unconscious, and the bear likely thought him dead, and left.

When the poor fellow came to, he laboriously dragged himself to the cabin, where his partner found him and went for help. They flew the victim to an "outside" hospital, where it took 280-odd stitches to sew up his wounds.

Later, friends in the Slana country took up a collection for him, raised over $600, and included a .357 Magnum revolver as future "insurance" against grizzlies.

The shortness of a grizzly's temper always amazes both the novice and the observant. "Hair-triggered" best describes it, and certain basic situations will habitually turn an otherwise "peaceful" silvertip into a raging fury. These include other things than food. A sharp noise at close range will often enrage this bear. Trivial annoyances will, also, as will surprise, old wounds, and any tendency of man towards pugnacity at close range.

I know of one grizzly which turned a pack string wrong side out, after the packer had moved far off the trail to avoid the oncoming beast. Having to kill the animal, despite all effort to avoid it, the packer found that the bear was full of old fight wounds, festering and alive with maggots.

Dalziel told me that many a time he'd studied a distant grizzly digging whistling marmots. All would go well until the bear found a rodent in a rocky crevice which he could not tear apart. The moment he found that he could not reach the marmot, the beast would "fly into a most awesome rage. He'd bawl, slap rocks, jump up and down like a child in a tantrum, then lope away, roaring and cussing himself out, you know."

Food itself has a bearing on the grizzly's ferocity. It is generally conceded that bears which live on berries and fish in the lower regions are not as mean and full of cussedness as those bears which, through necessity, have to live higher up and feed on rodents, roots, carrion, and meat.

Often bears which have to live on harsh diets, especially those made up mostly of roots and other unpalatables, are filled with large intestinal worms. I've been told by men who have killed such bears that these worms will sometimes reach a length of eighteen inches. The grizzly I killed in Alaska in 1958 had these worms—his whole intestinal tract was filled with them, we discovered while trying to retrieve the spent bullet.

These worms averaged six inches in length. They crawled like a mess of angle worms when exposed. Such a condition in any animal is conducive to short temper, and ill health. I am convinced that such a condition would greatly affect what a bear would do in any sort of contact with man.

Two brief instances involving Jake Butler will indicate the sheer awe and respect which the average northern Indian accords the legendary "horrible bear," and have a bearing on whether a grizzly might actually stalk or pursue a human being.

I have known and hunted with Jake for a couple of years. And while it is hard to tell what most northern Indians think, I gathered that his personal fear of a grizzly was based on legend, tradition, and his basic religion. To him, in some fashion, the live grizzly represented the reincarnation of a spirit which was his own brother-of-the-wild. To kill a grizzly, for him, was not only akin to killing a blood brother, but the departed spirit from such a kill would live on in the form of another bear which would take horrible vengeance.

This belief may have, in the first instance, accounted for what Jake did (or didn't do.)

At the time, Jake, as a guide, was left alone in a hunting camp. Many northern Indians, in such a predicament, simply won't stay alone, in bear country. Others, with greater control over their fears, may stay; but they'll sleep atop a cache, not on the ground where a grizzly can reach them.

Jake is not full Indian, but has part Irish blood in him. He was in the tent at the time, in a sleeping bag.

During the night, a big grizzly had approached the tent from the rear. Like the grizzly mentioned earlier, which ruined our British Columbia tent, this one, too, didn't bother to walk around. In one great swipe of his paw, he tore the tent's end out. Jake, rudely awakened, but fully inside his bed, watched the bear in horror as it walked straight through the "rag house," two feet from where he lay; and then, at thirty feet, just outside in the moonlight, it turned completely around. As if an afterthought, it regarded Jake in his bed—hungry-like.

By then Jake had his rifle, which always lay just outside the covers, in easy access.

"Why didn't you kill him?" I asked.

"I froze. I *couldn't* shoot," Jake said, simply, pointedly.

The other instance reached a far greater personal climax, and happened in another Alaska district adjacent.

It was late spring this time, and Jake had been shooting muskrats for their hides, with a repeating .22 rifle. The procedure was simple. During the long twilight hours of this season, he'd go to a lake shore, pull up a big pile of dry grass to sit upon on the bank-ice, and then wait for the rats to come out and play about at the edge of the ice. When the rats were shot and skinned, he'd discard the carcasses and go to another lake, to repeat the process.

In bear country, such tidbits would not remain long, of course. But shortly, Jake first got the "feeling," as he said, then the conviction that he was being followed in his operations by a certain big grizzly. Evidence showed that this bear, once tasting the flesh and appreciating the abundance of the rats' carcasses, had depended upon this food supply, and began tracking Jake from lake to lake.

Soon, the time interval narrowed down alarmingly. Jake no sooner would skin the rats and move, till the carcasses would be gone. Instinctively, he knew that soon the bear would show in his presence. It became a nervous battle of wits, and Jake was torn between the necessity of shooting more rats for a living and an unholy fear of that bear.

Sure enough, as he sat on the grass pile one evening at twilight, he saw the great hulking form slipping up through the shore trees toward him. He rose, shouted, waved his arms, and called the beast names. But instead of leaving, the bear began champing his jaws, and edging forward.

When the animal was within eighty yards, Jake could stand it no longer. Knowing any animal's aversion to fire, he quickly lit the grass pile. When the fire blazed high, the animal reluctantly left. Afterward, in full daylight, Jake circled his own tracks to find that the beast had followed him again from this lake.

Further evidence in the following nights showed that the bear persisted. Jake became convinced that the animal would never leave him or his skimpy outfit in the area, alone; eventually one of them would have to kill the other.

It happened soon, in fairly good light one evening just before dusk, as Jake made ready for the night's shooting. Without any warning, the grizzly showed up along the shore line. The only rifle Jake had for the rat season was the puny .22, and he hoped some way to do the job with that.

Pulling an arm load of dry grass again, and with matches ready to light it instantly, he began stalking towards the animal, which was at the edge of surrounding timber. His idea was to get reasonably close, try for an ear shot, but light the grass quickly if necessary.

As he slowly edged towards the animal, the bear showed no intention of leaving. At seventy yards, it simply crouched down in the grass, ears flattened.

Jake, knowing it was now or never, began shooting at the beast's head. Fast as he could, he emptied the tubular magazine of the old Winchester repeater at bruin's head. At the first shot, the animal rose and roared in rage. Squealing with pain and anger, it slapped at its head, then raced along the lake shore.

Jake is a professional dog racer, by trade, and used to

run the famed Fairbanks dog races. He told me that one such event was for a distance of 164 miles, in two heats of 82 miles each; and that his time was 18 hours and 30 minutes. To make such time, Jake usually ran one-half the distance behind the sled. I suspect that the speed he used now, after emptying the .22 rifle, greatly exceeded that, as he flew around the lake in the opposite direction. The distance he covered, too, before stopping, may have been similar.

Two days later, he tracked the big grizzly from where he'd last seen it. The bear was dead, a full mile away. Of the eight bullets which had hit it, one lucky little slug had cut the jugular vein, and the huge beast slowly bled out as it traveled.

Tex Purvis once told me of an example indicating that no matter how much contact a man makes with a grizzly, that bear will remain basically true to nature; and it will, under any of the above-mentioned aggravations or annoyances, immediately revert back both as to shortness of temper, and ferocity.

At one time Tex and a certain Major Hare were camped together at a summer camp in Yellowstone Park. They lived in a walled-up tent in an area frequented by bears. In fact, one old bear, a black, had become a camp problem. Invariably, she'd knock over the garbage cans, raid the kitchen tent if no one was around, and otherwise mess things up. This animal in some way, likely from a fight with another bear, had lost an eye. So, naturally, she was called "Old One-Eye."

On one occasion Tex was alone in the tent all evening, the Major being away visiting a friend some distance away. When the Major returned about ten o'clock, he was white as the proverbial sheet.

"I couldn't get a word out of Rabbit," Tex said. "We called him Rabbit, because his name was Hare. But he just lay there on the cot, studying the tent top. 'What the hell ails you?' I finally asked, half-mad that he wouldn't answer me before. And finally I got it out of him.

"Seems he'd been coming back to the camp along the main trail in. And maybe a couple hundred yards from the tent, he'd seen Old One-Eye sniffing along the trail. It was fairly decent light, and the old sow had her hind end towards him.

"Rabbit always hated her guts, for the trouble she kept causing the camp. And for some damn reason or another, he decided to get even a little. Anyway, he sneaked up behind her, pussy-footing along so she couldn't hear. And luckily, he made it. Hell, what happened then I'd have split a gut to see! Rabbit reared back like he was going to make a drop kick for Notre Dame, and kicked that old she-bastard full in the hinder. With everything he had.

"About then, Rabbit made a terrible discovery. It wasn't Old One-Eye at all. It was a big grizzly that had no business being that close to a tent, but sure was.

"When Rabbit booted him, he came uncorked even before he felt it. In a bound, he was up on two feet and swinging. His first swipe took off Rabbit's hat. And I guess the fact that Rabbit was a short man, or had sprawled off-balance when he kicked, was all that saved his head from sailing off along with the hat! And *after* that first swipe, Rabbit was long gone!"

CHAPTER 9

How To Hunt A Grizzly

The grizzly bear is one of the continent's most prized trophies; and the average red-blooded hunter wants one both for primal reasons bearing on the danger of the chase, and because of the grizzly's relative rarity as compared with other big-game species.

There are two fundamentals involved in getting that grizzly. First, one must some way get into country known to produce grizzly bears. Secondly, the visiting or non-resident hunter must employ an outfitter who knows the business of getting bears and further, who has a good hunter-success record on this prized species.

The actual hunting is done during two seasons—in the spring during the two to four weeks immediately following the bear's emergence from hibernation, and in the fall months usually from September first until the end of the fall hunting seasons (on all big game). Only at these two seasons is the pelage of the grizzly prime and suitable as a trophy. And with today's sparse population of these animals, that is the only reason the hunter, *per se*, should ever consider killing a silvertip.

Spring hunting for grizzlies is, generally, not so productive for the greatest number of hunters. There are sound reasons for this. First, grizzly country is often difficult of

A light spotting scope is being increasingly used in serious bear hunting.

access in that wet, cold period immediately after the bear's emergence from the winter sleep. There is usually remaining snow, mud, tough forest roads and trails (if any), and similar rugged conditions.

Next, other desirable species of big game are not hunted in the spring. This makes the grizzly hunt a lone, long shot. If the hunter fails on a bruin, he comes home with nothing else except the pleasure of the hunt—not another specimen or two, to help offset the necessary heavy expenses incurred.

Again, hunters are conditioned to the "feel" of hunting during the autumn months, with their complementary glories of better weather, a blaze of fall coloration, and an overall intangible, but very real, spirit of the chase. The "hunter's moon" was well labeled.

There are exceptions. In many areas of the Far North, the first spring slide areas, the new shoots of grassy slopes, and the wet basin bottoms initially bursting with new plant life and subsequent rodents, all produce grizzlies. Too, after the winter's erasing of all spoor, any evidence of a grizzly's workings are easy to detect, and his pattern of movement interpreted.

Here again the hunter must get into a region known to produce bears; and broadly speaking, he does this with the aid of a reputable outfitter. It is sufficient to say, in this respect, that in most of the better grizzly country, the services of a guide are required by law. This is true in Wyoming. It is true and has been for some years in Canada. It was once true in Alaska, but was discontinued for a few years; and currently, all indications are that this new state will soon reinstate the guide law. Even if a guide were not required by law for grizzly hunting, for purposes of hunter safety and law enforcement, the wise hunter would employ one. Otherwise he's a real babe-in-the-woods in a strange country, and his chances of success are small.

Once into a bear country, the smart hunter, of course, depends upon the judgment of his outfitter to get him up to bruin. This does not prevent the hunter, however, from being a real help in doing this, if he knows how to *hunt*. Two men's experience is broader than one's. Two men's eyes will cover more area, and with the same experience, spot more game. And in the very rugged pursuit of *any* grizzly, it is not good business to hunt alone. There are hazards besides the bear.

Areas to scout, study, and watch for include the first bare hillsides following snow avalanches; the first patches of tender grasses pushing up on the slopes after the first thaws and mud; the spruce "rubbing-trees" on which any grizzly in the region will make his mark, and will some time return to, in his circuit of travel, for enforcement purposes; the areas of old fallen timber which is rotting and whose logs show worm holes (bruin will tear them apart for grubs, ants, and worms); the semi-sandy, grassy bars along creek bottoms, where bears similarly root for grubs; any pronounced game trails, especially those high ones leading from one main drainage area to another; any country producing Adder's Tooth, or "dog-tooth violets" which bears like; and any winter-killed game which snow slides or melting snow leave uncovered. Too, the fresh spoor of any game animal which shows undue fright, or extended travel—old *Ursus horribilus* may handily be the cause of it.

One of the most productive ways of hunting a spring grizzly is, as mentioned previously, baiting with a dead

A lucky hunter smiles over his first small grizzly.

horse any bear known to be in the region. Placing such a bait is sheer art. It must be done at precisely the right time so as to be "ripe" for bruin to smell, not when he comes from hibernation, but at that period afterwards when he is conditioned on green grasses to where his digestive system will accept meat. This in itself is quite a trick, especially if any blacks are in the area. Many a $100 bait has been licked clean by black bears and yodel dogs, while the exasperated hunter waits for a grizzly, known to be close by, to make up his mind to come in.

Too, such baits must be placed with due regard for canyon winds which not only must "use" their rivers-of-air to fetch the scent to bruin, but must also prevent any man scent from being carried to the place where the bear is located.

Again, such baits must be placed to simulate a natural situation in which an old horse might die—not be placed with the obvious purpose of utilizing available cover or "blinds." Further, the bait must be placed with the knowledge that any grizzly will come in, not by crossing openings, but habitually inside a timber belt which will conceal his movements. Any open spaces in this route will automatically spell failure in the case of any wise old bear.

Years ago, I must admit, I was against such hunting procedure. It seemed unethical. But after watching it done, and studying the sketchy results it produces in an overall picture, my opinion has changed. I have never yet hunted and killed a bear over such a bait. But I have witnessed far more unethical hunting procedures (such as hunting *any* game animal with an inadequate "more sporting" smaller weapon than will produce a quick humane death) practiced in many types of accepted hunting.

One year's record of the "deadliness" of bruin-baiting may illustrate. In 1953, I killed Wyoming's first grizzly of the year, not over a bait. That same year there were not over six recorded grizzly kills for the entire state, including bait-kills. As practiced in that vast state, bear-baiting is still almost literally a needle-in-the-haystack proposition.

The fall hunts for grizzly have a greater potential and a bigger overall thrill. As with black bear hunting, the grizzly should always be hunted in conjunction with other species. Such species should be the "high" species, like sheep, goats, and caribou. In short, plan a grizzly hunt into an area where these alpine species are found not only in considerable numbers, but also in size or trophy-worthiness.

There are basic reasons for doing this.

First, the grizzly has been driven by civilization to the most remote areas left. These are the highest areas, also. And while it would be incorrect to say that the silvertip *lives* in the crags, spires, and peaks of sheep and goat country, he's usually not far below and indeed is often right among them.

This observation accords with actuality. Bill Jenkins, one of Don DeHart's guides, as one example, had killed a Dall ram high in the peaks above the Copper River in 1957 in several inches of snow. They'd caped it out, took the trophy to camp, and returned for the meat next morning. Since it was high, treacherous, and slippery, the two of them had left the rifles at camp and returned with only pack boards. When they were 24 paces from the caped ram, they saw a big grizzly coming in for the meat. Evidence showed, too, that *another* and bigger grizzly had during the night eaten a whole shoulder and the neck of the caped-out sheep. The "new" grizzly was just 50 yards away!

"My partner had a pistol," Bill told me, "and he shot it dry over that grizzly's head. I yelled to high heaven . . . and did we take off with that meat!"

Bill told me of another party which was back-packing out a ram when a sow grizzly came after the meat, while it was on their backs. They had to kill the bear in self-defense.

In these two instances, back-packing meant the country

was too high, craggy, and uncertain for horses to work. Also, no other game can go higher than Dall rams. Grizzlies were at the same craggy elevation.

In my own personal experience, my first grizzly was taken in ram country and as we hunted rams. So was my largest grizzly—we spotted him while working ram "saddles" at over 7200 feet and in the snow. Bruin was just below us, in an alpine meadow. Again, my last grizzly was taken in Alaska in 1958, not a mile from where Von Johnson killed a Barren Ground Caribou which will go into the Boone & Crockett records. Both animals were using and inhabiting the high plateau country above timberline.

The year before, my partner John Phillips killed the biggest grizzly to come from the Slana River country in years, far up towards the peaks of Gillette Pass. We were hunting prize caribou.

The range of the grizzly in fall overlaps the range of all these species, as well as the moose pastures lower down. Broadly speaking, where an abundance of these species is found, it means that they are largely unmolested. Since a grizzly now uses the most unmolested country left, it is but natural that their ranges coincide.

More, in such remote areas which have not been hunted too recently or hard, one finds the largest heads of the horned and antlered species. He's also apt to find the greatest abundance of large bears there, the real old high-country smarties.

While it is true that the hunter's bruin may not be found with sheep, goat, or caribou, there is a double advantage of hunting them together. First, in order to reach sheep and goat habitat, lower elevations have to be traversed. One may hunt bear both on the way up and when returning downward.

A second advantage is that after bagging that ram or billy, the offal and remains then become prime grizzly attraction; and a careful hunting of the "innard" for days afterward is a fine way to get a bruin.

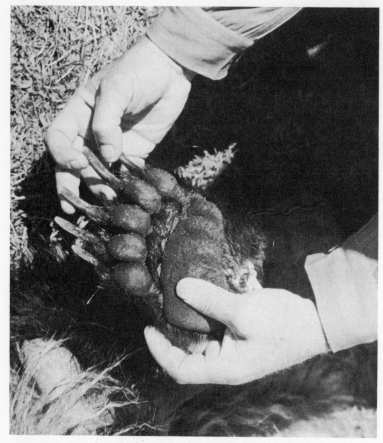

Forefoot of an average British Columbia grizzly.

Another fine way to hunt grizzlies is to hunt the elevation consistent with their current food supply. If any
salmon remain in the streams, then along the moose trails
bordering such creeks and streams are fine places to run
into a bear. If, later, the bears have left the fish for a blueberry diet, then it's smart to hunt at the elevation of greatest
blueberry abundance, and in the larger patches.

My 1957 Alaska grizzly came as a result of utilizing both
above procedures. I was being guided by Jake Butler at
the time. And as we stopped the horses high above timber-

line, to glass all country below, Jake suddenly said, "I see a caribou, maybe two miles up there."

As I tried to make it out, Jake turned and said, "Or would you rather try for that grizzly over *that* way?"

The caribou I was really after was promptly forgotten. We turned and headed slightly downward to where, two miles to the north, a medium-sized grizzly was methodically working the blueberry patches—a half-mile of solid fruit. Leaving the horses tethered over the ridge, we moved down on foot; and an hour later, from a position above, I shot the grizzly which had a mouthful and bellyful of the purple fruit.

If I were asked to state exactly what precise spot, elevation, area, or type of country I'd prefer above all others for grizzly, I'd unhesitatingly say, "The basin heads above timber line."

These great basin heads of the North country have several attractions for grizzlies during the late fall hunts. First, they are remote and unmolested—the grizzly isn't bothered there by lesser animals. Secondly, they are open areas which provide ease of movement, large areas to work, and a position from which anything from below can best be seen coming up.

Again, at this season, the whistling marmots inhabit this elevation in the rocks just under the patches of glacial snow. They are fat and ready themselves to hibernate against the rigors of winter. Their colonies are easily plundered by the grizzly, and provide his last fattening food. Consequently, most of his daylight hours are spent in digging them out.

On a single trip into the Cassiars, my one partner, Doc Jacobs, killed his grizzly by utilizing this knowledge. He simply went into the biggest basin head he could find, waited patiently until the shrill whistling of disturbed marmots told him that their agitation might be caused by a bruin, and spotted the bear with his glasses. It was no great trick to utilize the broken terrain to make a perfect stalk, and from 200 yards Doc rolled his bruin.

Our two other partners, Martin and Fairley, similarly spotted what they thought at first was a big moose, far up in the basin head at the west end of Rainbow Lake, just under the snow. Wondering just what a moose would be doing up there, they glassed the spot, finding it was two grizzlies. They came in that evening with the capes of both.

From the hunter's standpoint, the vast basin heads offer many hunting opportunities not afforded by the lower bush and timber levels. First he can see farther. His eyesight, aided by high-powered binoculars, becomes in these big open areas not only comparable to that of the quarry he seeks, but even better. In other words, in timber or bush country, he can see only a portion of the animals there because of foliage concealment. What he does spot at closer ranges is apt to detect him first because of keener vision, smell, and hearing. But in the highest open elevations, this is reversed.

Many of the best hunters now use spotting scopes in conjunction with binoculars for hunting grizzlies in these open basin heads. With a 20-power scope, all advantage of spotting and stalking are with the hunter, not the quarry. The problem used to be bulk in any spotting scope meant to be used by the horse-back, or foot hunter. Today, at least one manufacturer has solved the problem. Bushnell's small 13-inch Sentry spotting scope, together with a light stand or tripod, solves the problem perfectly. It carries handily on a pack board, or in saddle bags; and the steps it saves the hunter, in open regions of the "top" country, are legion.

Another advantage of hunting the basin heads is based upon any game species' liking for "edge" country. Grizzlies, like other game, may be found anywhere. But the bulk of their hunting for food is not done in heavy bush or timber. They may use the timber, bush, and "thick" country in traversing from one basin to another. But their most-used general level most always coincides with edge country.

The hunter at a basin head, and with a good spotting scope, is in command of the two best edge areas—the upper fringe of timber, and the low edge of the bush, where Northern bush and muskeg meet the shores of lakes. Game is relatively easy to spot and mark down at either. The quarry's probable intention may be interpreted, and a sensible stalk arranged.

There is another basic but little mentioned reason for hunting in the high basin heads. With the heavy fall frosts, such pests as black flies and mosquitoes are considerably thinned. But during September at least—and this is the heavy hunting month—these little so-and-so's remain in numbers. Game, like man, detests these; and game will range relatively high during the pest season, to avoid them and the heat.

Because of this, the incidence of game at higher elevations is greater than at low levels, such as the Canadian bush, which black flies love. From the hunter's standpoint, he can endure longer, less motionless, and happier hunting hours up in the top country where breezes thin out these biting, stinging pests.

The novice, who has never been in thick black-fly or gnat country, does not regard this as serious. Personally, I have been in Canadian and Alaskan bush where the swarms of these pests were so thick we'd inhale them. A few hours of that, for me at least, would not only discourage all thought of hunting, but would drive me crazy.

But perhaps the main reason for hunting grizzlies in the high, bare basin apexes, is the simple fact that by so doing, the hunter may hunt *down* on his game. For the veteran big-game hunter, this is fundamental. The reasons for this hinge on air, an animal's vision, his normal escape route, and the pattern of pursuit by enemies.

Briefly, warming air ascends, while cooling air decends. By making the day's climb to a high elevation the first

My partner, John Phillips, with big Slana River, Alaska, grizzly.

thing each morning the hunter hunts, he usually arrives at the game's elevation, or above it, by the heat of the day. This means that the numerous little fish-tailing "rivers of air" will from then on carry his scent above the game. More, at higher elevations, any scent has a tendency to dissipate itself to where it won't alarm game, more than the same scent when it comes from the hemmed-in bottoms, and coming up towards game.

Since scent is one of the grizzly's most usable factors, this is very important. A grizzly will detect danger much farther away with his nose and his ears (despite their small size) than he will with his vision. Remaining unsmelled then, is a great asset to the grizzly hunter.

Normally, in the big areas of grizzly terrain, the hunter and guide will begin to descend before the mountain air cools too much, creating a danger (in that the bear might smell them) going back downward to camp.

To the beginner, with his blunt sense of smell compared

with that of a bear, all this may appear trivial. It is not.
I have repeatedly claimed that if air were *colored,* so that
the hunter might see the movement, directions, and intensity of air which he practically doesn't know is in motion, his hunting habits and procedures would immediately
and violently change.

Again, the physical aspects of a bear's vision are such
that he detects danger, or any movement, far easier if it
is seen below him than if it is above. The bony orbits of
his eyes, at the ends of the zygomatic arches, protrude
farther on top than underneath his eyeballs. Too, his eyes,
like the black bear's, are closely set.

Couple with this the fact that a bear's natural stance
tends to point his eyes straight ahead at no more than
level, and even downward a lot of the time, as he sniffs
trails and scouts for food, and it will be seen that the
greater sweep of his vision is habitually below the level,
not above it.

It is similar with man's vision. Just as it is easier to locate
a bear when looking down, so is it harder for a bear to
detect a hunter when looking upward, and vice versa.

This is largely true of any big game. It is especially true
of a grizzly, since he fears nothing, can lick anything which
he contacts, has no mortal enemies from the skies (such
as the young of sheep and goats have in eagles), and therefore has no innate *need* of looking upward.

The basic matter of a game animal's escape route has a
bearing on the hunting elevation and terrain. From deer
and antelope, to elk, moose, and bear, all game animals
travel so that the areas where they stop, feed, bed down,
and shade up, will all be so situated as to leave an immediate escape route open. That, briefly, is why you will
find that most animals bed down or shade up on promontories over looking country *below* them; and thus have
possible three directions to jump, at the first signs of danger.
That's why deer love ridges, why mountain sheep lie
down on high shelving ledges, and why wapiti shade up

for the day at the end of timbered promontories.

While the grizzly fears nothing, he nevertheless is often aggravated by other beasts, and even individuals of his own species, and, of course, man. Grizzlies, too, have a perpetual escape route open. Startle one quickly, and he'll either wheel on a dime and romp back along the route he's come—and which he knows is open—or he'll retreat violently *forward!* I am convinced that many a grizzly which has been startled or annoyed at close range has chosen to fight partly because of the very position in which he has been startled. His escape route has been, to his way of thinking, obstructed.

With most game species, the enemy follows the species. Upon contact or threat of it, the pursued moves upward to rougher country, to less foliage which may impede flight, or to less concealment for the enemy. Sheep race wildly up into the crags to escape wolves. Wapiti climb to the high saddles and cliff bases to thwart man, who has less speed and ability to climb fast. Deer head for ridges and high country when spooked by cougar. And pursued grizzles get "higher and more remote."

The wise hunter takes advantage of this instinctive conditioning, simply by habitually approaching his quarry from above—the *unsuspected* direction.

These are the fundamental ways of hunting a grizzly bear. Other methods include the glassing of all trails, since the grizzly, like a black, prefers the easier footing of trails; the patient watching of any recent game-kill remains; and the actions of any horse he may be riding while in bear country. Once a horse, especially one used to game hunting, snorts, shies, points his ears, or refuses to go forward—*look out!* Whatever has spooked him in the adjacent bush may be that grizzly. It can be located by sighting exactly between the horse's ears, and down the plane of his face.

One general, overall hunting technique cannot be stressed too much. That is to have one's wits constantly about him, while in *any* bear country. Surprise may be mutual, as between hunter and grizzly. But it's smart to make any subsequent befuddlement be on the part of bruin, not the hunter.

Finally, once a grizzly is seen, there is that vital problem of getting the first shot into the most vital area. If at all possible to achieve, the best shot at a grizzly is a broadside shot through the shoulders. Such a shot, approximately

Typical northern cache on which gear is placed to make it grizzly-proof when hunters are away from camp.

mid way as to height, does one or two important things. It breaks the near shoulder, greatly impeding the bear's chances to move fast—forward or away. It also penetrates the lungs and possibly the top of the heart, causing relatively quick death.

If, at the time of the shot, the bear is unmolested but with the near fore-leg forward, then the best shot is broadside into the center of the "boiler-room." Such a shot, with an adequate bullet, is very apt to break the opposite shoulder blade, going out.

Only the coolest rifle shots should try for neck shots on a grizzly, and then only at relatively close range. Such shots, if they hit the spine, are quick killers; but it's easy to miss them. Brain shots, even on charging grizzlies, are best left to fiction. Not one hunter in a hundred can do it, and even then the chances are far better if a chest shot is attempted.

Once a grizzly is shot and drops, the hunter should *never* assume that the beast is fatally hit, until it has had time to die. Grizzlies have the often heart-stopping habit of dropping and balling up to any kind of a hit—even a hit in the fore-leg will make a silvertip do this. The novice, unless he is aware of the trait, is apt to be romping up to his "dead" bear about the time it gets to its feet again.

The matter of a suitable outfitter for that long-awaited grizzly hunt is very important to any hunter. The outfitting business, like any other, has its peculiar hazards, its ups and downs, its dependable personnel for the most part, and the occasional shyster. The hunter who has saved his shekels, often for many years, to go on a single grizzly hunt, does not want to have his time and his money wasted. He wants above all a grizzly bear. But when searching for an outfitter who can take him to his trophy, with a reasonable expectation of success, the novice is usually at a total loss as to where to begin.

Like the proverbial fence, there are two different sides to the outfitting business. It is extremely helpful for the hunter to understand both his own, and the outfitter's position, before he makes any definite arrangements.

First, consider the sportman's position. He's saved hard-earned money for the Big Trip. He has accumulated his time off. He buys equipment. He has carefully studied the available regions where he has his best chances for success, so far as he can tell. He fully expects to kill a bear.

However, before planking down his deposit, he wants definite assurance, or even a flat guarantee, that he'll get a shot at his grizzly.

The outfitter, from his viewpoint, knows that the hunter's fees represent his own bacon-and-beans. He, naturally, will put his best foot forward in all advertising, literature, and enthusiasm to the prospective hunter. The outfitter also knows that hunting seasons are constantly getting shorter; that remote and productive grizzly country is getting more scarce; that his average hunter is a sheer greenhorn, who likely can't ride a horse well, can't shoot too dependably when the chips are down; and is more than likely a lard-hindered man of middle age whose corpulency has come along with enough money for such a jaunt, and who can't walk the hills; and who likely will be miserable in the face of such rugged camp conditions as plain grub, wet weather, hard climbing, cold nights, and similar discouragements. Finally, most experienced outfitters know very well that, when the quarry is finally located, some men can hunt well, stalk quietly, and take advantage of a quick and reasonable opportunity; and many men would foul it up from the beginning.

For this reason, most reputable outfitters with the exception of one bear species, will *never* guarantee the hunter his game. The really good ones *will* do *this*: They will explain the region they will hunt, list the overall chances at different species of game, give references, and list satisfied clientele, to whom the prospective hunter may write. The outfitter will agree to meet the would-be hunter at road's end, take him into the hills with certain items like beds, food, tents, riding horse, guides, cook, wrangler, and specified items of gear all furnished. He agrees to hunt the individual in game country, show him a good time, and if at all possible get him his chances at game.

For this service, the outfitter charges a fee, at this writing averaging around $100 per day, per man, with everything except personal gear and rifle, furnished. The hunter agrees to pay a deposit to assure fulfillment of the contract, to be at a certain meeting place on a definite day, and to hunt a minimum number of days. After the hunt, the outfitter agrees to pack the hunter and his trophies back to transportation, at which time he completes the contract.

The very elasticity with which any big-game hunt into primitive country has to be conducted, often leads to misunderstandings.

For instance, weather is often too miserable to hunt with any hope of fun or success. If the outfitter decides to lay over a day in camp, the hunter sees a round $100 evaporate, and may complain. Or, occasionally a lucky novice will collect his quarry the first day out of camp. An occasional one, instead of being pleased with his outfitter for such good fortune, will actually say, "Why not me quit now and go home? Why should I fork over a hundred bucks a day for the rest of the minimum, when I've got my game?"

Such unforeseeables are always cropping up. The reliable and honest outfitter, and the sportsmanlike hunter, usually iron out such difficulties without trouble as they crop up. I know many outfitters who annually give a hunter an extra hunting day free if he hasn't got his game yet, if a delay has been the outfitter's, not the hunter's fault, and especially if the hunter proves himself a good sport.

Oppositely, I've several times seen a sportsman, when a temporary emergency came up, cheerfully take over such camp chores as wrangling, cording up wood, washing, cooking, or even guiding other hunters. All without any expected reduction in his fee, but simply to help out, and as an overall part of the fun.

It's sufficient to say that men with that attitude, on either side of the hunter-outfitter relationship, usually end up with a most satisfactory hunt to all concerned. My personal experience involving many of the top outfitters of the continent, has invariably been this: They'll bust a gut to show an appreciative, and understanding hunter a grand hunt, and make every effort to get his game. They won't do this for the griper, or picayunish person.

One nationally known outfitter simply tells the very few "lemons" he unwittingly books, after a hunt, "Please don't come out here again. You don't belong in the hills, and we have no business taking your money."

On the opposite side of the fence, the vacation hunter often has legitimate complaints. Since the reputable outfitter must charge heavy fees to survive, the shyster is always tempted to capitalize upon the honest outfitter's reputation. He'll, if possible, steal the other's hunting country; make exorbitant advertising claims which he never intends fulfilling; rake together a broom-tail outfit; haul the poor novice hunter into country that's never seen a head of game; dump him off with some second-rate guide who's idea of guiding is to get up at noon, and try to ride the hunter so hard the first day, over the toughest terrain he can find, that he'll give up and won't hunt the rest of his minimum; and, worse, suddenly find all kind of imaginary "extras" to charge the poor guy. Often the hunter has to pay through the nose, or he can't get back out of the hills.

Such chiseling outfitters, I am convinced, should be shot on the spot.

How then, to team up with a suitable outfit?

An outfitting service is a commodity and is bought and sold like any other item. Reputable outfitters advertise in the better outdoor journals. Many of the best make annual tours, lining up prospective hunters, and often showing movies of their camps, country, other hunters and their game, and giving an overall, visual picture of their operations. Such outfitters may usually be reached through some form of their advertising. Often they are contacted by a friend or acquaintance who has hunted with them.

Once a contact is made, then it's up to the hunter to decide how reputable the outfitter is.

One indication is the charges. In outfitting, as in a retail business, the buyer usually gets what he pays for, so long as the service or goods is reputable. Briefly, the expensive outfitter must charge high fees to keep him producing sufficiently so as to make his services attractive in the first place. Any claims of an outfitter to get the hunter a grizzly "cheap" should be regarded with suspicion.

Secondly, any reputable outfitter will furnish an abundance of names of former clientele who have been satisfied with the services, country, personnel, and results obtained. I have found that a correspondence with such satisfied customers gives one of the very best indications of the caliber of hunt he will furnish.

If the replies come back saying, "Had a grand hunt. Saw fifty head of big game altogether, three grizzlies, and got the last one—," or, "Had a whale of a trip with him, had my chance at a bear but got buck fever till I couldn't hit the broad side of a country back-house," then it's a fair gamble that the outfitter fulfilled his promises.

However, if the replies are non-enthusiastic, or even one saying, "Whatever you do, confidentially, don't ever get caught in the hills with that so and so" then one should be able to sort the kernel from the chaff.

There are two other near-certain ways of determining if the outfitter is reputable, good as his word, and will make every effort to show the hunter a fine hunt. These are both a bit hard on the beginning outfitter, who may be reputable but has not yet established himself; but the young outfitter, if he means to make a success of it, I'm sure won't mind and will some day overcome the obstacles.

First, ask any prospective outfitter for a definite breakdown of his hunter-success record, for the past three years. The good outfits will provide this information, if convinced

The author's 1958 Alaska grizzly where it fell and in the type of cover in which the big silvertips are ordinarily found. One liver-shot from a 200-grain bullet in Winchester's new .338 Magnum did the job.

you mean business. If they reply, "Last year we got 25 caribou for 30 hunters; eight rams for 10 sheep hunters; three grizzlies for six bear hunters—one hunter turned down one which he said was too small—; and all filled on moose—," then you know you're not dealing with a fly-by-night outfit. A good reputation and record "sells" them.

If, conversely, you get no reply, or a vague answer something about "there were millions of head of game in the region, but the disgruntled hunter wouldn't hit the ball despite *everything* I did to see they had a good time . . . however, years ago so-and-so's great step-half-uncle-in-law bagged sheep, elk, moose, bear—all record heads—all over the place—," drop such a guy with all possible speed.

Finally, ask any outfitter with whom you expect to hunt for an average of how many "repeaters" he has on his yearly list. Hunters who have a grand time and come back every year or so, are the life-blood of any reputable outfit. A high proportion of repeat hunters is the novice hunter's best assurance that the outfitter gives satisfaction.

As a final precaution, be sure that all agreements are understood between hunter and outfitter, and in writing, at least in the correspondence to which either might refer. It is not enough for the outfitter to write, "As to gear, you come on out and we'll take care of you, you bet." It's far more productive of good feelings later if he writes, "I furnish tents, guides, food, horses, saddles . . . you bring your own sleeping bag, rifle, scabbard, binoculars, and likker."

Similarly, it is not enough for the hunter to promise vaguely, "I'll be out your way around the 10th, unless something unforeseen comes up, and then I'll call you the last minute." It's better to say, "I'll be there at the Spruce Landing-Strip, at 10:00 A.M. the morning of September 7th. I'll have all items in the list you said for me to bring."

No matter under what conditions you hunt that grizzly, it's always one of man's greatest thrills when the guide nudges your arm, and whispers with excitement "There's your *bear!*"

Part Three

BROWN BEAR

CHAPTER 10

Biggest Bear

Sheer size has been a big factor in making the Alaska Brown Bear, *Ursus*, one of the most attractive trophies.

Until just a few years ago, the brown bear—erroneously called the Kodiak Bear because of his abundance on that island—was considered to be our biggest carnivore. The weight of these ponderous animals will run from 800 pounds, average, to an estimated weight of over 1600 pounds. Too, the skull measurements of recorded heads exceed those of any other ursine species as to total score.

The last few years, a controversy has arisen over this. Today, a few observers claim that the polar bear is even larger than the brownie, despite the obviously smaller skull measurements. The polar bear's head tends more to slimness, against the brownie's characteristic broad head. The polar, too, has a far longer neck, adding to the illusion of overall slimness, not to blocky weight.

Mounted specimens of the polar bear—full bear mounts, duplicated from field measurements, are enormous things; and in upright position, with neck extended, do often reach a greater overall height than the stocky brown bear and give an impression of greater weight.

Size is a thing hard to prove or disprove. The equipment for weighing our largest bear, of either species, while in bear habitat, is skimpy. The matter herein, however, does not make a great deal of difference until it is proven one way or the other.

Our brown bear have been here a long time. The history of this animal coincides in time with that of the grizzly. Both date back to the Pleistocene age. Present-day hunters, however, have known very little of the brown bear until the turn of the century, due to inaccessibility of the animal's ranges and lack of present-day means of transportation.

Brownie is distributed over a far smaller range than any other species of American bear. Broadly speaking, this range is the wet coastal area of the Pacific slope, beginning approximately midway of British Columbia, thence northward past Yukon and Alaska all the way to the tip of the Aleutian Islands.

His range extends inland a hundred miles or so on an average, overlapping the range and habitat of the grizzly. There are recorded instances of the two species interbreeding. Too, there are old-timers who will still swear that the brown bear is "nawthin' but a big grizzly that has et so many salmon that he's twice as big, and that's all." Game biologists, though, have not only classified them as two separate species, but have also broken the brown bear species down into over a dozen sub-species.

In order to keep the classification separate, at least as to trophies, the tendency today is to classify all these big bears taken within 75 miles of the coast as brown bear; those inland a greater distance as grizzlies.

Incidentally, the big grizzly John Phillips killed on the Slana River in 1957 had many of the characteristics of a brown bear—the big head, long broad snout, etc. Some of the guides swore it must have had brown bear blood in it.

In addition to the inland population, the brown bear inhabits numerous of the off-shore islands. Among these are Kodiak, Afognak, Admiralty, Chichagof, Baranof, and Unimak.

The population trend of this great animal has fluctuated considerably over the years. At the turn of the century, the brown bear was killed primarily for his hide. This was prized for two items popular at the time. One was for warm "lap robes" used around the lap and legs of people riding in the spring seat of wagons, and as protection against

Range of brown bear in North America.

winter cold. The other was for the big bear-skin coats so popular with men at the time.

Shortly afterward, too, fur prices were high, and foxes especially brought a good price. Many of the great bears were killed and their carcasses left to be used for fox bait. This, too, for many years tended to hold the bear population down.

Later, and coincident with the Great Depression of the 1930's, the fur market went down. By then the wagon was nearly gone as a means of transportation, and bear-skin coats were no longer popular. During this period, the brown bear population rose considerably.

About this time, however, the Alaska salmon pack began

to taper off until today the commercial salmon harvest is far below what it was in 1930. This factor had a bearing on the bear's numbers, since his staple food is salmon; and as with any species, the overall number is directly related to the available food supply. The dwindling salmon supply was particularly hard on the brown bears, since these animals, even under pressure, won't leave their salmon fishing during the months salmon is available.

Lee Hancock, Anchorage, Alaska outfitter, went to Alaska to outfit hunters in 1929, and has remained there ever since. His principal business is taking hunters to the Alaska Peninsula for brown bear. He has noticed these basic changes in bear populations, and also minor ones which have a bearing on the overall numbers.

For one thing, Hancock believes that the practice of novice hunters taking the huge old boars whenever possible has in itself tended to keep up the bear supply. This is true, largely, because brown bear seem individually afraid of each other. For instance, one sow with small cubs will usually high-tail it away from a spot at the sudden presence of another bigger sow and larger cubs.

Again, this larger sow and perhaps yearling cubs will run from the sudden presence of a large boar bear. These big boars, as with polar bears, will kill the cubs of their own species if they can catch them.

Similarly, this boar will run from a larger boar. Hancock once killed a boar brown bear which had evidently been castrated by a larger boar, during their fighting. Again, this man has observed a tendency towards cannibalism in the species. On one occasion, a large bear came and, with other bear, ate the carcass of a dead bear that was recently killed and skinned. This was unusual in that the old boars, like caribou, won't eat while rutting—they spend all their time looking for females.

When the oldest, biggest, and meanest of such a species is taken by hunters, it undoubtedly eliminates at least some inter-killing within the species.

The population of brown bears fluctuates in local and spot regions, too, due to hunter pressure. In a broad way, all brown bear country is remote and hard of access. A brown bear hunt is costly at best, and any hunter will go where he can get the biggest, the easiest.

Some of the largest bears have come from Kodiak Island, and this island also contains one of the largest bear populations. In recent years, Kodiak has been hunted more intensely than many of the other areas.

Bill Kvasnikoff has lived in that area all his life, and has observed the big animals he lives among.

Bill is pure Russian. He is not, however, the Communist type of Russian with whom the free world competes today, but as fine an American as the next guy. He is a direct descendant of a group of Russian exiles, dumped by the Czar into the Siberian-Alaska area and left to shift for themselves and live off the country.

This fellow's family became commercial fishermen, and successive generations have remained fishermen. Bill married a Scandinavian lady, and they've raised a fine family. Some of the enterprise and inventiveness which caused that first dumped band of exiles to exist, has remained in the strain all the way down to Bill.

In 1959, he showed me an old battered .300 Savage lever-action rifle, after he'd admired my own Magnum. "You see this old rifle? I've raised a family with it, and it's a good rifle yet."

"How did you raise a family with a rifle?"

"I killed moose with it. We ate moose when there was nothing else to eat. One shot, many a time, had to mean meat or we didn't eat."

His rifle had lost the rear sight, years ago. As a further example of his inventiveness, Bill had taken a plain table fork, and with no tool other than a file, had made a complete rear sight. The V notch was nothing more than the rounded space between two of the tines, which had been filed off short.

"Never missed a moose since I put it on," he grinned.

Kvasnikoff told me that while many people believe that the Kodiak Island bears have diminished, his experience is that they are on the increase. The west side of the island, being more accessible, is hunted harder, with a corresponding decrease in animals there. But the bears are on the upgrade in the island's interior and along the eastern coast.

"Why is the east coast hunted less?" I asked him.

"Too heavy seas to get there, often. It takes a 35-foot boat or bigger. Most outfits don't have that kind of craft."

All such factors have a bearing on the overall population.

Brownie's annual cycle is comparable to that of the grizzly, with several exceptions. These bears den in the highest, coldest periphery of their range in late fall. The cubs, like other bears, are born while the female is in hiberation, and are ridiculously small for so large a parent. They emerge with the mother in mid-May, and will run to around 15 pounds.

As with blacks and grizzlies, twinning is common. Three cubs are considered unusual, and four are rare.

John Belcher, noted California sportsman mentioned elsewhere, once observed four brown-bear cubs with their mother on the Alaska coast, while he was hunting for a big boar specimen.

"They were all about the same color," Belcher told me, "and exactly the same size. They traveled together, just like any family. The old lady bear treated them all just alike, and there wasn't another bear in the whole area at the time. I couldn't quite believe a brown bear ever had four, but I couldn't doubt it. Don DeHart, the outfitter, was there at the time and saw them, too."

In mentioning the incident to Lee Hancock, while talking bears, I asked if he'd ever seen four cubs. "No, but it must have been the same litter. A sow brownie won't adopt a stray cub."

The mating season begins soon after emergence. The females mate in alternate years. Under the drive towards reproduction, the boars normally spend all their time during this season hunting the sows. Other than the mating season, the brown bears are not gregarious by nature. They prefer solitude, except that the sows run with their cubs during the young's first summer; they den with these offspring the following winter; then they discard the yearlings the next spring upon emergence from hibernation.

The brown bear's pelage is in its best condition for a trophy immediately after he leaves hibernation. The oil from his summer's diet of fish leaves his coat glossy and long, and a trophy taken in late May is apt to be better than one taken in the fall.

The route of the brown bear's travels is more confined and static than that of a grizzly. This is true because his staple food is more concentrated. Salmon is the main item of the brown bear's diet, and the coastal streams provide this fish in abundance, and for most of the months the brown bear is out of hibernation. Like the grizzly farther inland, the brown bear conditions his digestive tract in early spring on the fresh green grasses of the hillsides, and the lower tidal flats.

While working the salmon streams in summer, each bear will concentrate on one certain area. Trails through the flats, used when traveling between streams, are often worn down as deep as horse trails in pack-horse country.

"While hunting the same general country from year to year," Hancock told me, "we get to see and know many a particular bear. If he's along a certain creek one season, and doesn't get killed, or chased away by a bigger bear, he's apt to be there the next year at that same time. In fact, we've got to calling certain bears by name, we'd see 'em so much."

The general assumption is that the brown bear is not so mean by nature as the grizzly. Invariably, except in extreme instances, the brownie chooses to run, or to leave the scene undetected, rather than to put up a fight. Not that he has any streak of cowardice in him; it's just easier to leave something he doesn't understand than to fight it.

Part of this may easily be due to his diet. Like the grizzly of the more mountainous country, when one is well fed on fish and fruit, he's far less likely to be looking for trouble than with a belly-ache from a diet of roots and marmots, and subsequent worms.

Whatever the relative ferocity of the brown bear may normally be, the fact is that he's a huge and formidable adversary. Once wounded without being fatally hit, he exhibits all the cunning, savagery, and tenacity of life, of the grizzly.

Brownie is, in short, a trophy for the sportsman who wants the "mostest," who is willing and able to spend the time and money necessary to go into his coastal habitat, and who intends to kill his specimen cleanly and without fail the first try, or leave him entirely alone.

CHAPTER 11

Hunting Brown Bear

As with grizzlies, no two brown bear will ever be taken in precisely the same manner. And the variety of experience, as to danger, difficulty, and excitement, ranges to the extreme on either end.

Take the case of Bill Kvasnikoff's big brown bear.

Bill was fishing at the time, in his 35-foot boat, and en route past the shore line of Kodiak Island. He had no thought of bear on this trip, so didn't have Old Betsy, with the table-fork sight, along. He did, as a matter of course, have a .22 long rifle rim-fire along on the boat, for the purpose of plinking in spare time.

While some distance off the shore, he spotted a big brown bear working the trail along in the grass. It stopped periodically, likely eating grass shoots and kelp.

Always wanting such a bear for himself (he hunts "dude" hunters on brownies when not fishing), Bill promptly set about getting it. Taking the puny .22 in the dinghy, he started rowing up to the shore, and almost in plain view of the moseying animal.

The average hunter would think Bill was a bit "off" in trying for a 1,000-pound bear with 40 grains of lead, or that he had no idea of the potential danger and ferocity of his adversary.

Quite the contrary was true. Bill had lived with the big

carnivores all his life. He'd guided others to them. He'd seen their power, tenacity, and awesome fury when aroused. He had, in fact, seen brownies fight their mightiest battles, and knew their full capacity as adversaries.

One such battle was fresh in Bill's mind, as he rowed out, and was a spectacle which few men have lived to see. It not only brought out the full potential of a brown bear's fighting prowess; it also was a revelation of the unbelievable scrapping ability of another humble beast, kindly of nature and one of man's best friends.

Some years previously, a surveying party had tried to land a bunch of horses on the Alaska mainland near Geographic Bay—this for use as transportation while doing their work. The horses had been loaded on a barge and had, during this last stage of the route, been towed by a boat towards the shore.

During the trip, the party had run into foul weather and high seas. The barge in some way broke loose from the boat,

Hunting for brown bear in Alaska's coastal range. Hunter's bear was located just after this picture was taken and at lower edge of glacier.

and lost its cargo of horses into the sea. One horse, however, swam to shore, and though exhausted, had wobbled up on the beach.

Occasionally afterward, fishermen working back and forth along the shore, would spot the courageous nag. Out of sheer admiration for such pluck, the fishermen would beach their craft, and give the steed bread, candy, and such tidbits.

As time went on, and the brown bears inland hadn't yet killed the animal, this got to be a habit. Each time a boat hove into view, the horse, now conditioned to the welcome change in diet, would come down the beach, meet the boat, and practically thank the anglers for the sweets.

Besides evading the great bears, this horse showed another remarkable adaptation to a difference in environment. He grew exceptionally long hair each winter season —nature's way of insulating him against the severe cold.

On one trip along the area, Bill came to witness what he called the "most terrific battle a man's mind can grasp." It came about because of the animal's habit of coming down to the open beach to meet the boats.

As Bill's boat came into view, he saw the horse. He also saw two adult brown bears. These hulking animals, forgetting for at least one time their desire to be alone, had combined on a single objective, the horse. Their obvious intent was to kill and eat the animal which had invaded their bailiwick.

It is likely—since the nag survived so long—that he'd had other battles with bears, and had accumulated some experience in the matter. Likely, however, with single bears.

But in sheer amazement, Bill watched the plucky animal. As the bears tore in, teeth grabbing and arms flailing, they were met with feet on each end of their adversary, and teeth almost equal to theirs. They were met also with a speed in whirling, ducking to knees, running, sun-fishing, and such tactics as are often developed to a high degree in "cutting horses" (ponies used to work cattle) which baffled

the bears and kept them off balance. Fur, hide, and feet
flew. Dust enveloped them all. The squeals of the furious
nag mixed with the roars and bawls of the bears.

"I had a ring-side seat on something most men can't
believe," Bill told me. "I hardly dared breathe for fear
they'd take him. But believe me, I was rooting for the
horse!"

Bill's admiration for the horse, incidentally, was born in
that moment, and was not a thing coming from long association with horses. In fact, I watched Bill Kvasnikoff ride
his first horse in Alaska in 1957, and remember his inno-
cence of horses to this day. Briefly, once in the saddle, Bill
poked the loose reins like one would ride a bicycle with
liquid handle bars, and talked to the roan animal like one
would to a child. "Now don't go that way, the trail is this
way." Or, "I asked you back there to stay up with the horses
down there. What you need in this muskeg is a fathometer."

And when once the animal had bucked Bill off, he explained to us later in nautical terms. "He put down his head,
got stiff in the front, and pitched me over the bow."

Now, as the rugged pony fought off two of the continent's
most powerful opponents, Bill's love for horses grew by the
second.

At last it was over. And the fight was ended by the horse,
ears flat and squealing with rage, chasing the two bears off
the open beach with flailing fore-hoofs. . . .

So when Kvasnikoff struck alone in the dinghy, with but a
.22 rifle to down the "mostest bear," he knew precisely what
he *might* expect. However, this hunt ended in a way incredulous to the average person.

As Bill rowed up, the beast spotted him. In such a situation, a brown bear will either discreetly retreat, rather than
bother with something which to him is so offensive (man-
smell), or it will ignore the human entirely.

The big beast did the latter. Putting its great broad head
down again, it continued sniffing in the grass. Bill rowed up
to within 50 or 60 yards of the animal, waited until it

turned exactly broadside, then shot it twice in rapid succession just behind the shoulder. The great bear bit quickly at the sting, jumped a couple of times, then headed back along the route it had come.

Bill, his hunting over, heaved on one oar, turned the dinghy, and rowed back to the big boat. There, he set the pot on the galley stove, brewed himself a couple of cups of coffee, then got back into the dinghy. He once more rowed out, this time going fully ashore to get his prize.

The big bear had gone only 70 feet from where he had shot it. There, it had lain down in the grass and died—bled out to the puny lead pellets.

A more nerve-tingling brownie hunt happened to a "dude" Lee Hancock had on the Alaskan Peninsula in 1956.

Hancock had taken his hunter in to a known bear-producing area, arriving at his old camp site at dusk. Bear sign was everywhere, and camp was set up as noiselessly as possible, to avoid spooking any animals in the immediate neighborhood. A small wall tent was quickly erected, and all gear stowed inside. The bags were laid out and soon the men went to bed.

Before they were asleep, however, they heard a noise outside. Without a word, Hancock reached for the flashlight, and shined the beam out the tent flaps. There, a measured thirty feet away, a huge old boar brownie was chomping on a coffee can and watching the men inside the tent. The hunter reached for his rifle.

There, to the average hunter's way of thinking, was a sure thing on brown bear. At the distance, the hunter couldn't miss. And the light on the animal's face made a perfectly illuminated target.

Hancock, however, knowing what might happen in case of his sport's nervousness, told him not to shoot. "I want no bear fuss at night."

As soon as the beast moved off, not liking the light in his eyes, Hancock got up and lit the gas lantern, hanging it to the ridge pole. He'd barely made it back into bed before

An adult, boar, brown bear is an enormous thing. This one will rank well up in the records. Lucky hunter is Willie Peyton.

the animal came again. Round and round the tent it went, crackling the brush and growling menacingly.

In his many years of experience with the beasts, Hancock had many times had the animals come up to a tent like this at night. But the others had all come silently, as their spoor showed next morning. This one made no attempt at stealth. Rather, it growled and snarled, at mere yards distance, its obvious intention to fight. All during the night, it didn't leave the tent clearing. But each time the enraged animal came close, and each time they thought it surely would attack, it reluctantly changed its mind.

"We had this tent near a salmon stream," Lee told me, "and I think the bear figured we'd stolen his property. It was the very first time I've ever had one threaten me inside a camp at night. But there could be no doubt that he was spoiling for a fight. I'm convinced that the only reason he didn't knock the tent down and take us, was that the eerie light and hum of the gas lantern was something he couldn't quite make out. It was the one thing that kept him off till we got out of there at daylight."

The poor hunter, who'd saved his money for years and had come so far for his chance at a brownie, shook all night with the forlorn hope that the bear might possibly go away; and remembered with each breath the poetic truth that "distance lends enchantment." By morning, he'd *had* it!

Between these extremes is the more likely manner in which the hunter will get his brownie. A typical example is the way Willie Peyton bagged his bear in the spring of 1959.

Willie, a cotton rancher from New Mexico, had booked a brownie hunt with Don DeHart the year before. When spring arrived, Willie and Don flew to Kodiak Island, set up camp on Uyak Bay, and started hunting.

Peyton, knowing Don's methods and being acquainted with his high success ratio, did all his hunting in a simple fashion. He propped his hat over his eyes, lay down on a huge grass hummock, and went to sleep. Don began glassing the entire area from tidelands up to the patches of glacial snow on the surrounding mountains.

An hour of this did little more than to make Willie sleepier. So they moved on. At one point, in traversing the deep trails made by recent animals, and moving through the grass from one area to another, they actually spooked a brown bear "out of his bath tub." Willie didn't get a whack at this flying, wet animal as it made it through bog, grass, and foliage in a bounding run.

So later, they hunted some more—Don glassing, Willie snoozing. Within minutes, DeHart spotted the long-awaited trophy just under the snow line of the nearest mountain, and called Willie. Peyton hated to be disturbed, but agreed to a short stalk. At the close of it, Willie, at reasonable rifle range, sent a 180-grain Nosler bullet out of his .300 Weatherby Magnum and into the bear's heart. The animal simply wilted, rolled 50 feet down the hillside, and was dead as a last year's bird nest when they reached him.

This prize was bone-poor, but weighed an estimated 1100 pounds. Willie quit yawning long enough to measure the skull, which ran 10½ inches across the zygomatic arches and 17½ inches lengthwise of the skull, for a total score of 28. This puts the "hard-fought-for" trophy well into the records.

There is but one successful way of getting a brown bear for the average sportsman. That's to team up with a reputable outfitter who has a good success-ratio on brownies; pay the necessarily high fee; then hunt according to the outfitter's procedure, and trust his judgment.

The brown bear hunt is largely a one-specimen hunt. That is, it can't be combined with several other species of game in the same general region. Some outfitters do hunt brown bears in conjunction with Rocky Mountain goats, which are in the coastal mountains and may be reached in the same hunt's duration, and at some distance.

A most popular way to hunt brownies is to hunt them

Peyton and the head of his brownie which came the easy way.

This beautiful brown bear trophy came from a bruin whose hide had been ruined by rubbing, thus demonstrating that most any trophy may somehow be saved.

from the coastal inlets and around the bear-populated islands, using the boat as the base camp. Boats used for the purpose are usually large, sea-worthy craft, complete with galley and living quarters. The boat is anchored in a bay or cove, the immediate areas glassed and hunted (including in-coming streams), then the boat used as a camp for the night.

Much of the tide land is semi-open country, and the bears are often spotted at extreme ranges, then stalked down. For this purpose, both a spotting scope and good high-powered binoculars of 8- to 10-power are necessary. Bears are often literally picked up miles away in this fashion, then a stalk and campaign outlined.

Oppositely, big bears are just as handily come upon at short range along the salmon creek beds. Here, the long, patient stalk gives way to a knowledge of woods hunting, and quick, cool decisions must be made.

As in any endeavor, the experience of a specialist is a far greater assurance of ultimate success than the efforts of the inexperienced. The experienced outfitter, with a good record on brown bear, is the average hunter's best guarantee of a good trophy. In exchange for this skill, the hunter should be willing to offer his own patience and co-operation under adverse weather conditions, so often necessary to achievement of the final goal—the brown bear trophy.

Regardless of the way in which your brownie does come, it won't likely be as easy as the grizzly trophy came to a certain hunter at Alaska's Mankomen Lake. He'd flown 3,000 miles to kill a bear.

The hunter there recently had killed a caribou and had hung the meat just outside his cabin window. Knowing grizzlies to be around, he simply tied the end of a fishing line to his caribou, threaded it along the ground, through his window, and left the reel intact just on the floor by his breeches. This, the night after.

During the night, his fly reel began to sing. Awakening to the fact that he *couldn't* be fast to a trout, he looked out the window. There, an adult grizzly was in the process of acquiring himself a steak dinner. The fisherman lifted his .300 H&H Magnum, poked the end out the cabin window, and cinched his grizzly trophy at 30 feet!

Part Four

POLAR BEAR

CHAPTER 12

The Great White Prize

Until the last few years, there has been comparatively little interest in the polar bear, *Thalarctos maritimus maritimus,* by American sportsmen. It was generally considered that this great white bear lived in an untenable climate; was inaccessible to the current modes of transportation; and the overall cost in money, hardship, and discomfort was too great.

Three allied factors have recently combined to change this picture. One was the increase of sporting dollars following World War II—a war economy and subsequent inflation created many well-heeled sportsmen who turned to trophy hunting.

A second and even more basic factor was the improvement of aircraft, the opening of Arctic mail routes, landing strips being whittled out for such use, and a system of military installations made along the Arctic Coast. The increased use of aircraft in the North largely erased the time-and-distance barrier, and served to put the visiting sportsman within striking distance of this huge, last-remaining trophy area.

A secondary outgrowth of this mushrooming increase of air travel in extreme cold weather was the war development of suitable clothes, food, and survival gear for use in below-zero temperatures. Down parkas, down mitts, down sleeping bags, food concentrates, and emergency-survival equipment all became adaptable to the sportsman's use, and reduced another age-old hazard. In short, with such equipment the white man could endure the Eskimos temperatures.

The third factor was a natural outgrowth of a trend

Off-shore areas of the far North is the range of polar bear distribution.

which has gradually come over the sport of hunting, since the settlement of the country. Where hunting was once purely for meat, it is now largely for sport and trophies. And to the trophy hunter, nothing is ever quite so appealing as the *biggest* of anything.

For many years the so-called Kodiak bear was considered the biggest of the American carnivores. The sight of huge polar bears in zoos, however, and the occasional report of a huge polar being taken, caused men to wonder and investigate. Such reports were augmented by the tales our military men brought back, after service up north.

At this writing, as hinted previously, many informed people now consider the polar bear the biggest carnivore on the North American continent. Bigger as to body, that is.

As one indication of this, I was told by the Eskimos at Point Hope last February that polar bear which weighed up to 1500 pounds there have been taken by native hunters. My Eskimo guide Ookeelah (Run Fast), as a parting gesture of good will, gave me the penis bone of his own largest polar bear—and he's killed many bear. This prized object, which I intend making into the handle of a letter-opener, came from a polar bear male which squared eleven feet, four inches!

That's a lot of bear, even for a brownie.

At this Eskimo village, the six- and seven-footers are considered cubs (which run with their mothers as long-yearlings), or small sows. An eight- or nine-foot bear is good. A ten-footer, which they hoped to guide me to was a *Nanook Puk*—big polar bear.

As concrete examples of a polar's relative size, the male bear which John Belcher killed in 1958 off Point Hope squared ten feet. It scored 28 under Boone & Crockett measurements, and the full-mounted trophy stands upright at approximately ten feet in height.

The polar bear which Roy Weatherby killed in April, 1959, similarly scores 28 in skull measurements, stands nine feet tall as a full mount, and ranks eighth place in the world's records.

I was told by the professional outfitters in Kotzebue last winter that the polar bear which beat both these bears was no larger of body than Belcher's bear, but had a larger skull, as is often the case. And up to now skull measurement has been the criterion of size.

Like other bear species, the polar bear lives mostly a solitary existence. Boars, especially, travel and live alone, and, according to Don DeHart, will kill their own cubs if and when they can catch them.

The females are good mothers. They den up in pressure

ice and snow along the rocky Arctic coast line, where the young are born. Like other bear cubs they are naked and tiny when born. They live inside the shaggy warmth of the female's fur, suckle, and grow to where they are large and hair covered enough to travel outside the snow-and-ice den.

Some observers say that both sexes of polar bear hibernate. Some claim that only the sows do. Others maintain that the boars never leave the ice pack in their cycle of living, though there is evidence to contradict this.

The mother cares for the cub, or cubs, with great consideration and protectiveness. As with grizzly sows, they will fight man, the only real enemy they recognize, with ferocity when their cubs are endangered.

When traveling polars are seen together, it is habitually a sow and her offspring. I've been told by Eskimo hunters that often it is difficult to tell by the size of the long-yearlings which is the mother, as the cubs will be of an approximate size.

In color, the polar is a creamy white. This coloration changes slightly from winter to summer, turning to more yellowish in summer with the shedding of the winter coat. Part of the yellowish color of a polar is due to stain from the oil, or blubber, of the hair seals which he eats.

The polar's diet is mainly fish, hair seals, and waterfowl which he can slip up on. All he eats of the hair seal is the oil; and often when a polar is killed, his stomach will be full of it. He is omnivorous, however, and will eat grass and similar shore vegetation when it is available, likely for a conditioner.

There is no species of bear which travels farther or wider in search of food than the polar. He is well equipped for travel on either land or water. His white fur blends perfectly with the ice floes and pressure ice. His feet are all haired, except for a slit of exposed pad on the fore paws, and a similarly small pad on the rear feet, making "insulation" on the ice, good traction, and promoting stealth in his stalking. He walks over the ice with a shambling walk which covers ground deceivably fast.

Between ice floes, or in the continually-forming open leads of water, the polar bear plunges in and swims. He is a most excellent swimmer, and moves silently along with only the black snout and eyes above water line.

These bears have been seen by aircraft pilots twenty or thirty miles out at sea, swimming in open water. It is hard to determine whether the bear is crossing between two ice floes, hunting, or simply enjoying himself.

One case indicating the extreme distances a polar bear might go in open water, is a matter of record. The father of a well-known Alaska outfitter, during his lifetime in the Far North, killed a walrus and one polar bear along the shore line of Kodiak Island.

Kodiak Island is, of course, in the extreme south of Alaska—not northward in the recognized polar bear habitat. Any way that bear approached this island would necessitate a swim of around fifty miles across the Shelikof Strait.

From the hunter's standpoint, the incidence of polar bears in any area is dependent upon the combined factors of food, prevailing winds, ocean currents, and season of the year.

In summer, the bears stay with the floating icepack well northward of the continent, in the Arctic. The main diet is the delicately-spotted hair seal. This Arctic inhabitant weighs from eighty to nearly two hundred pounds, and itself works the region of moving ice floes.

The bear's hunting technique is to spot such a seal, resting or sunning itself on the edge of an ice floe. Bruin then slips cautiously into the water, and swims noiselessly up at an oblique angle. Pulling himself quickly upon the ice edge, the bear makes a short rush, and knocks *nahchik* in the head with one swipe of his big forepaw. Then he feeds on the two-inch-thick blubber.

In winter, the young ice forms off the shore. If the prevailing winds during November and December come from inland, or the east, they are the "bad winds" from the hunting standpoint, especially at such popular bear-hunting take-off points as Point Hope, Kotzebue, and Point Barrow. Such winds keep the ice pack far out at sea, and keep intervening water opened up between them and the anchor ice formed solidly along the shore. Because of this, the bears are kept far out on the Siberian and Arctic sides.

Tricky ocean currents often aid the winds in this. Miles of flat ice will break loose from the shore, drift out to meet

Lucky polar bear hunter with trophy.

the main ice pack, and build up into pressure ridges and shifting ice fields.

Where untold billions of tons of such ice come together, it becomes an awesome, grinding, squealing spectacle which can be heard for miles, and whose immensity is hard to describe. Literally worlds of ice come together, groan and convulse, split and separate—either piling into great pressure ridges or tumbling in yard-thick blocks into a sudden opening in the sea. This phenomenon tends, with inland winds, to build up far offshore.

But in the tumbling, crumbling process of ice pushing up into twenty- or thirty-foot frigid windrows, the ocean surface is kept constantly in a breaking-up stage. This creates shifting, new leads of open water as one ice field moves from, or towards another. The hair seals work these open leads for fish. This furry animal can remain submerged for ten to fifteen minutes, but does require oxygen, and has to surface periodically.

As a consequence, seals either have to do their fishing near the open leads, or else keep "air holes" constantly open under the layer of relatively thin but solid ice. These inverted funnel-shaped cones, incidentally, are kept open by a constant pushing up of the forming ice by the seal's nose from below. These air holes may be detected at considerable distance by the hunter or his dogs, since each time the seal breaks open the hole again, he forces water up through the dollar-sized aperture. This water runs down the cone, and builds up like the small cone of a tiny Yellowstone Park geyser. Eskimo sled dogs, by the way, will break direction and head for such cones at a high lope unless restrained, once they scent them. The dogs live largely on the chocolate-colored seal's meat, and know that such a hole often means groceries.

It is obvious that these seals will work the open leads more than the layer beneath heavy ice—simply for convenience in breathing. So long as the inland winds and prevailing currents keep the moving ice ridges and open leads off-shore, there is where the bulk of the seals will be.

However, in January and February, the winds usually change in the Point Hope-Barrow region to northerly or north-westerly winds—the "good winds."

These bring the ice pack closer to shore. It permits farther travel out to sea with dog teams. The ice movement near shore creates a constant supply of opening leads. When coupled to favorable ocean currents coming in towards shore, this also brings the fish; and all elements— water, ice, fish, seals, and bears—concentrate just off such finger-like capes as Point Hope, Barrow, and Lisbourne.

The sequence is progressive. The currents bring in the fish. The seals follow the fish. The big bears come in from the Siberian and North Pole sides, to work the seals. And it is then that the great white trophies are close enough in to reach via dog sled and aircraft.

Hunting in open leads is to a bear's liking. Hunting when the seals are beneath solid ice takes more patience. A bear will find a recently used air hole, cautiously approach, and lie motionlessly by it for an hour. Often before lying down for his patient wait, he'll enlarge the cone's aperture, with rakes of his paw.

Later, if and when the seal surfaces, one swipe of his razor-like claws and husky forearm will practically decapi- tate a seal, as its fuzzy nose comes up through, for air. Then bruin dives onto it.

Ooyahahlook (Big Rock), another skilled Point Hope Eskimo hunter, told me that he'd often watched such a hunting bear take his stance at a seal hole; but before lying on his belly in wait, bruin would curl a hairy arm around his whole face up to his eyes, completely covering his black nose-tip. Then he'd remain immobile.

"Him smart maybe I don't think," Ooyahahlook explained in his questionable English. "Him know nose maybe only black spot I guess on bear. Cover it so seal can't see I guess maybe not."

It is odd that in this frigid land of extreme scarcity, the

polar bear will eat only the seal oil, or *okruk,* which comprises nearly fifty per cent of the seal's weight. The dark flesh beneath the layer of blubber is left for the scavengers.

In the frozen Arctic, as in other hunting regions, there is a true brotherhood of the wilds. Just as the magpie finds offal and carrion from the air, and cackles his discovery to the coyote which watches him from below, so does the

Belcher, a large man, looks small by comparison beside a full-mounted beast.

white Arctic fox follow the muted pad marks of the traveling polar, and from a ridge of pressure ice, watches him
hunt. When the bear leaves a seal, the white fox takes over
and cleans the landscape.

To the Eskimo hunter, one of the first and most favorable
bear signs after the first week of the "good winds," is the
presence of fox tracks coming closer to shore line from the
ice pack.

With spring and a breaking up of the ice, the polar bears
stay with the ice floes and move farther out to sea again.
A prize catch for the bear is the finding of any whale carcass which may have been washed ashore with the new
water. Such huge carcasses are, of course, stayed with by
bears until they are cleaned up. Ookeelah told me that one
spring native hunters killed seven separate polar bears at
one such whale carcass.

The flesh of polar bears, due to their diet of seal oil, is
not palatable to the average white man. Eskimos, however,
relish the meat and save every pound from bears taken
by themselves or game hunters. Should one Eskimo kill a
bear which another has been following, he's morally bound
to give the other hunter a hind quarter.

Bear skins are used as barter by the natives. Their year's
supply of staple goods, in the Barrow-Hope section, is
brought in during mid-summer on the *North Star's* single
northward voyage. Dried polar bear hides are sent back
with it, on the boat's return to the "outside," where they are
sold by the governmental agency "Anaca," coming from
the words "Alaska Native Arts And Crafts." The proceeds
come back to the village, partly as credit at the co-operative
store, itself financed by "Anaca." Strips of dried polar bear
hides are in big demand among fly tyers for making streamer
trout-flies. The rate is $1.40 per lineal foot of bearskin.

In actual numbers, the polar bear is hard to estimate.
The species ranges from near Kotzebue on the Bering Strait,
northward and eastward along the entire length of the
Arctic Coast.

Much of this region, off shore, is explored very little. This fact, plus the bear's tendency to travel far and wide, and much of the time as "singles," make an accurate estimate impossible. A bruin spotted here today, especially an old boar, may be fifty miles away day after tomorrow.

One observer lists a possible 3,000 polar bears off the Alaska shore line. Another estimates the total bear population as around 17,000 bears.

One thing is important, at this writing, to the total bear population, whatever it is. The popularity of polar bear hunting has catapulted overnight from casual interest to fever pitch. Due to the bear's relative scarcity, enormous size, and the cost in time, effort, money, hardship, and real danger necessary to bagging one, the polar bear has suddenly become to many trophy-minded sportsmen the continent's Number One Trophy.

CHAPTER 13

Hunting Polars *a la* Eskimo

One of the things which has fired the imagination of sportsmen, and added to the urge to hunt polar bears lately, is the amazing yet true yarns of how the Eskimo hunts *Nanook*.

These stories, filtering out of the frigid north and heard or read by a warm fire in a temperate climate, tax the credulity of man. Many a hunter, unused to extreme hardship, will hear such a tale and exclaim, "Horse-feathers! Who do you think you're kidding?"

My own reaction to some of these recent occurrences was similar. However, in February-March of 1959, I had the pleasure of living in an Eskimo village for a month, hunting for 700 miles via dog team over the Arctic ice with the best Eskimo hunters, and witnessing the unvarnished way in which they confront Nature in the raw every day, and literally take their lives in their hands with each hunting hour.

My conclusion had to be that while tales of the Eskimo's courage, skill, and ability to survive where a less hardy race would surely perish were certainly awe inspiring, they were by no means unusual. The Eskimo lives largely by hunting. And in the matter of polar bears, the encounters come about incidental to the hunting of other game, largely, and not through bear hunting *per se*.

189

This takes some explanation.

Most of the larger Eskimo villages today are serviced at least once each summer by boat from Anchorage and Seattle. Many of the staples are left at the village co-operative store. The products of the Arctic, such as seal skins, ivory carvings, caribou and bear hides, native parkas, and so forth, are used in a round-about manner as a medium of exchange. "Anaca" disposes of these items on the "outside," and the money, or credit at the village store, is given to the producer of such wares.

This takes care of but a small part of the Eskimo's needs. His basic food supply, and its by-products necessary to his day-to-day existence, come from his daily hunting.

Nothing, in this hardy land, is wasted. The quarry ranges from salmon and other fish in summer, to caribou back inland, whales in the spring, and seals, water fowl, and polar bears in winter.

Part of this food supply is stored against the annual "starvation period"—the late-spring season of little game. Storage is made in the Eskimo "deep-freeze," meaning as far into the frozen earth as handy to dig, and beyond the reach of dogs. Stored meat consists largely of caribou, *totopeak*, and *arkgruik*, or whale. Whale meat, or *muktuk*, from the animal's tail, is a prized food. In storage, it "ripens" until it gags most white men, but the Eskimo loves it. He'll take an inch-square strip, feed it into his mouth like carrots into a food grinder, whacking off each small hunk with a scything motion with his razor-sharp knife, in a stroke between nose and fingers that leaves you breathless.

I swore, upon leaving for the Arctic, that I'd eat some *muktuk* or bust. I was never quite able to get it past my nose.

The prized portions of the caribou are the ribs and breast meat. Ookeelah told me that Eskimos consider the hams fit only for white men and dogs.

Another item of summer diet is the eggs of the Murr, or crowbill. This bird nests in the high bluffs along the rocky coast line in certain areas such as the cliffs above Cape Lisbourne, and Dyer. The two big ear-like mountains there—*Evanyik*, or breasts of a woman—are an especially productive rookery.

In these nesting places, the birds lay their eggs by the thousands. In July the Eskimo hunters make pilgrimages to these areas by boat—the big, 28-foot whaling boats made of wooden frames and five to seven skins of the bearded seal, or *oogruk*, sewed together for a covering—and collect the eggs.

This "bird-fruit" is approximately the size of chicken eggs, and, to the Eskimo, is as palatable as the domestic egg.

Ooyahahlook told me that one trip a few years ago, they "—maybe got eight box *ukba* eggs I don't hardly think."

"What kind of boxes, Ooyahahlook?"

"Blazo maybe."

A Blazo box is a wooden crate in which two five-gallon cans of white lantern gas are shipped.

Egging there is simply done. The hunters climb the high bluffs, fill their summer parkas full of eggs above the belt, then descend with them. "I climb down once Blazo box enough eggs in parka," Big Rock assured me.

The staple, day-to-day quarry of the Eskimo, however, is the lowly hair seal. The brown flesh from an average seal will feed a team of eleven dogs for one day. The two-inch layer of blubber surrounding the flesh will provide either seal oil for food, waterproofing skins, etc.; or be sufficient for a day's heat in a tiny oil-burning stove. The blubber is simply chopped into hunks and fed into the smoky stove.

The hide from the same 80- to 100-pound seal may be used in a variety of ways. Tanned with the hair left on, it may become half of a pair of insulated pants for the hunter. Or, it may be sinew-sewed into *mukluk* tops—hair boots. Or, after being native-tanned, it may be shipped "outside," sold, and fetch $2.75, currently.

Such a hide is also apt to end up in a parka, *mukluk* bindings, or as reinforcement for the innumerable joints of a 12-foot hunting sled. The punishment which such a sled takes while being pounded over and through rough ice, especially loaded, is awesome to behold. Solid wood junctions alone will not stand the terrific strain; and they must be strengthened by the semi-rigidity of tight sealskin bindings.

Seal oil itself cannot be over-estimated as a basic item in the Eskimo's diet. One instance will indicate this. While hunting polar bears, Ookeelah and his brother took me fifty miles from the village, out over the ocean and northward up the coast line. We were to be gone several days, so the sled not loaded with me was filled to capacity with food and supplies. The outfitter, Don DeHart, had sent along all kinds of choice food, together wth gasoline stoves, tent, snow shovel, axe, lantern, and other hunting equipment.

It was 26 degrees below zero that March day, and we huddled in a miniature hut pit which Ookeelah had dug the summer before into the side of a rocky hummock along the coast line.

During supper, which Ookeelah cooked over the gasoline stove, I noticed him fidget about the food. His brother, whose name I never could pronounce, and practically broke a jaw trying to, also seemed concerned. Neither ate too much.

After I'd finished supper (all white man's grub), Ookeelah could stand it no longer. Blushing, like a guilty child, he fished into his own sealskin war bag, and brought out a lard can which he'd filled on the sly with seal oil.

"What are you going to do with that?" I asked, with the peculiar smell of it already reaching my nose.

"You laugh at me."

"I won't laugh at you."

"You tell DeHart."

"I promise I won't tell DeHart."

"Then," he grinned, "I show you Eskimo steak."

Unknown to the outfitter, he also brought along a piece of the fat breast meat of a caribou he'd killed some weeks

Ookeelah and one of the tiny, single-skin skin boats, made from one oogruk hide split up the belly and lashed by the edges to the gunwales of a 7-foot wooden skeleton. On two occasions this boat saved his life.

before. He cut some of this into inch-sized chunks, and boiled the meat in an open kettle. When it was done, he salted it, then lumped the boiled meal onto two plates. He and his brother would then each take a lump with a fork, dunk it into the warmed, yellowish seal oil, then eat it.

This procedure was followed until the pot was empty. Happy now, Ookeelah explained, "Eskimo steak. Eskimo has to have seal oil." Likely the fat produces body heat, or supplements other items of their meager diet.

The government recognizes the Eskimo's dependence upon the hair seal. Until about 1951, there was a $6 bounty on the hair seal, off the Alaskan coast. Hunting them, by visiting white hunters, became so popular that it threatened the local Eskimo's food supply; and the bounty was removed. However, such a bounty still exists from Sealing Point, near Kotzebue, on down the coast southward. This is because the seal eats many of the edible and usable fish, such as the Shee, Tom-Cod, and others.

Oddly enough, it is this day-to-day dependence upon the hair-seal (and his larger cousin the bearded-seal, or *oogruk*, which comes less often to the hunter) which has caused the occasional hair-raising experiences with polar bears. The excitement and lack of certainty of the outcome is usually caused by the hunter's often puny hunting equipment.

The early Eskimo killed his seals largely by waiting over a seal air hole, with poised spear. After a most patient wait, he'd spear the seal as it surfaced for air. The occasional polar bear which came along had, of necessity, to be dispatched with the same weapon, or the battle lost.

With the coming of rifles, the Eskimo turned to the more certain weapon. Today's Eskimo hunter, despite an often old and salt-water-rusted rifle, is an excellent shot. The younger hunters are rapidly acquiring modern rifles, with scope sights, and are going to hand-loading, due largely to economic advantages.

At Point Hope, as an example, the village council has saved from its meager income enough to buy a reloading outfit, with which the village hunters may reload ammunition at no cost. It's interesting that the five dies they have (for the most-used cartridges) are for the .30-30, .30-06, .22 Hornet, .222 Remington, and .243 Winchester.

Because of the value of the seal, plus the animal's habit of swimming with but its head above water, only head shots are taken at the quarry. This is true largely of the *oogruk*, too. The *oogruk's* tough hide is priceless for making bottoms for *mukluks*, for covering for their whale boats, and as a single-skin covering for the tiny kayak-like skin boats, used to retrieve seals from far out in open leads of water. Anything except head shots would spoil the *oogruk's* hide for these purposes, and isn't tolerated.

The flat-shooting .22 Hornet and .243 Winchester, mentioned above, are popular. The .222 Remington, too, is increasingly being used. These three cartridges reflect the Eskimo's real need in rifles.

This brings us to the crux of the matter, as it relates to polar bears.

Eighty per cent of Eskimo hunting is done for seals and *oogruk*. Small caliber, high intensity, inexpensive cartridges are ideal for the necessary head shots on these two species. Polar bears, which are contacted occasionally, are really incidental to seal hunting. And when such bears are contacted, they are stalked down, and shot with the ordnance which the seal hunter has on hand, and with little thought

Ookeelah making a 60-yard cast with the bobber-and-line to hook a dead seal in open water.

of possible danger or probable outcome.

What happened to young Kahpooyoo (Good Spear) in March, 1957, is a fair example of what happens on such an encounter, which the hunter, unused to why an Eskimo hunts as he does, often does not believe.

Whenever possible, two Eskimo hunters will hunt together for sheer safety amid a multiple of dangers. On this particular day, Kahpooyoo was hunting with Ooyahahlook. This older, more experienced hunter had a white "dude" hunter along in his sled at the time, and was trying for a big polar bear. Kahpooyoo traveled alone with his own dog team, keeping just in sight of the other team as they loped along over the flat ice. The ice, in some areas, was newly-formed young ice, lying between the mountainous windrows of pressure ice, which the winds were driving towards shore.

Suddenly, and most unusual, Ooyahahlook ran into sight of three polar bears, close together. They did not appear to be a sow and cubs, but rather three adults, which possibly had been attracted to the area by the blood of recent kills.

Kahpooyoo's first inkling of the presence of game was the sudden barking of Ooyahahlook's dogs, then the immediate fuss of his own team.

At the sound, all three bears at once reared upright and looked. Then, like most ursines, they began to run away, not from the fear, but the annoyance of the dogs.

Kahpooyoo quickly drove the iron anchor spike of his sled into the ice, to hold his own team from entering the chase, then raced over the young ice in an effort to intercept one of the bears, which at first he estimated to be a nine-footer.

The angle of the chase led him to a position within 200 yards, and he began firing. He used an ancient .25-35 Winchester, and at one of the shots he got off, the bear's hind leg went out from under him, obviously broken.

The big bear angled away, breaking over a tumble of mixed pressure and young ice. As the beast ran, and likely partly due to the broken leg, it fell through the new ice and began floundering about. While struggling, the animal enlarged the hole, but kept trying to pull itself upon the more solid ice edge. All that showed as it sank back each time was, of course, its head and nose, in the water.

This was a problem which the Eskimo faces often. To finish off the animal while it was in the water meant losing it. Indeed, as Kahpooyoo ran up, the tender young ice flexed dangerously under his own *mukluks*, and he wasn't so sure but what he'd fall through himself. With rifle ready for a finishing head shot, he waited and hoped the beast would first pull himself up onto the ice. Then the animal could be killed and retrieved. Kahpooyoo estimated the animal at 800 pounds.

Suddenly, the bear reached heavier ice and pulled itself from the water. Then, spotting its tormentor and the dogs, it started in a crippling run for them.

This was what Kahpooyoo wanted. But before he could fire, the heavy beast again broke through the young, rubbery ice. This time, in its efforts to get out and to the dogs, it broke a larger hole, in the shape of a rough triangle. Unable at first—due to the broken leg—to get back onto the ice, the beast kept swimming about in the ice-piece opening, mostly at the triangle's apex.

The struggles, after a time, became less vigorous, and the young Eskimo hunter feared that the beast would give up and go down, rather than make it onto the solid ice once more. This would have meant a heavy loss, both in meat and fur.

Gingerly, with the cocked rifle in one hand and the six-foot hunting pole, *oonok*, in the other, Kahpooyoo edged up closer. His only chance now was to prod the bear into sufficient anger, to make it try again to get out of the water.

At a distance of 8 feet (as Kahpooyoo paced it off and showed me in the village hut when recounting it), he poked the beast with the out-stretched pole. One end of this hunting staff is equipped with a hook, for dragging seals from the water. The other ends in a sharp spear, the principal use of which is to test dangerous ice, and the treacherous "snow-holes" which are unfrozen beneath a shell of covering, in advance of walking. It's the foot hunter's life insurance.

When the bear felt the point of this spear, it snarled with rage and made a prodigious effort. In a motion, "quicker than I know," according to this fellow, the beast succeeded. One second it was swimming in salt water, the next it was clearly a'top the edge ice and heading hell bent for Kahpooyoo.

Wheeling on a dime with change left, the hunter raced away, presenting the bruin with only the view of departing *mukluks*. However, no man can outrun a polar bear. As Kahpooyoo poured it on, he kept his head turned. He hoped for some such miracle as the dogs interfering, or that the beast—heavier than he was—might again go through the ice. But no such luck.

Within a few bounds the enraged bear had closed the gap to a mere six feet! It was now or never. As he ran, Kahpooyoo poked the rifle barrel back over his shoulder, and jerked the trigger—still on a dead run.

The shot miracle happened then. The bullet luckily caught the animal in the throat, temporarily knocking it down to the ice. As it sank, dying, Kahpooyoo emptied the other 117-grain soft-point bullets into it. To make sure.

Of this young hunter's five polar bears till then,—"he was one I remember I think," Kahpooyoo assured me with a grin.

Ooyahahlook (Big Rock), mentioned above, is one of Alaska's most renowned hunters. He is, at this writing, fifty years old. Several times during his life he has been "outside" to places like Fairbanks, supplementing his annual income by working as a carpenter during the summer season.

While working there, and from the English-speaking younger generation at Point Hope (product of the current

After lining in a seal, the hunter hooks it from ice edge with his
hunting pole, oonak, and drags it to his dog sled.

school taught by a white teacher and his wife, and where
English is a required subject), Ooyahahlook has acquired
a working knowledge of the tongue, of which he is very
proud. Except while in the company of white men, he
lapses, of course, into native Eskimo—a language difficult of
spelling and pronunciation because it is purely a spoken,
not a written tongue.

Big Rock is also proud of the fact that he is a movie actor.
He starred in the Hollywood movie, "The Eskimo Hunter,"
made in the Arctic about 1948.

Each time I wanted to take a picture of Ooyahahlook
doing anything, he'd pose proudly, disdain the simple action
I wished, and remind me, "I know. I was been in pictures
I think maybe."

As one of the Far North's most experienced hunters, his
whole life has been colored with danger. Had not these
daily hazards been met with extreme care and good sense,
Ooyahahlook would never have reached the age of fifty
years.

His experience with polar bears began when he was a small boy. At such a tender age, he was once out hunting alone and got onto thin young ice at its periphery where the heavier ice was moving. Before he quite knew what happened, the thin ice began to break under him.

From watching his elders and maybe partly instinct, he dropped to his belly, spreading all fours out like a flattened bearskin over the hunting pole. This never-without item he lay upon, paralleling his small body.

This, of course, spread the weight until the young ice would support him. While flat on his belly, he paddled, as in the water, with all fours until he'd worked himself to the more solid blocks of ice. Crawling gingerly onto the first big block—itself floating in the moving, grinding ice field—he cautiously stood up.

At this point, the ice block, thinner and less stable than he'd hoped, turned over. In a great leap, and covering a distance he'd never before considered possible, he made it to the next block. As *it* turned over, he kept racing across the block tops, jumping intermittently here and there, and off each block before it sank with him into the ocean. Finally he made it to solid anchor ice.

His intention, upon reaching home, was to say nothing. However, his wet *mukluks* and pants gave him away. His mother asked, and he told what had happened.

It is indicative of the rigors of the hardy existence there that no one appeared glad he'd made it. Instead, a few days later two of the village's wisest and oldest men bawled him out thoroughly for being careless!

When I hunted with Oooyahahlook last winter, he'd killed a polar bear for each one of his fifty years.

"Sometimes I was kill seven, sometimes I was kill eight, sometimes I was kill three in year," he told me, when asked of his biggest annual score. In addition, this hunter has killed eight Arctic wolves, 15 wolverine, 48 *oogruk*, and more seals and "caribous" than he can count with his limited mathematics. Probably thousands, combined.

When I asked Ooyahahlook what he considered his most dangerous polar bear encounter, he laughed in his happy, serious way. He was at a loss, however, to tell whether any one single incident stood out from any other. Here's the one he finally related.

While hunting one day off Cape Thompson, Ooyahahlook spotted a ten-foot bear traveling toward him. He crept up into the pressure-ice ridges, and angled towards the beast, eventually coming into decent rifle range. At that time he was using a .30-30.

When the bear approached within a matter of rods, Ooyahahlook let him have it, trying for a head shot. The first shot, however, simply clipped the bear's chin.

As the beast reared up, looking for him, he shot again. This bullet hit the beast squarely between the eyes, and upon the up-slant of its forehead. As Ooyahahlook had expected, the beast dropped in its tracks.

Instead of beginning the skinning chore, the hunter left the bear and climbed upon a pressure-ice ridge, to scout for further game. He knew that, under certain conditions, these bears traveled loosely together.

Ooyahahlook was gone for an estimated thirty minutes. Then he came back and began the heavy work. First he rolled the beast by its hind leg over onto its back—this, to make the first belly and leg cuts. That done, he went to the front end, picked up a forepaw, and began.

"When knife touched Nanook he plenty alive I think maybe. Him was rare up and look me in the face ready to take bite out of me I think maybe."

The second bullet had simply knocked the bear cold. It had not penetrated the skull but had glanced off, upward. Now, discovering that he shook hands with a live, ten-foot polar bear, Ooyahahlook hastily dropped the paw for the rifle. Before the beast could struggle to its feet, he shot it at the base of the ear.

"Good place I was plenty scare!"

He likely was. This time he left the beast, before attempting again to skin it, until the legs were stiffened like timber from the 20 below zero temperature.

As if I might not consider this unusual enough for my purposes, Ooyahahlook told me of a second polar, largely in afterthought.

This animal, too, was a large one. Ooyahahlook was hunting seals at the time with a .22 Hornet. This bear was moving away, presenting him with only a rear-end shot. But in that hardy land, no opportunity is ever lost.

"I was shoot him in the gluteus-maximus (Ooyahahlook, with his great affinity for brief English, used a far shorter word), this didn't kill *Nanook* I don't think maybe, next I shoot in shoulder, bear died."

Not more than a month before we arrived in the Arctic, two other Eskimo hunters had experienced what they considered a run-of-the-mill bear hunt.

Seymour Tuzroyluk and his partner Peniluke had been hunting seals. As often happens, the open lead and winds were wrong, and no seals had bobbed up for an hour or so. This period of quiet, likely, caused the two polar bears traveling down the open lead's edge to reach their position in the ice maze unobserved.

Suddenly, Seymour looked up and there the animals were, coming head on. Each hunter took a bear, and they began firing. Both hunters carried their current seal rifles—.222 Remington's, and 50-grain ammunition!

At the short range, both tried for head and neck shots. Seymour had no trouble killing his. Peniluke's bear, however, was only enraged with the sudden pain of a flesh shot. Immediately it charged Peniluke.

This hunter, having experienced this sort of thing before, didn't give ground or attempt to run. Rather, he fired the four cartridges in the magazine, trying desperately for a brain hit.

None of his shots, though, were effective; and from the position behind him, Seymour couldn't fire without hitting Peniklue.

As the bear and the hunter came to grips, Peniluke swung the empty bolt-action rifle, splintering it to several pieces upon the bear's head. This didn't faze the enraged animal. It reared upright, grabbed Peniluke by the shoulders, and tried to bite through to his throat.

A polar bear's claws are razor sharp. Only the thick, skin clothing the Eskimo wears against the cold saved him. At each swipe of the claws and at each bite, hunks of Peniluke's parka came away. There was only one possible outcome, unless in some way, Peniluke could have an assist from Seymour. It came several breathless seconds later.

Between swipes of the paws, Peniluke shoved with all his strength against the bear's neck. And at one point he succeeded in moving the big white face several inches away from his own. Seymour, waiting for the opportunity, shoved the barrel of his puny .222 rifle at the bear's ear and shot him.

This bear measured eight feet square. When asked how he felt about the encounter, Seymour admitted to me that he was "awful nervous." He didn't say how Peniluke felt!

Perhaps the most astounding true polar bear incidents which have come to my attention are the ones involving an Eskimo whose English name is Rocky, and to another Eskimo whose English-Eskimo combination name is Patrick Attunganah.

Rocky likely holds some sort of record on polar bears, having reputedly killed 32 bears in a single year, in the Point Hope, Alaska section. I got to know this mild-mannered hunter quite well, while blizzard-bound in Kotzebue for over a week. We'd been talking whaling—in fact Rocky wanted me to find out for him some place "outside" where he could obtain whale bomb-harpoons which would surely function. Only last year, in the April-May whaling season, he'd had his chance at close range at a 70-foot bow-head whale. He'd hit the animal well with the harpoon gun, but the ancient black-powder bomb, which had been driven into the whale, had failed to explode.

The loss of these tons of *muktuk* was a serious one for his village, and Rocky was most concerned that new, active bombs could either be obtained or made. Incidentally, in his area that same year, at least eight of the old bombs had not fired.

Partly because of this conversation and mutual interest, and partly because of the prompting of his friends, Rocky was inveigled into telling me about his bear encounter, which happened in the winter of 1937.

Rocky had been hunting off the cape near Point Hope, and had killed a medium-sized sow bear. Her cub—actually a two-year-old and still running with the sow, and of similar size—immediately started for him.

At the time, Rocky hunted with an old octagon-barreled .32 Special. As the young bear came on, he emptied the remaining shells in the rifle at it. He tried, as was usual, for head or neck hits.

The last shot from the rifle succeeded only in breaking the beast's lower jaw. The shattered jawbone dropped, making it impossible for the bear to bite him. He had no more cartridges with him.

Having nothing except his hunting knife, with a five-inch blade, Rocky decided to finish the job with this skimpy weapon.

The only vulnerable spot that he might successfully reach with so short a weapon was the animal's eye—a small target indeed, especially with the target fighting back and to the death. Anyway, round and round they went. The angered bear, partly because of its wound, and partly because the young of any bear hesitates to leave its mother, even though dead, stayed and fought it out. Each time they came together the beast would rear up and rip at the hunter with its fore-claws. In order to get close enough for a possible stab into the beast's eye, Rocky had to do close-in fighting.

Time after time he struck, doing no damage whatever except to further enrage the animal. And each time, the bear would swipe wickedly at his head and upper body.

Eskimo hunter scouting for bear after taking two hair seals for the dogs.
Note height of the ridge of pressure ice.

"How long did the fight go on?" I asked.

Rocky hesitated, trying for an accurate estimate. "I think maybe fifty minutes."

"Fifteen minutes?" I asked, thinking even that an incredible length of time for such mortal combat.

"Fifty minutes," he corrected me. "Maybe fifty minutes, not hour."

Finally, he got lucky. With a single knife stroke, he plunged the blade through the bony orbit and into the beast's brain. All during the life-and-death struggle, the 7-foot animal never left the ice for escape in the open lead of water. Neither did it try to get far from the vicinity of the dead sow.

Rocky's heavy parka was ripped to pieces and completely off him. The sharp fore-claws, too, had reached his shirt and had taken most of the front from it. Other than that, he was barely scratched.

This modest man was actually embarrassed while recounting the affair—that such an ordinary event should be considered noteworthy. I have no doubt that he spoke the unvarnished truth; and indeed, most of the yarn had to be pried out of him with repeated questions.

Attunganah's bear experience was largely with a constant but incidental hazard to the Eskimo hunter.

This hunter is 49 years old, and at the time, in late winter, was hunting on foot. In the Arctic a hunter's prowess and worth are often estimated by the quality of his dog team—this means of transportation being essential for hunting offshore any considerable distance. However, many hunters not owning dog teams—largely because of the heavy expense of feed—hunt on foot. In late winter especially, the bears come close in from the Siberian side, and the seals work the ice-edge, itself moved by the offshore currents and winds. When the foot hunter kills a seal, he can easily drag it to the village using his *oonok*, with the hook into the seal's head. Similarly, when a polar bear is taken by the hunter on foot, the hide is packed in, and the meat gone back for the next day with another's dog team. The Eskimos are very democratic in such matters, and in all their community life. What one hunter takes becomes community food. The next day, another hunter may be the lucky one.

While a short distance in miles offshore, Attunganah killed his polar bear without undue incident. The temperature that wintry day stood at 30 degrees below zero. Since he hunted alone, Attunganah's immediate concern was to get the hide off his bear before it froze stiff.

With his attention on the skinning job, he failed to notice a shifting in the breeze, and a different sound to the grinding ice pack. However, when he'd finished peeling the bear and had started back, he discovered with dismay that a lead had opened between him and the shore.

Such a lead may extend for miles and miles, in a broken, zig-zag course roughly paralleling the shore line. There is ordinarily no walking around it, within the space of twenty-four hours.

As the horrified Attunganah watched, the lead grew steadily wider. It was now several rods in width. The freshly-exposed water, under the frigid temperature, already smoked black and dirty with rolling fog, like the fumes from a witch's cauldron.

Here at last the Eskimo's Great Danger had caught up with him. He had misjudged the wind and current. He had no skin boat, no means of subsistence on the ice pack. His entire equipment consisted of his rifle, knife, his seal-skin bag containing the seal-retrieving line, and the bear hide.

The choice was simple. Attunganah could either choose almost certain death on the ice floe already drifting out to sea, or he could risk death by exposure in the open water.

Quickly he took off his clothes. These he wrapped inside the seal-skin bag, and tightly tied the bundle inside the green bearhide with the end of the seal line. The other end was equipped with a bobber and hooks for fishing dead seals out of open water. This end he heaved across the open lead, to where it landed on the solid ice opposite. Then, with the knife in his teeth, he slid into the icy water and swam in sheer desperation.

Reaching the opposite ice, he chopped rough hand holds into the surface with the knife. With fingers digging into these, he somehow pulled his numb body up onto the solid ice. Then, jerking the bundle across the water with a few swift strokes, he untied the near-dry clothing, dressed, picked up the bear hide, and walked the five intervening miles back home!

It was as "simple" as that.

That happened 29 years ago, when Attunganah was twenty years old. When I was in the Arctic, he was still alive, healthy, and braving the hazards of the ice pack.

Attunganah will likely never have a closer brush with death until he actually meets the Grim Reaper. Certainly it was but the stamina of his youth and his great courage which saved his life.

CHAPTER 14

Hunting Bears by Dog Sled

I have had the personal good fortune to have hunted big game for 34 years. In this span of time, I have been lucky enough to have taken a total of 125 head, of virtually every species of North American game. The hunting has been largely in the best areas for each species, and habitually in the company of good men.

If one type of hunting were to be picked out of this extensive experience as thrilling beyond all others, I'd say it was the hunting of polar bears with Eskimo guides, native dog teams, and in the hardy, simple manner in which these people customarily hunt *Nanook*.

This is true not alone because of the ultimate prize. It is equally true because of the allied factors of danger, extreme cold, the sporting chances afforded the quarry, the incidental hunting of seals and *oogruk*, and above all, the sharing of the day-to-day experiences of another race of people.

Truly, polar bear hunting via dog sled is an experience with another civilization, in virtually another world.

There is only one feasible way of taking on such a hunt. That is to book reservations with a capable outfitter who has personal connections with the Eskimos of an Arctic village, and whose services he can employ. This includes the leasing of skillful guides, who not only are excellent

208

hunters, but who have the necessary dog teams, sleds, and other basic hunting equipment. It also includes the rental, lease, or purchase of necessary living quarters for the hunters while stationed in the village, and the arrangements for air or boat transportation of the necessary groceries and supplies.

In our own case, the outfitter had arranged for us to stay in a 16x16-foot military Jamesway hut, complete with insulation and board floor. Tables, chairs and bunks were built by the native guides by arrangement with the outfitter in advance of our arrival. The hut was also equipped with an oil stove—which incidentally had to run continuously night and day—and barrels of oil arranged for in advance. This hut was also furnished with a tank-type toilet, and igloo-type entrance of sawed ice blocks, in an L-shape, to shut out a portion of the cold.

This was all done previous to our arrival, by arrangement from the outfitter. All food, dishes, lanterns, beds, and personal gear were flown in—in fact, came in on the plane with the hunting party. The dog teams and guides had been employed for a year, and met us at the Arctic air strip, just outside the village.

As a final act of preparation, one of the natives took his dog team and hauled us our supply of fresh drinking water —a 12-foot sled load of fresh-water ice blocks from an inland lake, five miles away. This "water" was stored outside the hut, at a height preventing the village dogs from hoisting legs and leaving their calling cards.

Such basic preparation takes time and is very costly. As a single instance, air transportation of fresh meat to such a village from the "outside" runs around a dollar per pound, as it does for much of the other supplies.

The overall costs are, of course, transferred ultimately to the hunter. This, any way you figure it, means an expensive hunt. So, as with other species of bear, the only outfitter the hunter should choose is one with a good hunter-success ratio on polar bears. This, however, does not mean a one hundred percent record. With polars, hunted by dog team, the hazards of wrong winds and currents, the incidence of too much pressure ice for dogs to negotiate, and similar unpredictable factors, are all beyond the outfitter's control. Often the hunter will not get his bear despite all the outfitter, guides, and himself can do. However in many other ways, the hunt will be well worth the price anyway.

A big share of the hunting via dog teams and Eskimo guides is done from small villages off the Alaska Coast. Point Hope and Point Barrow are two choice areas. The only way for the novice to make arrangements for his first Arctic trip is to contact the professional outfitters who advertise in the sporting journals, or to hear of their services from a hunting partner or friend. From such a contact, plans may be arranged.

In such an arrangement, the outfitter usually has a flat fee for a specified length of time. For this fee, he agrees to furnish such basic items as listed above. The hunter is required to provide only his personal gear such as rifles and sleeping bag, clothes, cameras, binoculars, and transportation to the native village at the point of take-off. At least the last leg of this has to be by air.

For hunting with dog teams, the period from early February until April is best.

At this season, with favorable winds, the ice is usually thick enough offshore for dog teams to travel from the anchor ice out many miles over the ocean. By then, too, the great white bears have come south and eastward enough to travel from the major ice pack onto this newer ice near shore. This is necessary to bring the quarry and the hunter into proximity, and doesn't usually occur until early February. The native hunters usually don't see many bears until that late in the winter season.

Hunting with dog teams after April is not recommended. By then the plane hunters are usually working the coast line offshore, and spooking the game farther out again. Too, with April, at both Point Hope and Barrow, the native

hunters are turning their attention to whaling—whaling with
skin boats and harpoons still being done at these two places.

This is an offshore operation, and the best hunters are
then no longer available for the bear hunter.

The biggest handicap to be overcome by the hunter from
a warmer climate is the perpetual cold at this season of
year. On an average, temperatures will range from around
zero to 30 below. These temperatures, due to the low-
slanting rays of the sun then, remain fairly constant both
night and day. Periods of moderating temperature may send
the thermometer to above zero for a few days. But the
visiting hunter had best not figure on it.

Most experienced hunters of other big game are used to
this amount of cold for brief periods. They are not accustomed to it for a continuous period of, say, three weeks.
And in dog team hunting, the frigid temperature is with
him twelve hours per day, day after day, and with no
opportunity for him occasionally to get into any form of
shelter where he can warm up. Briefly, he takes the cold
or else. His one method of warming up, is to pile off the
dog sled, and run behind.

Recent developments in Arctic clothing have largely overcome this basic handicap of cold, and only with suitable
clothing is it ever wise to hunt in the Arctic. The clothing
which a man has on his back not only must keep him reasonably comfortable during the long hours of each day's
hunt; it must provide his literal life insurance if he's unfortunate enough to be caught beyond an open lead, necessitating his staying on the floating ice pack for several days.

The survival period at 30 below zero, should a man
happen to fall through into the water, is considered to be
three minutes. This is a far shorter length of time than
Attunganah took to swim that open lead written about in
the previous chapter. The survival time of a man in open
air at this temperature, and without his clothes, would also
be but a matter of minutes.

One example of this I will mention. At one time I snapped

three successive color pictures of Ookeelah and his dog team, later to be used as a magazine cover (The American Rifleman, December, 1959). This necessitated taking my hand from the mittens, and adjusting the metal lens ring between shots. In those brief few seconds, I froze two fingers and thumb to where the flesh all came off later. Metal touched at such temperatures, with the bare hands, burns rather than feels cold.

Suitable clothing for the Arctic begins next to the hide. First, the hunter should wear a suit of light cotton underwear of the "union suit" shape. This garment is easily laundered and prolongs the usability of the heavier underwear. Otherwise he becomes a literal stinker.

The basic underwear should be one of only two materials, dacron or down. Each will suffice, but down is the better material, especially if one is so unfortunate as to fall through young or moving ice into the water. At least one recent case is on record where the hunter survived a dunking largely because he had down underwear, plus the other necessary insulated garments.

These two-piece garments are quilted, light, and provide great body warmth. Often, back at the hut, they are worn as outside garments when the heavy outside pieces are removed.

A light woolen shirt. worn on cold days and left off on warmer days, is a necessary item. This is worn over the insulated underwear.

The outside garments are most expensive, equally important, and should be chosen with great care. Down pants are ideal. The new military-surplus, glass-insulated, double-thickness pants are also adequate, though more bulky. The heavy woolen pants made of rugged 30-oz. "mackinaw" material are worn by some, and will often suffice if worn over down underwear. Any pants should be loose fitting, and of ankle length. The ankles should be small or tapering so as to fit well down inside the necessary *mukluks*.

Only a coat with integral parka hood will do. It is impossible to keep the head and neck warm with any kind of coat and cap. The Arctic cold will seek out any gaps and freeze one immediately.

Such a parka coat should be loose fitting, of down filling, and of adequate length to go well down over the buttocks and thighs—at least half-way from waist to knees. The arms should be amply long, with knitted inside wrist bands. It should be zipper closed, as well as button closed on the flaps. Too many big pockets, for the hands and small items, is just right.

The hood should be down filled, also, and quilted. The fur ruff, which goes around the wearer's face, is indispensable. This ruff should always be made of wolverine fur. Each exhaled breath at extreme temperatures condenses the mouth spray into frost, which collects on this fur ruff at the edge of the face. On wolverine fur, it becomes frost which may be brushed off with a mitten. With any other fur, the moisture becomes ice, and will build up.

The best Arctic parka I have seen to date is one developed especially for Arctic wear by the Eddie Bauer Company. It has taken years and the experience of many men to reach its near-perfection.

This garment has all the qualities listed above. The fur ruff next to the face is of wolverine, but also has an outer ring of wolf-fur whose longer hairs are most useful in breaking the impact of the wind.

Many hunters wear only the parka on their heads. However, a down-filled cap, with firm poke in front, is most necessary for the man who wears glasses. It keeps the fur out of his eyes, and allows him to see out front when the parka is tightly closed.

The Bauer Company makes the best down mittens also. These big oversize mitts have several needed Arctic features. They are long enough to prevent cold getting to the wrists. They have an extra inside hand pocket into which the fist may be doubled for added warmth. On their backs is a layer of fur on which the nose (always on the run in extreme cold) may be wiped. This moistures immediately freezes and may be brushed off.

A necessary complement to down mittens is a pair of inside gloves—these to keep the hands partly warm when handling a rifle, and other items necessitating the use of the fingers. A pair of rabbit-lined driving gloves works fine. A pair of tight-fitting nylon gloves works even better when actually shooting, but are less warm.

The feet, in extreme cold, are most critical areas. Especially when riding for long hours on a dog sled, the feet are prone to freeze before the hunter is aware. For this reason, special care must be used in the choice of footwear.

For Arctic wear, no form of shoe, or combination shoe and overshoe has ever been developed which will successfully work. The bulky ones which keep the feet fairly warm are no good for the intervals of necessary walking on ice.

The only successful footwear is the *mukluks*, which the natives habitually wear. *Mukluks* are made in two pieces. First is an inner boot of 10-inch height, made of summer caribou, usually, with the hair side turned in, and sewed up without sole into a form-fitting shoe, with split caribou sinew. The pattern for these which the Eskimo has developed is such that, when sewed, no hard "corner" exists to rub the foot. This inner boot, worn over a pair of woolen socks, and containing a half-inch of fur all over the inside, provides extreme insulation.

Such insulation is increased by the outer boot which is worn over the inner element. The outer boot, or *mukluk* proper, is made of a length to come just below the knees, for hunting purposes. Dress *mukluks* are made shorter. A variety of furs and hides is used. Mainly they are made of the sewed-up shank hair-and-hide of caribou, sealskin, or wolf hide. Their tops are held firmly down upon the pants (tucked inside) by a draw-string run through a leather or fabric loop, itself sewed all around the *mukluk* top. The leg of the outer boot is left large, to go over the inner boot loosely.

Such tops are made with the grain of the hair running downward, to drain off ice, snow, and possibly water. A strip of sealskin with the fur turned inside is sewed all around at the bottom, and is used to join the tops with the bottoms. Sort of an all-around, leather hyphen.

Mukluk bottoms are made from the thick, tough hide of the *oogruk*, or bearded seal. The hair is scraped from the hide, then the native-tanned leather is shaped into foot bottoms.

These bottoms, with vertical sides approximately two inches high, look like miniature row boats. They are patiently formed to shape in a unique way. Tiny serrations are formed into the leather from the foot part outward—these are at both the toe and the heel ends. Like the puckering on a moccasin, these draw the flat leather together and upward, forming the *mukluk's* sides at the foot.

Most people would swear these serrations were made by some pliers-like tool. They are not. The uniform creases and ridges are made by Eskimo women chewing them into the leather!

On the outside bottom, longitudinally, a small "keel" is similarly chewed into the leather. This serves in a small way to prevent side slippage on the ice.

The bottoms are sewed on to the circuitous caribou-leather strip at the base of the uppers. Lastly, two ¾-inch binding bands of tanned seal skin are sewed on at the ankles, for tying the *mukluks* snugly at the ankles, and they are complete.

There is no warmer foot wear, and it is surprising how much cold these ingenious boots will turn. There is a trick to walking in them on ice which the novice must learn. Start out with long strides as with shoes, and you'll land sprawling on your backside. The trick is to make tiny, mincing little steps, with the legs close together, as the natives have learned to do.

The visiting hunter may be able to have a suitable pair of *mukluks* made to his individual foot size, after his arrival at the village from which he'll hunt. A far better way is to send the individual "hoof print" (an outline drawn around the foot in a heavy woolen sock) to the outfitter, who will relay it to an Eskimo friend or employee. This fellow will have his wife sew-and-chew a fine pair which will be certain to fit. Incidentally, the natives like such an additional source of income, and will be happy to accommodate. Ookeelah's wife made my own *mukluks* after I'd sent the foot size three months in advance, and had them ready for use when we arrived. She charged $25 for the set, and I wouldn't take three times that amount for them today.

These are the vital garments for survival and enjoyment while going it via dog team in the Arctic. Other items include a pair of sheep-lined house shoes for use in camp at nights, and while the inner boots of the *mukluks* dry out. A leather thong or nylon cord which will go around the neck and tie down to each mitten is also necessary, so as not to lose one, which would be disastrous. Such a cord is used outside the parka, and secured against loss by a cross piece tied across at the arm pits. A tube of lanolin is good for the face against frost and sunburn, if one's skin is tender. Colored glasses against the glare of the sun on ice and snow are necessary.

Another most useful item is the recently-developed pocket hand-warmers, which burn lighter fluid or even white gasoline used in lanterns. These gadgets will run almost all day on a filling. They are lit and made sure to be burning before leaving the hut in the morning, and provide extra heat for the hands, when carried in an outside parka pocket.

For the older person, who simply can't keep his feet warm no matter what he wears, a pair of electric socks, operated from small batteries carried at the belt, will often save the day. I used to snort uproariously at the notion of plugging in one's tootsies. But after an elderly hunter, with a heart condition and poor circulation, got his polar bear last spring largely through the aid of a $14-pair of electric socks, I've changed my mind. This change, incidentally, was assisted by my own 17 straight days out over the polar ice with a dog team, in bitter temperatures.

Lastly, as to clothing, a pair of felt gaiters, inside a pair of 4-buckle dress overshoes, or arctics, are mighty fine for riding the plane after one leaves Fairbanks. Some of the planes making the final hops into Eskimo land are unheated. Felt gaiters save a lot of foot misery. In conjunction with this, a pair of heavy woolen pants and the parka should be left as a carry-on package, or in the duffel where it can be gotten, also to wear on these final hops, Suffice it to say that the hostesses on the planes from Fairbanks north, also wear their dress parkas and woolen, bi-furcated breeches, plus *mukluks* or flight boots. So do the pilots.

The Eskimo dog sled is also a specialized, highly adaptable piece of Arctic equipment.

The best sleds are made of hickory. They have a bow front-end; up-swinging sides which end at the rear in handles, with which the driver manipulates the conveyance through pressure ice; a slatted bottom, with runners which extend behind far enough to be ridden with a foot on each side; a slatted back; and a brake consisting of a 1x6-inch board running the full length of the sled beneath it, and ending in a set of down-turned steel claws—the brake, which is driven into the ice by a foot, to stop the sled.

There are numerous joints in this sled, largely where the standards join the runners, and the side rails. Each wooden member is hand cut and worked to shape from hickory planking shipped in on the *North Star's* lone voyage. They are fastened together with mortise-and-tenon joints, reinforced by sealskin bindings.

The most usable sleds are between eleven and twelve feet in length and approximately two feet wide. The length is most suitable for hauling heavy loads, yet being sufficiently short to be worked through "impossible" mazes of pressure ice. The width allows one rider to sit inside, with feet extended flatly out before him, his arms on the side rails, and his spine against the hard sled back.

For purely ice-running, hickory runners are often used. But where the going must be upon bank ice, where winds drive the snow off and leave rocks, then the runners are steel-shod.

Finally, the dogs' lead line is attached, a caribou hide is tossed onto the slatted bottom for the rider to sit upon, a sealskin bag is tied behind the sled back for small items of gear, and the sled is ready. Making such a piece of equipment takes several weeks. In the rough Arctic use, such a well-made sled will last for three years.

The teams of dogs are marvels of hard work, skill, intelligence, and the physical capacity to work fourteen hours a day on a single three-pound feeding of frozen seal meat. This is usually given them upon completion of the day's work, as an incentive to get home safely and quickly.

A big percentage of the Eskimo dogs are of Siberian Husky origin. Most drivers today, however, will admit that their string has a most democratic ancestry. All dogs, though, are heavily haired, average from forty to sixty pounds, and live entirely outdoors. At night they are tethered separately, otherwise they'd kill each other from sheer savagery.

The better dog teams number eleven dogs as "standard." This means five span, or pairs, working on opposite sides of the rope "line," plus the leader. That number makes a dog for each foot of sled length, a hundred pounds of capacity load for each dog, and the longest combination of team and sled which can be worked handily through and over bad pressure ice.

All dogs frost over when working in extremely cold weather. This is especially hard on any thin-furred animals. To prevent freezing of their flanks during such extremes, folded caribou-hide strips averaging four inches wide by fourteen inches long, or "dog brassieres," are tied around them, and worn.

The way my guide Ookeelah broke his dogs, handled them, and worked them in hunting country is typical of the best dog team hunters.

One morning at sunup, Ookeelah came to our hut. "Today we break the pup," he announced simply.

The "pup" was a year-old dog which, in his customary wild nature, had broken from his tethering-stake some months previously. In order even to catch him again, Ookeelah had to set a fox-trap by his food one night. In the harsh but necessary treatment of capturing him, the pup had lost two front toes. He limped, but was otherwise all right. I promptly named him Shorty.

When being harnessed, Shorty, like the others, was dragged from his stake under protest, and a round leather dog collar pushed over his head. His hand-made harness consisted further of two tugs of heavy, tight-woven webbing, coming together well behind him; a belly-band; and a back-strap. An "X" of crossed straps, over the back, finished it.

The tugs of each dog were attached to a ring tied into the lead line. This same metal ring also becomes the anchor to which the pair of dogs immediately behind is tied by their necks, with a short length of rope. All dogs except the leader, and the pair of experienced "wheelers," are tied by their necks in this way. Neither the leader nor the wheelers have neck lines. The leader, of course, must have complete freedom of movement. The wheelers also must have more freedom than the others, both to keep themselves out of the way of the sled behind them (as it swings and is bumped off-course), and also to "curve" sidewise around ice obstacles, thereby pulling the sled along the leader's course—not allowing it to cut through on an arc to the curve of the course.

The dog team was otherwise hitched before Ookeelah started on Shorty. Shorty, with all the savagery of his

breed, coupled with fear of what was to happen, fought
furiously. Ookeelah, with heavily-mittened hands, choked
him down until the collar could be shoved over his head,
and the line attached.

During this, Red, another sixty-pound brute, and one
of the best imaginable wheelers (I know because I rode
700 miles immediately behind him, with his black peep-
sight always aimed at me) could not stand the delay. Red
barked eagerly and jumped three feet up and down. This
tangled the lead-rope and harnesses, to where hitching
Shorty became impossible.

The author, whom the Eskimos named Avik Puk (Big Walrus), on a
recent polar bear hunt via dog sled.

Ookeelah, a most practical man, fixed this in a hurry. Seizing the snow scoop from the sled, he batted Red fully over the head with an equally savage swipe. Red went down with a yelp and lay stretched out in a heap. By the time he'd regained consciousness. Shorty was hitched and cowering on the snow. Red, however, held nothing against his master for such treatment. Regaining his feet groggily, he did nothing further than actually "smile" at Ookeelah, wag a couple of times, and jump eagerly up and down. He didn't, however, bark.

"Ready," Ookeelah told me.

I piled into the sled, Ookeelah released the brake, and the team was off into a high lope within the second bound.

Shorty, however, reacted as any dog will. He pulled back in his collar, lay down, and skidded along the ice which was hard-packed at the edge of the village. Such a skidding was hard on Shorty's feet, and he promptly rolled over on his back.

I'd estimate that we were going between fifteen and twenty miles per hour. Shorty was still on his back after fifty yards, and plainly choking down.

"What if he won't pull?" I asked Ookeelah.

"I shoot him."

It was that simple, The overhead in feed is enormous for dogs there, considering how difficult it is to obtain in any fashion. Once a pup has reached a year, the vacation is over and he then works each day till he dies.

By the time we'd raced away a full hundred yards, Shorty's attempts at fighting the collar were noticeably feebler. I expected Ookeelah to slow the team, to give the pup a chance for breath. He didn't. Shouting at the leader, he swung the team into a straight-away, and the speed was increased if anything.

At this, a miraculous thing happened. Shorty somehow regained his feet, and feebly lunged forward, undoubtedly getting his first breath since we started. Again he lunged, again being jerked back by the tugs. A few such jerks, with the air he got into his lungs, gave Shorty a whole new insight into dog sledding, and so help me, within the next hundred yards Shorty was pulling his share.

That day, we covered a full sixty miles. The distance could be measured, since we passed well down the cape beyond Cape Thompson—a known distance—and came back another circuitous route of known mileage. The only difference I could detect in Shorty and the others was that each time Ookeelah shouted, the pup would lunge forward with fear. Occasionally he'd turn his flattened ears behind, as if trying to find out what it was all about.

That night, Shorty came in completely exhausted and with no tension on his tugs. His feet were badly sored up from the ice. Ookeelah's one deference to Shorty's status was that he gave him the next day to recover, before hitching him again with the string.

"What about Shorty's sore feet?" I asked.

"If they get too bad, I make him boots."

Leather boots, tied around the dog's ankles with thong, are often used, and are about the only cure used for sore feet. These are most often used on the leader, who has of necessity to travel each hunting day.

The leader is the real marvel of the dog team. Dogs are driven entirely by word of mouth, and under the command of the driver. No line of any kind is attached to the leader. He goes where the driver dictates, and the team members all follow him.

Only five words, so far as I could tell, are necessary to driving a dog team. The younger Eskimos have adopted the white man's English in part, and commonly used shouts of "Gee" and "Haw" to turn the dog leader right and left, respectively. "C'm gee! C'm gee!" will turn the leader *sharply* to the right, often mid-stride on a high lope, and virtually at right angles. "C'm haw! C'm haw!" will similarly turn the team sharply to the left, or even in a hair-pin turn, back the way they came.

In the mountainous ridges of pressure ice, I've watched

these drivers literally worm the lead dog through chunks of ice the size of pianos, and up-ended into thirty-foot "windrows" . . . often changing courses at each yard or rod, and at violent angles. And all with but the above commands. Plus a swinging, prying, and helping with the sled.

For fast going, out on open ice, or where the driver wants the dogs to run, he simply slaps his mittens together and shouts, "Gudo! Gudo! Gudo!"

I have been told that in the Eskimo's language there are no words with which one may curse a dog or person. I am, however, convinced that Ookeelah, at least, spoke to his dogs in a combination of English, Eskimo, and Western Grammar. When I asked him what "Gudo!" meant, he grinned and said that as near as he could translate it into my tongue, it meant for the dogs to "get the hell out here you sonsofbitches, and on your way." Likewise, when an occasional dog would get on the wrong side of the lead rope, Ookeelah would trot forward (after braking to a stop) grab the beast by the collar, lift him to a man's height, throw him as hard as he could to the ice in a resounding plunk and yelp . . . all the while muttering something in Eskimo which I'm sure couldn't be printed in this volume, but whose import the dog understood.

Ookeelah's lead dog for nine years was Avik. This brilliant 70-pound beast was one-fourth wolf and looked it. A single low word from Ookeelah would make Avik change course, stop, run, or lie down. Sheer intelligence was in those wolf-slanting eyes—Avik could practically talk.

"Many time," Ookeelah told me, "I be 20, 30 miles out on ice when blizzard come. Couldn't see five sleds ahead. I turn old Avik loose. He never lost course. Always bring me home. Maybe the wolf in him."

After nine years, Avik became too old. Now, Son of Avik leads Ookeelah's team, and the old dog is relegated to a place farther back in the team, where vision, hearing, and responsibility are less.

Of all the small honors which I've had bestowed on me,

none was ever intrinsically greater, more sincerely given,
or more greatly appreciated than the Eskimo name those
people gave me—Avik Puk. Eskimos are smallish people.
Bundled in my down clothes, and great fur-ruffed parka,
I did look like a big walrus, which the name meant. But
also, I was named after a dog I came to love—Ookeelah's
team-leader, old Avik.

The lead dog has one advantage, besides a change in
scenery, over the other dogs in a team. The driver will
allow the leader the privilege of stopping to urinate and
evacuate his bowels. All other dogs must do this "on the fly."

To the uninitiated, this perpetual performance is at once
hilarious and pathetic. It is something to see dogs on a
swinging trot or high lope veer out to each up-ended ice
block adjacent to the course, and try to sprinkle it, mid-
stride. It is an even bigger revelation to witness a loping
dog, keeping full pace while running on but his fore legs
. . . with the rear half of his body carried above the ice,
hind legs way up under his chin, and attending to the
wants of nature.

Since the seal meat these animals eat is mildly cathartic,
it makes the dog sledder wish for a wind shield, partly
to ward off the smell.

The actual technique of bear hunting with dogs is similar
to other open- and broken-country stalking. The hunters
like to leave by daylight, since the early morning hours
are best both for seals and *oogruk,* and for polar bear.

The direction for each day's hunt is determined the
evening before, and then checked the following morning.
The visiting hunter usually cannot tell whether there will
be wind that day, or whether it will blow from north or
south, or change during the day. The Eskimo hunter, living with daily hazard, and having reached adulthood, has
demonstrated this skill. Each day's hunt is arranged so as
to hunt offshore into the wind; then return with it to shore.

I once asked Ooyahahlook how he could foretell which
way the wind might blow for the day. "I show one way

I think maybe not." He pointed to a low pocket in the distant shore line. "Grandfather and father was tell me if fog there morning south wind sure that day I don't think."

From such signs, experience, and, I think, a near-animal instinct, these indomitable hunters seem to know what weather to expect.

Basically, each day's hunt is a pattern of getting as far out onto the anchor ice, and towards open water, as possible. This involves threading the dog team through the endless windrows of pressure ice, and following the flatter ice between these ridges. Crevices, often six feet across, are simply jumped with the dogs and sled. The dogs are shouted into a dead run parallel to such a crevice, often,

The amount of drifted snow and the degree of freshness are both good indicators when a polar bear track is examined.

then swung abruptly with a "C'm gee! C'm gee!" or oppositely. Each dog in turn leaps the crevice, and momentum carries the sled and rider across.

In the mazes of pressure ice, blocks up to the size of small houses are tumbled together, often to a height of 20 or 30 feet. The dogs are urged up over, through and between these, with the driver twisting and "working" the sled through afterward. And what a beating those sleds take!

Periodically, at each of the highest ridges of ice, the Eskimo guide will climb and survey the entire country for miles, usually with the best available binoculars. This minute scrutiny tells him the course where dogs may go, how far he can travel without the ice maze stopping him, the incidence of open water, and if any game is within the first few miles.

Open water, in Arctic temperatures, literally smokes with dirty-colored fog. In the distance, it looks like the black smog from a city. Open water, of course, means the presence of seals, and the possibility of a bear. The polar bear's coloration is creamy, and against a back-drop of white, he shows up well for long distances. This is especially true when he's walking, and is caught in sunlight. On his shadow side, such a bear and his leg shadows will appear as blue, and distorted because of mirages.

In this travel—climb ice-ridges—scrutinize manner, the hunt goes on. Between stops, the dogs lope on flat, unimpeded ice and snow, and trot through broken, twisting areas.

When first a bear track is spotted, a lot may be learned. If the spoor comes toward shore, it means the game is moving from the pack ice. If the tracks follow an open lead, it means hair seals are likely near and the bruin is hunting. If the bear leaves the ice edge of a long open lead and swims, it likely means that the presence of other seal hunters have spooked him and he's going out to sea to another ice floe.

The pads of this bear are mostly haired over. But on the frothy salt-water ice and intermittent snow, they leave a clean imprint. If the tracks are thin (hind foot) and sink deeply, it means a bear in poor condition. A wider, pudgy track indicates a fat bear.

My partner John Phillips and I were hunting with two dog teams the day we first saw a polar bear track. Ookeelah and Ooyahahlook studied it intently.

"Eight-foot bear," Ookeelah said.

Ooyahahlook agreed. "I was think eight foot maybe not."

I measured this track. The hind foot made a clean print 11 inches long by 7 inches wide. This was considered a medium or small polar bear.

The dogs, too, do part of the hunting. They sniffed these tracks eagerly, knowing a capture meant meat. Similarly, they'd take off course, unless shouted back in Western Grammar, at the sight of any seals in open water, or the smell of fresh air holes made by seals.

Once the bear's intention is determined as well as possible, a stalking campaign is outlined. If the beast is plainly traveling, then the driver plans a long chase in the hope of overtaking or intercepting the animal. If the tracks are meandering, then the Eskimo guide tries to locate the beast from a vantage point on high ice. If he's successful in this, then the dogs are anchored by driving the steel anchor hook (attached to the sled with a rope) into the ice, and the stalk begins.

Most Eskimo guides equip their hunters and themselves with white cotton stalking jackets. These effectively conceal their presence from the quarry, and are put on over regular parkas.

Often such a stalk will take an hour or more. Any bear's actions are highly unpredictable, but the skill with which an Eskimo hunter unravels a bruin's intention is highly incredulous.

John Belcher, who killed the Boone & Crockett ranking polar bear in 1958, described the actual stalk as well as

I've ever heard. His guide's English name was Antonio.

"When we left the dogs anchored," John said, "Antonio told me to do everything he did. 'If I stop, you stop,' he told me, 'and if I go on my belly, you go on your belly. If I stand up, you stand up.'

"Soon we'd made it up to still another mess of ice ridges. Antonio climbed up again and stayed a long time. Then he came down quickly. 'You set down here,' he told me. 'Bear come out in that open, seventy-five yards or so.' I did just like he said. And after I'd waited until there didn't seem to be a bear in the whole Arctic, out walked Mr. Bear. Just like Antonio had said, and in the very spot he said. All I did was set there on my fanny and let him have it!"

All during the hunt for a bear, seal hunting continues also—this partly to supply horsepower for the dog team, partly for something to do.

An important item always carried on the sled is the seal line. This is usually 100 feet long, cuttyhunk, and with a 600-pound breaking strength. With it, an Eskimo can retrieve a hair seal, *oogruk*, or even a Beluga whale from open water.

To the line's business-end is attached a wooden bobber, of maple wood if possible (as it won't split), which weighs about 1½ pounds. In an ivory stem leading from this bobber are four hooks, ¾-inch shank, and filed razor sharp.

The entire outfit is coiled around a tiny hunting stool. This stool has a top about ten inches wide, is kidney-shaped, and into it are hand mortised three driftwood legs measuring seven inches long. Along the concave side of the top, a thin strip of walrus ivory is attached with whale-baleen "nails." A hole, or socket, is also cut into the top board.

Besides serving as a spool for the line, this tiny stool also keeps the hunter dry as he sits or stands upon it while seal hunting. The ivory strip won't build up with salt water, as the hunter scrapes his *mukluks'* bottoms free of wet. And in an emergency, the hunting pole, *oonok*, is shoved through the board hole, making a temporary paddle for a skin boat.

Seals killed close off the ice edge are retrieved with this line. I watched Ookeelah bring in seals up to 60 yards in open water, often with but one cast of the bobber hooks. He'd stand on solid ice, and start the bobber swinging around his head, gradually lengthening the line. When he had 15 feet of line out, he'd heave the bobber out and over the dead seal, much as one throws a rock from a sling. Straight as an arrow the heavy bobber would sail out over the seal, "plunking" down oppositely. With a quick jerk, Ookeelah would set the hooks, then bring in the animal hand over hand.

He hooked one seal at a full 60 yards, the first attempt; and I never saw him make over three casts, even in heavy wind, to hook any such seal.

When two or more Eskimos hunt together (without sled passengers), one of them always takes along a skin boat. This puny but sea-worthy craft is made from a single *oogruk* skin, sewed all the way around a wooden skeleton, usually of driftwood, at the gunwales. The result is a chip-like craft of seven-foot length, which weighs little and is adequate for retrieving seals too far out to be hooked with the seal line. It is always life insurance, also, for the lone hunter, should a lead open up between him and shore when he's far out upon the ice.

Alternating the climbing and looking, and hunting seals, the bear hunt goes on. By mid-morning, the moving edges of the ice have been reached. There, at the shifting line where ice meets water, is where the good hunting and the danger are.

It's an eerie sensation to sit on a sled, have the dogs urged into a run, then break sharply to the side and jump six feet of open water, with a 12-foot dog sled, having the new "edge" slowly sink beneath the racing sled runners. It's equally hair-raising to race along, with the dogs never permitted to slow down from a high lope, over "young" ice, a mile in extent, and which you can see sink in a sickening, perpetual arc under the runners of a companion's sled to a depth of four inches all the way across the mile, to stronger ice. When making such necessary crossings, the two sleds are never allowed to come close together, lest the weight send them both through. Only momentum of the racing dogs carries the sled over.

It's also awe-inspiring to be loping along, over moving ice, and watch a flat field of oppositely-moving ice, of five acres extent, coming towards you at four to five miles per hour. One 12-inch ice field skidding over another right at you—and watch the dogs vault upon the new, shifting field, and feel the sled bump upon it!

Again, it's humbling to the human soul to see a 10-acre field of ice, some of it piled 30 feet high, all squealing, and grinding against the edge of anchor ice with sounds of fury and under the force of millions of tons pressure; to see that field move one way, suddenly grind to a stop, shift, and go the opposite way with no more than a second's pause. Maybe the moving field, upon which you intended to take the dogs, might move out, opening a rod, then two rods of murky-purple, fog-wreathing water between. Maybe it will move oppositely, upending thousands of tons of ice blocks in a new pressure ridge at the break, instead.

It raises the neck hackles to hunt upon, across, and along this frigid, living line between life and death.

At noon, the dogs are stopped in a safe ice area, and out of sight, for lunch. Each time the dogs are stopped, they immediately lie down, curl their noses to their backsides, so that what warmth exists at 20 below zero can "circulate."

Lunch, for the bear hunter, consists of fresh ice carried along on the sled being melted over a gasoline stove for tea, and cookies. Kerosene pot stoves used to be used, and "tea" was the broth left from boiling caribou into "Eskimo steaks"—nothing in that harsh land ever being wasted. However, the modern gasoline stove, and the white man's tea, have improved the lunch situation. It is, though, an experience to gulp scalding tea from one mittened hand, and poke a frozen cookie into your parka face with the other. Any cookie-filling "bites" just like case-hardened steel—you wolf the entire cookie and melt it inside.

Hunting for the afternoon follows a reverse pattern. The dogs can make from 40 to 60 miles per day, and are eager to get back to their evening rations. Often in flat, open-ice stretches, the enthusiastic beasts really take off. Then, as the conveyance without springs bumps over the contour of the frozen snow, dog-sledding becomes an unforgettable experience in itself.

Personally, in the interests of hunting, I've ridden every kind of vehicle from airplane to raft, wagon to train, and boat to pack mule—even to these "bray bunnies" equipped with nothing except a decker pack saddle. But one Arctic dog sled ride, surpassed all else. Bucking horses included, it was the wildest thing I've yet been on.

While waiting for young ice to freeze solidly enough to continue hunting polar bear, Ookeelah said, "We go inland and look for caribou."

This entailed climbing the small mountains inland for five miles, and up to their very peaks, with the dog team. We found no caribou by mid-afternoon, however, and decided to go back. Instead of Ookeelah taking the twisting, mildly up-grade route over which we'd come, he looked straight downhill towards the ocean. "We try down canyon," he announced.

The snow in these coast-line hills had been mostly blown off by the violent winds. While many side hills showed their black rocks, the canyon bottoms lay drifted with from three to ten feet of hard snow. The howling, fish-tailing winds, in sub-zero temperatures, had laid this snow in a most uneven, intricate pattern. The whole valley below us looked like the meringue topping of some giant cake, its surface in folds, piles, and innumerable hill-like humps. In more open places it all lay like some vast tufted mattress, with humps and crests up to four feet higher than the sunken "buttons."

All side canyons converged into the main canyon, down which Ookeelah obviously intended to drop off. The very steepness left me gulping. The canyon simply "fell off" below us, towards the ocean.

But without hesitation, Ookeelah shouted, "C'm haw! C'm haw!" The dogs swung. Already they could almost taste the three pounds of frozen seal meat each would get, if and when he made it back to the hut camp.

In the instant before Ookeelah lifted the brake with his foot, I'll swear that Son Of Avik knew his intention, and actually jeered at us. Tongue point out, and slanting eyes laughing, that canny beast seemed to say, "*I'll* make it back down that way. But five will get you ten none of these other bastards can keep up."

Ookeelah lifted his *mukluk*. The brake tore loose and with a jerk we were off!

The snow beneath was hard as linoleum. The sled, as yet containing me, weighed 400 pounds. The steel runners were slick as a baby's bottom. And the angle downward was quite like the half-pitch of a shingle roof.

From the instant the dogs leaped, there wasn't any question of their pulling the sled. It was going to be a sheer race to see if they could keep from being run over by it. Like some long, furry, rippling angle worm, the line of dogs shot out, ears laid back, legs pistoning in one blinding blur. The lead rope suddenly ran up on them in a loose loop. *Ta-da-lump! ta-da-lump! ta-da-lump!* Like a bullet fired from a gun, we were off with no stopping possible.

At first all dogs held their own. But gradually, Shorty, next ahead of the wheelers and smallest dog in the string, lost air speed. As his tug rope loosened, his neck rope inexorably became taut. Failing to maintain the pace, Shorty gradually was stretched out, rolled onto his back, and "rested" while skating on his spine. A hundred yards of this, plus the unevenness of terrain and his rolling motion, gave Shorty the necessary encouragement and again he made his feet. This alternating routine of up, then down, then up continued periodically, as hair, snow, Shorty, and sparks flew.

Big Red, the slower of the two wheelers, wasn't doing so well either. Ears flat, brush floating well behind, he ran for everything in him. Each 10 seconds he turned his head to read the score. His original six feet of line gradually slackened, as we gained even more speed, until it bounced on a slack loop under the sled's bow. Being untied by the neck, he lacked this "incentive" the other dogs had; and inch by inch, Red's furry hinder crept back to the bow of the flying sled. Rather, it over-ran him.

Watching from a position just behind—partly upon the sled, partly above it—I felt sure that Red would surely lose, and be run over by the bouncing sled. But as his rump touched the sled's bow, he gained reserve encouragement, and again, by fractions of an inch, he lengthened the hand span separating him from instant death.

This process, too, was repeated over and over. Each time it seemed for sure that Red could never quite out-run the bounding conveyance, with the sled's bow apparently biting at his tail, some slight variation in the humpy surface of the snow would impede the sled to where Red could gain another inch.

On the sled, things were little better. The humps in the hard-packed surface averaged maybe a rod apart. The sled, like skijoring over a jump behind a horse, would rise, sail out into space, than *wham!* back down into the next depression in a sled-creaking impact. Each time the hickory horse would vault up and over the next crest, I'd have the temporary, peaceful sensation of being again on the airliner, though looking downward upon the flying backs of the dogs. This welcome respite lasted but a fraction of an instant. Then, three feet of unimpeded fall, and we'd slam down, with ear-shattering bang, to meet the next up-coming surface. Bang, bang, bang!

At each free fall, I came down with the sled, onto my

spine, as though someone had hit me on top of the head with a sledge hammer while I sat on an anvil. Each time, the vertebrae were "accordioned" into a shorter overall length; and this series of pile-driving motions was augmented by the fact that while I could go *up* with the sled at each incline, in the air I had more of a tendency to float, and could not follow it downward as fast. This provided more leverage.

Before we'd flown a quarter-mile, I swore that even my ancestors must have been jarred from the impacts.

Ookeelah, masterful driver that he is, suspected shortly that he'd bitten off more gravity than he could chew. Spraddle-legged, a foot securely anchored on each runner, and hands gripping the handle-bar ends, he looked like nothing else than a plowman, part of the time on earth, largely plowing in the air towards Heaven.

Each banging contact with the snow gave him just sufficient traction to steer the sled. Periodically, he'd chance lifting a *mukluk* long enough to try the brake. This steel-clawed appurtenance will stop a dog-team on ice or hard snow as though the string had suddenly been riveted. But the same brake, vigorously applied while sailing three feet in space, is far less effective.

Finding that braking was impossible, Ookeelah concentrated on keeping the sled upright, and this we both did by leaning with it, both in the air and upon the snow, much as one rides a bicycle, or neck-reins a horse.

The dogs were doing their utmost, feet scissoring like sets of outside pistons. But the best expedient for keeping the sled, now planing over the snowcrests like a motorboat racing on choppy waters, from running over them was even more speed.

"Gudo! Gudo! Gudo!" Ookeelah shouted, still clinging to his aerial plow handles.

Son of Avik seemed to sense that old Avik's honor was at stake. He bent deeper into the lead rope. The others, possibly noting the rapidly increasing proximity of the seal meat, gave their all, Even Shorty extended the distances between his periodic "rest" periods, when he was skidded by the neck over the undulating course.

There was one thing in our favor. Within two miles, the steepness of the slick descent *gradually* leveled off. And at a time when the sled was at last precariously nosing its fatal way up between the wheelers, the rippled surface temporarily smoothed out. Ookeelah, in addition to yelling more "Gudo," at last got the brake into the snow. This, plus the gradual leveling out of the canyon bottom, slowed the sled. Somewhat.

I've talked with professional dog drivers who say that such a team can make 30 miles an hour on the flat surface of easy snow. I'm positive that within but a few more minutes, we'd decreased our own speed to approximately that.

These are, briefly, some of the thrills of hunting polar bears via dog team, Eskimo style.

Other aspects, which are worth the price within themselves, include the living with another fun-loving, hardy, courageous race of people in a different land; of hearing their legends; seeing their colorful dress; watching them carve ivory with hand drills held by their teeth and bow driven; worshipping with them in their tiny churches; and marveling at brave men who pursue 60-ton whales in 28-foot skin boats. All this is an experience which no man can forget, or wants to.

I think of all the aspects of this colorful form of bear hunting, the element of sheer danger is at once the most thrilling and the most awesome. There the Great White Danger is with the hunter every second of every hunting day. This Big Danger is most intense in that tenuous region where solid ice meets moving ice and water. There is the hunting country. There is the region where life and death is separated by but a single mis-step, the wrong guessing of a wind or ocean current, or the mis-judging of an acre of young ice.

The Eskimo hunter is prepared for, and accepts this. Two
hunters work together whenever possible. A lone hunter
always takes his skin boat along. The six-foot *oonok* is as
much a part of an Eskimo on ice as his pants, and with
it he prods ahead of him for the treacherous thin spots—
snow-covered and unfrozen beneath—or of thin ice. His
snow shovel and saw go on the sled, too, as do emergency
rations. If, as inevitably must happen within his hunting life
span, he gets caught on floating ice, then with the saw
and shovel he makes an ice-block hut and weathers the
temperatures until the offending lead again freezes solidly
enough to cross. Or help comes.

There are exceptions. Ookeelah told me a re-told tale
his people have handed down for 90 years, since it occurred
in his own hunting country. A hunting party was caught
adrift for days on an ice floe without fresh water. Death
from thirst and exposure was imminent. One hunter wore
a big handle-bar mustache, and drank the melted frost
which accumulated on that. Another of the party offered
this more fortunate hunter two wolverine skins for the
"water" off half his heavy mustache. The second hunter
refused—and it is significant that only the man with the
mustache survived that ordeal.

In my own brief stay there, I had the commonplace, but
heart-stopping experience of having our dog sled break
through thin slushy ice, with me on it, a-top a load of six
seals. Only Ookeelah's quick thinking, plus the fact that
those wonderful dogs won't back up, but stood straining
at the lead rope as the sled went down, saved me from a
sudden death in the Arctic Ocean.

Three weeks before this, a neighbor Eskimo, Ahknacheok,
lost his entire team of eleven dogs and his sled, in a similar
breakthrough.

A significant fact is that all these hardy hunters spend
much of their hunting time listening. Ooyahahlook explained
this to me. Three quick shots fired out on the ice do not
mean "hunter lost," as in most hunting areas. Rather, this

means, "A lead has opened up between us (you) and shore. Race for your lives!"

If anything were needed to pinpoint the real and constant danger of hunting bears via dog sled, it was what happened upon two different occasions to Ookeelah. Twice, while of necessity hunting alone on moving ice, this man has had sizable leads open up between him and shore. In both instances, having his seal-retrieving line with him saved his life.

Each time, as he came to these open leads separating him from shore ice, Ookeelah did the same thing. Tying one end of the line to old Avik's collar, he then would paddle the puny skin boat across the lead, using the stool mentioned earlier as an emergency paddle, and un-coiling the line behind him.

Safely on the opposite ice, he'd jerk Avik into the frigid water, pulling him and the other unwilling dogs along behind. In each instance, the sled was loaded with seals, which at that season were fat enough to float, thereby helping the sled to stay sufficiently near the water's surface so the dogs didn't drown. One lead was 100 yards across!

Ookeelah mentioned these incidents, not because they were unusual for him, but rather to indicate the value of having a seal line and skin boat along. "Without them I not be here."

Awed at the daily hazards he faced, not without fear but with great courage and caution, I asked him, "Ookeelah, how do you *always* overcome these real day-to-day dangers?"

He answered simply. "I 32 years old."

CHAPTER 15

Hunting Polar Bear via Airplane

There are two ways for the hunter visiting the Arctic to get his polar bear. One is to hunt via dog team and Eskimo guide, as detailed before; the other is to hunt the quarry by the aid of an airplane.

Of the two, hunting with an airplane is approximate as to cost, is less sporting, and is far more certain of result.

At this writing, the most popular jumping-off place to hunt via airplane is Kotzebue, Alaska—at least for the states-side hunter. There are several reasons why this is true. First, it is the closest good polar bear area to the United States. Next, it is serviced by the major air lines, the only winter transportation from the outside to this outpost. And again, Kotzebue is within striking distance of the bears, within a single day's flight.

Other reasons why this little settlement is a popular jumping-off place are that it boasts a fair hotel, where hunters may lay over during the terrific Arctic storms. Many good outfitters use the hotel and cafe as the actual base-of-operations, and many of the needed items of supplies necessary to such a hunt may be obtained right in the town itself. These include such articles as *mukluks*, parkas, and similar Arctic gear.

Kotzebue itself sets just inside the Arctic Circle, and is along the coast. The urban sportsman doesn't know what desolation is until he flies for hours and hours, and miles and miles, over nothing but Arctic white—and then spots the small, snowed-in buildings of Kotzebue beneath the plane. It is an Eskimo town of 900 people, of which approximately 40, currently, are whites. The others are all Eskimos, and there is an effort there to keep the town "Eskimo," and not allow it to be exploited by the white man. Besides the main hotel, there are a couple of stores, a small hospital— which is soon to be enlarged because of forth-coming military necessity in the region—and, of course, the school.

Within the village, there are a few cars, one of which is used in decent weather as a taxi from the landing strip to the village. In winter, most transportation is via Shank's Pony and dog teams. The hotel has its own well, of course, but many of the natives haul a dog sled load of ice, sawed into blocks from an inland lake, for their fresh-water supply. "Selling ice to an Eskimo" there is no joke, but an actual fact, and there are several ice vendors.

Within the village, there is still much of the authentic Eskimo color (in their dress, living quarters, off-shore ice fishing, and racial characteristics); but the "outside" influence is rapidly being felt because of the Eskimos' daily connections with it, due to the incidence of the air lines.

Arranging a polar bear hunt is simple. The best outfitters for bear regularly advertise in the big outdoor journals, and may be contacted by correspondence. As with reputable men in other lines of business, they will furnish the prospective hunter with names of satisfied clientele with whom the novice may also correspond. Such customers include many well-known American sports figures, and the hunter-success ratio is very high. In fact, it is the one form of hunting wherein the outfitter will actually guarantee the hunter a bear. At this writing, there are several outfitters headquartering in Kotzebue (during the bear season at least) who will give the hunter a guarantee of no charge unless a bear is taken.

The best period for this form of hunting is from late February on through March and even later. Until late February, the offshore ice is not stabilized sufficiently to be set down upon safely with aircraft. Also, after late February, the winds are not quite so perverse. More, the bears are then moving down from the north.

At present, the standard polar bear hunt is 10 days, and the best outfitters charge an even $2,000 for the trip.

Two factors make airplane hunting inherently dangerous. First, and perhaps the more dangerous of the two is the incidence of Arctic "white-outs" all during the winter months. A white-out consists of some fog, some snow, and a major part of frozen ice crystals—all mixed together. This dense, white, fog-like phenomenon either lies like a shroud of white death over the ocean and inland, or it drifts with the prevailing winds over the ocean ice. Visibility, once into a white-out, is often but a matter of yards; and white-outs are the bane of a flyer's existence.

To the average pilot, these fog-like banks of invisibility are difficult to detect at distances. When flying, one often comes into a white-out without warning. And once into the mass of frozen, white crystals, it is almost impossible to differentiate just where one stops, vertically, and where the ice and snow of the terrain begin. In that area, only one pilot recently has been able to fly white-outs, when actually caught in one, without cracking up. This fellow happened to be color-blind, and to him, the coast line appeared another shade of dark-and-light, allowing him to differentiate between them.

Couple this factor to such natural elements as blizzard, storms, and fish-tailing winds, and they make flying extremely hazardous. It is said that the fliers in the Kotzebue-Point Hope-Barrow section are the world's best pilots. After having flown considerably with them, I agree.

Several run-of-the-day incidents occurring on our own hunt are indicative of the flying hazards due to weather.

When coming into Kotzebue on the small airliner, we were caught by fog and white-out, incidentally, with not enough gas supply to take us back to any other distant landing field. We circled the village just one hour and ten minutes, waiting for a possible break in the dense white bank, through which we might descend. The only time we ever got a glimpse of the village was once when the landing-gear skimmed only a matter of feet over the hut tops, and then only for a second. Everything was white, eerie, ghostly.

Only sheer guts on the pilot's part, and a last desperate dropping through the fog bank (which covered 200 miles of area) over the place he hoped the town to be, saved our necks. The hotel manager told us that night that most of the village, hearing the circling plane but a few rods above them, but invisible, were in the street praying for the plane to make it.

Or again, with the mail plane scheduled to take us on the next morning, we sat in the hotel at Kotzebue exactly nine days before the white-out lifted enough, or the blizzards subsided sufficiently for us to leave. Once, during this enforced stay, a local pilot took off in a two-place plane to see just how far the invisibility reached. Ten minutes later the fog closed in again to where visibility was limited to a few feet. This pilot got back to the ice landing strip, out on the sound before the hotel, only because his fellow flyers poured a hundred yards or so of yellow "sea dye" in a line mid-way of the strip, so he could see where the fog ended and ice began.

That evening, during supper, this pilot said to me, "I circled one helluva while without seein' nothing. Till I spotted that dye, I just flew by the seat of my britches."

The eighth day, we tried to reach Point Hope. After making 70 of the 140 miles, we came without warning into a vast white-out again. As if we'd run into a white wall, visibility was cut to the width between the two motors on the small plane.

"We'll drop down and see if we can follow the coast line," the pilot said.

Dropping to 200 feet, we continued on up the coast. But

even that low, none of us could tell where coast line began and white-out ended; and we had to return.

Finally, on a clear day when it looked like no fog was in the area, we flew for 100 miles towards the Siberian coast line, trying to spot a polar bear. But almost at the same time we reached the good bear country, another white-out, coming up out of nowhere, blotted out all definition, and again we had to return to Kotzebue.

Such a hazard, in bear hunting, is very real to both pilot and hunter. The good bear country from Kotzebue is approximately 100 miles north and west towards Siberia and Point Hope, and the area separating them. Not only must the small plane get that far before being able to spot a bruin, it must also have to fly sufficiently far to track down the bear from the first spotted spoor, and have enough time, gasoline, and flying weather to return.

The probability of an intervening white-out, after the plane is 100 or so miles out, is eternal and very real. In this, the hazard approximates that of a lead opening up between a dog team hunter, and the shore ice.

The second big hazard is the ice itself. Once a bear is spotted from the air, or fresh spoor is followed until the traveling bruin is seen, then the plane must set down in order for the hunter to make his final stalk. This in itself is a tricky order. The craft must land closely enough so the hunter can approach, or overtake, the bear before he moves away. Yet such bears hunt the edges and brinks of the open leads and moving ice, and the half-mile or so of ice upon which the craft lands must not only be smooth, but must be sufficiently strong to support its weight. Smooth ice often means young ice, and from the air, the pilot has no *oonok* to prod its thickness. He has to estimate, and one guess is all he has.

Because of these dangers, an occasional plane and hunter are lost. A single misjudgment on the part of the pilot is all that it takes. Death is usually quick, but always certain in such a case.

Other hazards are common, but incidental to these two basic dangers. Extra gasoline must be carried in the light plane in five-gallon cans. Due to the uncertain nature of the flying, there's always danger of running out. There's danger that the unmarked international boundary line may be crossed, due to hunting enthusiasm or getting off course; and that one may become a permanent, shot-down resident of Russia. Once safely down and a bear taken, there's a possibility that the plane will freeze up during the skinning (in 30-below-zero temperatures) and won't start again. There's a possibility that ice upon which the plane has set down isn't right for it to take off again. Or that a lead will open up mid-way of it. Or that unobserved leaks in the surplus gasoline may cause a plane fire.

As if all this wasn't enough, there is the constant, overall possibility, too, that the pilot may simply become lost. Landmarks at this season in the Arctic, simply aren't.

Because of the real dangers, the best outfitters now make a practice of hunting with two planes. These are usually light two-place aircraft, equipped with either ski landing-gear or wheels, Each pilot of the pair takes a hunting passenger, together with the gear necessary for one day's hunt.

Long before daylight, the plane motors are warmed with an oil burner and air compressor—the heat being driven through a canvas tube into a closed motor-covering.

Warmed up, the planes are loaded with the hunters, and fly in two-altitude pattern. One plane flies low (upon reaching the good bear country) its occupants scouting for spoor and game. The upper plane watches the actions of the lower ship, and further watches the conditions of weather, ice, and direction. Neither loses sight of the other, *ever*.

If spoor or game is spotted, then, by signals between pilots, a campaign of getting the hunter down upon the ice and into stalking position, is determined. The second plane, of course, doesn't land until the first is safely down—one lost plane still being better than two gone through the ice.

It is at this point in the hunt that ethics take over, and

hunting sportsmanship becomes either real or just a word.

Reputable outfitters will endeavor to have their hunters finish the hunt with a thrilling stalking of the bear through the pressure ice, and giving the game an equal chance in the game of hunting wits.

Others are less conscientious. They set the hunter down in the general proximity of the bear, then, with some low flying, actually herd or drive the beast up to within rifle range of the waiting and concealed hunter. Often this is accomplished after a long chase, in which the bear, having no place to go, has been run to near-exhaustion.

The outfitter's excuse, of course, is that he has guaranteed his hunter a bear, or it will cost him $2,000; and that the average desk-bound hunter who can afford such a hunt, is usually a pot-bellied, lard-hindered hunter who couldn't walk, or stalk, for 100 yards in pressure ice if his life depended upon it. And that even if he did, at any range of over 50 yards, couldn't hit the broad side of a barn.

From the "dude" hunter's standpoint, he's a long ways from home. He wants a polar bear or else, and he's way out on the ice where no one can tattle. Whether he walks up to a traveling bear, or has a winded, plane-run bear herded into short rifle range, is often something he can lie and ease his conscience about, after he gets the beast mounted.

I had one outfitter tell me frankly, "I don't advertise it, but that's one reason we use two planes. Between us, we can usually *manage* to get the bear and hunter close enough together."

Hunting polar bears via airplanes is at its heyday right now. "Dude" hunters have found that, except for the severe cold, hunting from a heated plane is not much tougher than hunting out of a camp for deer; and overnight at the hotel is just as comfortable. More, the chances of success are very high, during a 10-day hunt.

Because of this, polar bear hunting will mushroom. Just how much airplane pressure these bruins can take and their numbers survive, is becoming open to question. Alaska's recent admission as a state has caused added interest in such resources, with an eye towards the future.

After observing the entire situation as objectively as possible, I am convinced that restrictions on taking polar bear with airplanes, and indeed the overall "take," are both going to be tightened.

The necessary hunter's equipment for airplane hunting of bear is quite like that necessary for dog-team hunting. There is always the possibility that emergency may overtake the hunter and/or plane; and that if one survives, he must stay out upon the ice pack a day or more until help comes. His clothing, therefore, should be as adequate as for dog-team hunting, and of the same type. Some form of emergency rations should *always* be carried in the hunting planes. Such planes are, of course, radio-equipped and carry survival kits.

One item has been purposely left till last. That's the care of the bear hunter's shooting and camera equipment.

Special care for both categories is necessary in these extreme temperatures. My partner, John Phillips, discovered this the hard way, as regards cameras. He took a two-thousand-dollar movie camera, and several thousand feet of color film, expecting to make a documentary film of hunting bears in Eskimo-land. John's first shot was to be of the igloo-type hut entrance, where we'd stay for a month. He broke out the camera, got all ready, and turned it on. The shutter started, but gradually purred more slowly and finally stopped. The Arctic cold had frozen it solidly, and on that entire jaunt, John didn't get a single yard of footage.

I discovered the relationship between cold and rifles in a similar, though less wasteful manner. As I lay down to shoot the head off my first hair seal, Ookeelah said, "You shoot low."

"Why?"

"It 26 below zero."

Knowing the rifle to be sighted dead-on, I cut loose anyway. All I got was a water spout approximately three

inches below that seal's head. This went on for three shots
—until I admitted he was right. Briefly, cold decreases the
intensity of powder, causing less velocity, and more conse-
quent bullet drop at a given range. For rifles of the 3,000
foot-second class, this amounts to about one minute-of-
angle drop for each 25 degrees of temperature. My rifle had
been sighted in at around 50 degrees, back home.

Both cameras and rifles should be de-greased before being
taken into the Arctic after polar bear and seals. Any good
camera-shop can de-grease both movie and still cameras, so
that their shutters will function in extreme cold.

Once into such low temperatures, the only hazard then is
moisture forming on the lenses. This can be avoided if in
some way the cameras are allowed to heat up, and again
become cold, *gradually*. I solved the problem by habitually
putting all cameras under the down parka, and actually
wrapping them inside it, immediately as I'd enter the heated
hut. This allowed the lenses to warm slowly, avoiding condensation. The down parka released the outside cold very
slowly.

Bolt-action rifles may be easily de-greased before leaving
for an Arctic trip. All heavy grease is removed from the
bore, receiver, and magazine by wiping these parts. The
bolt itself is cleansed of all grease by soaking and rinsing
in ordinary white lantern gas. Do not use regular gasoline
for this, as it contains harmful additives.

With all grease removed, a very light coating of thin oil
is applied to the metal parts outside, and a patch run
through the bore having only a drop of the same thin oil
on it. Make sure that no oil gets into, or on the bolt, however, as that will tend to make it "freeze" up later in the
severe cold.

The de-greased bolt is subject to rust, and will be in salt
air over the ocean, which will speed any rusting. This may
be prevented by again oiling the bolt, once the trip is over.

Some Eskimos use a drop of kerosene both at the striker
end of the bolt and upon the firing-pin bushing. This serves

to lubricate the firing-pin mechanism and make certain the rifle will fire. Kerosene won't freeze until approximately 50 below zero. However, this isn't necessary for the duration of one trip. A rifle will fire with certainty every time, with just the simple de-greasing described above.

A most valuable item of equipment is a full-length scabbard of heavy leather, big enough to completely enclose the whole rifle and scope—this for both plane use and for carrying the weapon on a dog sled. In the planes used for bear hunting, there is a minimum of space, a lot of gear, and considerable squeezing together of equipment. A heavy scabbard protects the rifle during all this.

With a dog sled, the rifle is slung alongside the sled, usually in two loops. Into tumbled pressure ice, where the rifle would be subject to breakage between the ice blocks and the sled itself, the entire scabbard and loops are simply swung over and into the sled, riding for a time either upon the passenger's lap, or on the inside if he walks. When riding in normal outside position, the rifle is instantly available.

Once into the extreme cold, it's a good thing to let the rifle *remain* cold, rather than bring it inside at night, causing it to be alternately warm and cold. We did this by leaving all rifles in a shed outside the hut.

Where this isn't feasible, then it's always wise ·to allow a rifle to warm up, and cool off, slowly. Ookeelah showed me how he did this—he wrapped the rifle in a blanket each time he brought it inside. The insulation of the blanket not only kept it from heating up too fast and causing heavy condensation on the metal, it also soaked up what moisture there was on the rifle's outside as fast as it formed.

There's one other constant danger in such extreme temperatures. That's the danger of ice forming inside the bore, due to any warming-then-freezing. Ice in the bore can easily blow up either the rifle or the shooter the first time it's fired. A periodic check, by looking through the barrel, is advisable.

During the excitement of actual shooting, most hunters

not used to bitter cold weather make the same mistake. With the face on the stock, they breathe so as to let the warm mouth-spray contact the ocular scope lens. This does not fog the scope—it simply freezes it over with solid ice. Many a seal, *oogruk*, and occasional bear has lived to a riper age because of this one fact. The trick is to breathe downward, away from the scope, or actually hold the breath while shooting.

With most game, the greatest hunting thrill comes when the excitement of the stalk is at its climax, the trigger is squeezed, and a prized trophy falls to a clean kill.

This is true with polar bears. However, exceptions make a rule, and occasionally the biggest excitement comes later. Consider the story they told me in Kotzebue of a recent state-side hunter, used to a warm climate, *after* he'd bagged the great white prize.

Sensibly, this fellow paid his fee, then put the problem of getting a bear entirely in the hands of his capable outfitter. Wanting his "dude" to get as fine a specimen as possible, the outfitter turned down several "medium" bears—actually grown cubs and sows. The suspense grew as they hunted for most of the trip's duration without finding anything reasonably large.

By then the hunter was panicky. He began to complain continuously, and was ready to bust anything wearing white fur and padded feet. But as luck would have it, the final day they flew, the outfitter spotted a nice boar, set the plane down, and the lucky hunter killed it the last minute. He had no idea of the actual size, only that it was a "dandy one," to which the outfitter fully agreed.

Back at Kotzebue, they put a tape on the green skull and practically fainted! The bear would rank well up in the records!

Realizing this, and with pardonable pride, the suddenly-excited hunter immediately reversed himself. By leaps and bounds, he began "enlarging" all that happened. Those days when they actually couldn't find hide nor hair of a bruin abruptly became days in which "—the outfitter here showed me dozens of medium and big bears. But not big enough for *me*. I wanted a record or nothing." The boar they'd come luckily upon and bagged was, of a sudden, one which the proud hunter "*knew* was a record, a *real* record, or I'd have turned him down, too!"

Such enthusiasm is understandable. However, from this point the fortunate hunter really turned loose his imagination. To each listener he detailed all the dangers, the misery, the excessive cold, the breath-taking suspense caused by landing upon thin, treacherous ice, the failing gasoline supply, the long distances they'd had to track down that great bear, and the moral certainty that the beast was just crossing into Siberia—where they'd surely have been detained forever as salt-mine workers—and allied discomforts and hazards. With each re-telling of the yarn, bravery and courage grew.

In short, he was the hero of the age; and no lesser man would have possessed the stamina, intestinal fortitude, and moral courage to have braved and endured what he braved and endured.

For all this, he could reasonably have been forgiven—even by the outfitter and folks around Kotzebue who knew the score. But at this time, just a day or so prior to his departure back to a more temperate clime, the poor fellow fell sick. His skin turned pimply and green. He bloated.

At once the unhappy fellow was certain he'd been poisoned. He blamed the food at the hotel. He blamed the extreme cold. He blamed the desolation and the country. Within a matter of hours, all his previous courage and bravery in bagging the bear dissipated. In actual tears, he begged, "Get me to a doctor, quick! I'm dying!"

Quickly, they took him to the small hospital. But with their limited facilities, they could not diagnose his disease.

At this, the poor man went entirely to pieces. Not waiting for his own flight to take him home, he had the air lines radio to "outside" for a special plane complete with pilot.

His last request was that his bones be gotten out of this horrible, desolate land, which even God had forgotten, before they turned to ice.

The chartered ship arrived from "outside," loaded him in without pause, and flew him again to the "outside," virtually non-stop. It was, without doubt, the village's most expensive mercy flight to date.

Rushing the frightened, babbling patient to a hospital before death closed its icy fingers, the specialists quickly diagnosed his malady. He'd had a recent change in diet. He had a simple case of hives.

Part Five

1

RIFLES, TROPHIES, CONCLUSION

CHAPTER 16

Rifles and Ammunition For Bear

The question of a suitable rifle and ammunition for bear hunting is an interesting one, and is made more so because, with any species from black to brownie, a wounded or aggravated bear is apt to fight back. In many instances, such an animal is certain to fight or even to attack.

Because of this, the proper choice of ordnance becomes a two-way proposition—the bear rifle is both an aggressive weapon and a defensive one.

Before getting into the matter of what constitutes a good outfit for bear, let's see what has happened, under hunting conditions, with various rifle-cartridge combinations. Here are some actual field examples which I have either experienced, witnessed, or had recounted to me by members of our own hunting parties.

Bear number one was an average-size black bear, caught in the act of carrying twigs for a hibernation nest in a hollow log. A 139-grain expanding bullet in a 7X57 Mauser caught it through the chest, broadside, at around 100 yards. This animal bounded two rods out of sight behind some fallen logs, and was dead when approached ten cautious minutes later.

The second bear was a huge old blackie, shot through the heart as it stood upright at 30 feet facing the hunter, with the same 7 mm., but with a 175-grain soft-nose bullet. This bear snarled, balled up like a cat, rolled three rods downhill, and was similarly dead when approached.

Another large black bear was shot directly through the back, at 175 yards, with the same outfit as the one above, as the beast climbed straight up out of a canyon. The bruin rolled over, wiggled the chaparral, and was thought to be dead. As the hunter crossed the brushy, intervening canyon, the animal regained its feet (indicating that the spine itself had been missed), climbed to the top of the ridge, tumbled and plunged down into the opposite basin, was tracked a full mile, and was lost.

A fourth black bear was shot at, with this same 7 mm. and 175-grain bullets, at 300 yards, and completely missed because the hunter couldn't estimate the bullet fall at that range.

A fifth black bear was similarly over-shot, at 200 yards, with the same rifle and load, by a hunter who held over, not believing so mild a rifle would "carry up."

The next black was shot as it ran broadside with a 150-grain bullet from a .270, through the lungs. This bullet was obviously defective, didn't open up and sailed on through taking bits of lungs with it. The wounded beast ran, characteristically, into the thickest canyon downfall, and was lost mainly because the two husky men in the party did not dare to help the youngster who'd shot it, by following the bear into such a maze. They insisted he give up "such a fool notion."

Another medium blackie was missed once with a .257 Roberts, at easy range, then dropped dead in its tracks by a neck shot with a 117-grain soft-nose bullet.

The final black bear was seriously wounded by a 150-grain bullet at 300 yards from a .30-06. It was tracked down by the guide to 30 feet, but rose on its haunches, facing him. At this range, the cool sportsman tried to knock its eye out with a .30-30, with which he'd killed every species of big game including grizzlies. The bullet here, too, must have been defective. It hit just inside the bony eye-orbit, spattered completely, doing little more damage than to pepper the hide with bits of lead. The bear still stood upright, and the guide killed it with a shot through the throat. I later photographed this skull.

The first grizzly was shot *at* 14 times by a sheep herder, at close range, in the full moonlight, as it bothered the sheep. The man used a .30-30 Winchester. At the first shot, which was a hit, the beast discarded its interest in the mutton for an intensive interest in the human. As it bore down on the herder, he emptied the rifle, loaded it again, and shot it dry. This bear dropped at his feet. In the morning, he found nine different holes where he'd hit the animal.

A British Columbia grizzly was hit broadside through the lungs with a 180-grain Silvertip, from a .300 H&H Magnum, by a hunter in prone position at 200 estimated yards. The bear went down, rose, and headed in the other direction. Another shot hit the same area from the opposite side, completely pulverizing the lungs like hamburger (as they found later). This bear lived 20 minutes while the smart hunter and guide waited, and was still up on its hind feet, but not the front feet, as the shoulders were broken, when the hunter finished it with a neck shot at 30 feet.

A small Wyoming grizzly was shot broadside through the heart at 92 steps with the same outfit as above. It keeled over, kicked all four feet in the air for several seconds, then tipped over onto its side. As the happy hunter approached, this animal regained its feet, raced fast as a horse into the timber for 125 yards, died mid-stride, and lay on its belly with all four feet stretched out fore and aft.

A Canadian grizzly just above Rainbow Lake was fired upon by two hunters, one using a .270 with 130-grain loads, the other using a .300 H&H Magnum with 180-grain loads. At each shot, at 125 yards, the animal went down. Oddly enough, it always got back to its feet, but somewhat at a distance in the heavy bush. When down, this bear couldn't be seen. Each time it arose, both hunters fired, trying to finish it off. They shot over 20 times. When the beast was finally killed, they approached, to find *two* dead grizzlies. At each shot, almost, the other grizzly would leap up to find the source of the pain. Both hunters were still scared stiff upon reaching camp.

Another British Columbia grizzly was hit three times completely through the lungs with a .300 Weatherby Magnum using 180-grain bullets, at 110 yards. Each time the beast would drop, but quickly regain its feet, and sway its broad head, trying to find the hunter who was shooting from behind, and over, a large glacial boulder. At the third shot, the animal stayed down. All shots had made a hand-sized group over the lungs. All bullets, having exceptionally heavy jackets, had sailed on through without too much expansion.

One polar bear killed in 1958 and which is currently entered in the record books, was killed with one shot broadside from a .300 H&H Magnum, using a 180-grain bullet. This bear simply slumped on the pressure ice, completely dead.

The same year, a hunting partner using the powerful .378 Weatherby Magnum wounded another polar bear with a shot in the leg, then finished it off with a second in the bear's geometric middle.

A third man of this same party killed his small polar bear with a .270 Winchester, using a 110-grain load he'd hand-loaded for use on seals. This animal, shot at reasonable range, came bounding towards the hunter at the shot, but died mid-stride a few rods later.

These are actual instances, recorded without embellishment. Unlike those extreme cases of killing large bears with puny cartridges, or of losing bears because of over gunning mentioned elsewhere in this book, the above instances may be considered average. By and large, they are comparable to the field hunting conditions which the average novice hunter may find himself in. The cartridges listed in these incidents are those commonly used, over a wide range of country, individual hunters, and time span.

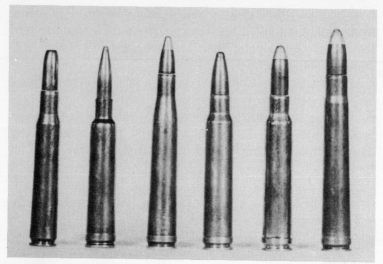

Popular cartridges for the bigger species of bear. Left to right, .30-06 with 220-grain bullet; 7X61 Sharpe & Hart, 160-grain bullet; .300 H&H Magnum, 180-grain bullet; .338 Winchester Magnum, 200-grain bullet; and .375 H&H Magnum, 300-grain bullet.

A close scrutiny of these field examples will indicate some apparent contradictions, as regards a suitable cartridge and rifle for a given bear species. Before making any conclusions, let's dig a bit deeper.

There are today two basic schools of thought on the matter of a suitable cartridge for bear. One group approaches the matter from a standpoint of theory, fact, and science. On the broader basis of what all cartridges have been able to do with deer, say, over all the decades of shooting, with all sizes of deer, and in the hands of innumerable hunters, these fellows make a blanket conclusion for the species of black bear.

"A black bear," they conclude, "is similar in size to deer. It is shot at comparable ranges. It is thin skinned, and at least partially susceptible to shock and the hydraulic action of bullets at high velocities, when entering semi-fluid tissue. Therefore, the cartridges suitable for deer, will be suitable for black bear."

The minimum for deer has long been considered nothing

smaller than .25 caliber (which assumption is giving way today in favor of the new, hot 6 mm. cartridges); nothing less than 100 grains of bullet weight; and nothing slower than 2300 foot-seconds velocity and/or 1300 foot-pounds energy. In short, the old Winchester .25-35 has long been considered the minimum for deer, the country over.

Similarly, these advocates line up suitable cartridges for grizzly, brown bear, and polar bear. The criterion has habitually been a similarity in animal size, when compared to another species. In other words, if a .30-06 is suitable for a 900-pound bull elk, these men say, then it should be equally fine for a 900-pound grizzly.

The opposing faction base their conclusions on the more abstract factors of individual hunter capacity. In a broad way, their conclusion is simple: "The best rifle and cartridge for the bear hunter is that outfit with which he does his best shooting, which he can handle without fear of recoil, and which he likes to shoot. It's the man behind the gun that counts. And *any* bullet that hits the vital spot is adequate for the job."

Like the blind men who touched various parts of an elephant, and assumed he was like a spear, fan, or rope, both groups are partly right and partly wrong. In each case they have omitted vital matters which are pertinent to the *hunting condition;* and which have long been totally neglected in favor of the more tangible aspects which could be set down with greater definition on paper.

To begin, a bear, any species, cannot be patently compared to any other species, as to what is necessary to kill him. First, in many an encounter, it is not only necessary to kill a bear, it is also necessary to stop him, virtually in his tracks. Wounded bears are apt to maul the hunter. They are as likely to maul the luckless guide whose job it is to follow up and finish what his greenhorn has begun.

Again, a wounded bear immediately makes for the most inaccessible terrain, if only wounded, to avoid pursuit. With blacks and grizzlies, such animals are often lost in heavy foliage. This is due not alone to the fact that such terrain is most difficult to negotiate; but also to the fact that a bear's fat, and the small entrance holes which bullets always make in a bear's hide, both tend to seal over a wound within but a few short bounds. Blood spoor becomes extremely sparse. And this fact, plus difficulty in tracking in the heavy maze into which bruin goes, combine to make finding him next to impossible.

With polar bears, the difference between bagging an expensive, life-time trophy and having one make open water and disappear, often lies in only a small difference in the cartridge's horsepower.

Too, the sight picture presented by a bear does not make for the ease of sighting and accuracy of shooting offered by many another species. Bears shot for trophies are in their prime. Prime bears have long hair, which tends to drop with gravity, and roll as they move. Peel down such a beast, and there's far less, vertically, at which to shoot, than the average hunter believes. While walking, or standing, the vital area of a bear, under a prime coat, is not at all where it seems to be. Further, when a bear stands, he's usually sniffing or rooting, and his body length is, more often than not, all bunched together, with the vital area either covered by that deceptive front leg, or difficult to place with certainty.

At a quartering angle, such a vital spot is usually covered by a heavy hind quarter, or a thinner front quarter, deceptive as to contour.

On a run, with front paws far out behind his hind end, and rear feet way up under his chin, a bear represents a scissoring, stretched-out, lanky length of horizontal target one instant; and by the time the rifle's sight picture is established on that, he's but a round ball of bunched-up fur, flying through the brush. More, when so spooked, the hunter's only target is often the bear's backside.

In looking back at the black bear I have shot (and shot at), I don't recall a single animal which presented the clean-cut contours, and vital-area definition which a deer gives. Similarly, I've yet to see a grizzly, under hunting conditions, which presented me with as "clean" a picture for the scope, as the thirty-inch body of a bull elk. This has a definite bearing, when making a comparison in actual shooting of a bear, with a similar-sized animal of another species.

Relative toughness, and tenacity of life, as compared with other species, is another often-neglected factor to be considered. Many a time I've heard a novice say, "Any rifle that can bust as big an animal as a moose, would surely kill any grizzly bear dead as a mackerel."

Actually, a moose gives up the ghost easily. In proportion to his immense size, a moose is not harder to kill than a deer—which he is. A grizzly, however, is just as apt to rise, once he's down from a heart shot, and either run a hundred yards, or kill his tormenter before his unbelievable will to live runs out.

These are some of the reasons why one can't say simply that a certain size of bullet, from a certain cartridge, is adequate for a species of bear.

Similarly, those who state flatly that any cartridge is enough, if the man behind it can place it with certainty, are only partly correct. The blunt fact is, ninety-nine per cent of all shooters can do their *very best* shooting with the lowly .22 rimfire cartridge, with other considerations such as rifle fit, weight, accuracy, trigger pull, and sights being equal. A shooter always does his best shooting with cartridges of the least recoil and bang. And certainly the .22 rimfire is no bear cartridge, despite the fact that bears have been killed with it.

What are some of the other vital but neglected factors which should influence the proper choice of a bear rifle and cartridge?

One is the hunter's age. Bear hunting is tough, rugged work. When the opportunity does finally come for a shot, the younger hunter, or the one with the good sense to condition himself beforehand, can shoot better—with far more accuracy and confidence—than the lard-hindered hunter who's panting for lack of oxygen, and is literally pooped. Accuracy in the placement of the shot—and especially that critical first shot—has a direct bearing on the needed horse-power behind a bullet.

Again, hunter temperament has a relationship between what will do the job and what won't when the chips are down. Some husky men who wrestle trucks, spud-sacks, and livestock all season and think nothing of physical rough housing, simply quake at the mere thought of twenty pounds of recoil against their shoulders, and a smoke-pole which is surely going to go *bang*! Other puny little gents, looking as though a hearty belch would knock them off their feet, simply soak up recoil and love to lay 'em in there with a magnum rifle.

Likewise when actually confronted with dangerous game, some men remain cool and shoot with precision. Others go all to pieces. Often the matter of just what a man will do is hard to estimate.

In British Columbia once, we'd stalked a grizzly for a half-mile or more. Tension was high, and both my blood and the guide's pounded with excitement. As I lay down to let bruin have it, I passed the guide a handful of magnum cartridges (my levi breeches have tight pockets). I'd been tangled up before with a grizzly in the bush, and wanted those extra shells right handy. If I needed them.

"I don't know what'll happen," I whispered. "But if I need 'em, you hand me them shells mighty fast."

"Sure, sure."

When the shooting was over and the grizzly down, the guide was a full seventy yards up the hill behind me. His fist was clutched over those cartridges, his face white, and he shook till the shells sounded like castanets. Had I missed, he'd be going yet.

The type of terrain, too, has a bearing on what kind of cartridge is necessary for bear. Often the species determines this. For black bear in wooded country, a big-caliber, heavy-slug, slow-velocity outfit would cut through brush and do the job best. That same black bear, climbing out of a high bare canyon in Idaho's primitive area, would require a far different kind of ordnance. He'd need at 300 yards what the first rifle had at the muzzle.

Similarly, that unmolested, slow-moving grizzly digging marmots far up under the melting glacier may handily be taken by the hunter after sheep, with a .270. There's time to get his breath. To assume a solid prone position. To wait for the bear's stance to change to broadside. And more, there's ample intervening distance for more shots and time for the animal to die before it can reach the hunter.

It's a far different condition later to meet that same bear, at mere yards, around the bend of the brushy muskeg trail and with mutual surprise, as the same hunter lugs the ram trophy down on a pack board. In the one instance, leisure aids a certain kill. In the other, fast action (of one kind or another) is all there is going to be. And one of them—we'd rather it would be the bear—must be *stopped*.

This brings up the matter of distances. It is impossible with any species to tell in advance how far the animal will be away when the opportunity for a shot comes. However, most hunters choose their bear rifle on the basis of muzzle energy and velocity. If one cartridge has a muzzle energy comparable to that of another, the uninformed person considers them equal. They may be *if* their bullets have similar weight, sectional density, shape, and initial velocity.

However this is ordinarily not the case. One bullet may be long, spitzer-pointed, and relatively small of diameter. The other may be blunt, large of caliber, and with a poorly-shaped ogive and low sectional density.

At the muzzle, they may be equally good on bear. At 200 or 300 yards, one may still have ample power left, and the other be almost "pooped." And with bear, as with any other species, the determining factor should always be: What efficiency has this cartridge and bullet got, out where the game is?

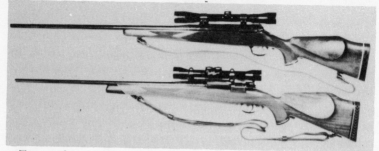

Two modern high-intensity rifles and calibers suited to most forms of bear hunting. Top, Schultz & Larsen rifle with 7X61 Sharpe & Hart cartridge and Leupold scope; bottom, Weatherby .300 Magnum and Weatherby Imperial scope.

Another allied factor is the accuracy potential of the hunter when balanced against the probable outside range at which a certain cartridge-rifle combination is still efficient. I have constantly maintained that, with bear, the hunter should *never* shoot unless he is reasonably certain that any or all bullets will "group" within a 12-inch circle. That is, he should not fire at a range, or while in a position, or under the stress of excitement, wherein he cannot surely place his shots within a foot circle.

Some men can do this while prone at 300 yards, when sitting and calm at 200 yards, and off-hand at 100 to 150 yards. Others, lacking the experience, co-ordination, and shooting skill, cannot do as well at half the distances.

The sure killing area of a bear's vital "boiler-room," under average hunting conditions, does not much exceed this 12-inch circle. To shoot with a potentially wider "grouping" of any possible shots, would usually mean only to wound the beast. Therefore, if one man can't keep his shots within twelve inches at over 100 yards, then why does he need, or why should he ever use on game, a cartridge with sufficient power for bears at 300 yards? He doesn't. Neither should he *ever* fire at a bear (lacking the added power and skill) at over this limit of 100 yards.

Another factor affecting the decision as to the right cartridge for bear is the hunter's weight, in connection with the rifle's weight, and the transportation means he'll use while hunting.

Briefly, lighter, older hunters should not lug around the same weight of rifle that younger, huskier men do. The old rule-of-thumb is: The rifle's weight should equal one-twentieth the hunter's weight. That is, a 160-pound man should use a rifle of around 8 pounds.

That's a good beginning, but, of course, the rule must be taken with a grain of salt at either end of the weight scale.

However, the matter of recoil enters the picture. Higher-powered rifles, especially the "magnums," have necessarily higher recoil because of the intensity of their cartridges. Light rifles accent the recoil effect; and often to stay within the recoil an unseasoned hunter can stand, he drops to an ineffective cartridge.

If, however, the hunter intends to do most of his hunting on horseback for blacks and grizzly, from a boat (except the final stalk) for brown bear, and from a dog sled for polars, then he can safely upgrade the rifle's weight. In short, then, for a light bear hunter, a heavy rifle is not the burdensome thing it is when foot hunting after other species of big game.

Another thing affecting the choice of rifle is the matter of hunter experience. Ordinarily, the man who has stopped ten grizzlies cold will tend to use a lighter rifle on the eleventh bear than on the first. Experience has given him confidence. It calms him in a crisis. His aim becomes better, and usually he won't fire until dead certain that the vital first bullet is going into the spot where it will do the most good.

Still another factor is whether the hunter will hand-load for the bear rifle. With modern rifles, in good condition, it is often possible to develop a huskier load for a given caliber than the standard factory ammunition. Factory ammunition must be loaded to reasonable pressures, to be used in rifles of a wide variety of condition and servitude. More, the hand-loader can often experiment with bullet types, until he finds one which suits his particular rifle and cartridge, and perform ideally on the game he expects to hunt. It often comes as a surprise to the novice to learn that no two rifles shoot the identical cartridges meant for them with the same accuracy, velocity, or energy. Indeed, no two factory rifles, of identical caliber, model, and barrel length will shoot the same ammunition with the same velocities. Often there will be several hundred foot-seconds difference.

The hand-loader, however, can always bring his own cartridges and rifle up to full potential by working up adequate loads a step at a time.

Up till now, we've talked of rifles and cartridges for bear. This is incorrect. Neither the rifle nor the cartridge kills a bear. All they do is to send a bullet on its way at a certain speed, rotational twist, and degree of accuracy. Once the bullet has left the muzzle it is on its very own; and it either does or does not do the job of killing.

In the matter of bullets, we've lagged far behind. By that I mean that in a broad way we do not have as fine a development in bullets as we have in instruments to fire them.

The problem involved in suitable game bullets is simple of objective, but difficult of execution. To perform ideally, a bullet must, upon impact with flesh, immediately expand to approximately twice its caliber; lose no weight; retain the rearward one-half (or thereabouts) of its length in solid form and without expansion, to penetrate deeply into an animal's vitals; and expend all its energy by the time it reaches the skin on the opposite side of the beast.

To manufacture bullets within the pocketbook of those who shoot considerably, the procedure has been fairly common. Brass or other kinds of metal tubing are drawn into tubes, filled with lead cores, and pointed at the forward ends. The amount of exposed lead, the jacket's thickness, the bullet's shape and weight have all been correlated, and calibrated to a certain probable velocity—all with the anticipation of a given amount of resistance, upon impact.

When all such ideal conditions jibe, the result is often about as intended. However, once the range, the velocity, or the amount of impact is altered—often by only a minor amount—the results are disappointing. Bullets drill completely through game without expanding, because the initial velocity was too low; because the range was too long and the speed fell off; because the animal wasn't hit in a highly-resistant spot; or because the bullet was used on a lighter species than intended.

Oppositely, bullets blow up and mangle outside tissue rather than expand and kill properly because the jackets were too thin for the species intended (game was shot with a varmint bullet); or a "standard-caliber" bullet was hopped up in a magnum cartridge, exceeding the velocity the manufacturer intended being used.

Perhaps the biggest obstacle is the fact that over the trajectory arc of any bullet's flight, its energy and velocity are never the same at any two given points. Every rod, a "new" bullet situation exists.

The problem has been how to make ideal bullets on a production basis and without the cost becoming prohibitive.

Currently, at least one custom bullet has approached the ideal. That's the Partitioned Nosler Bullet. This is an H-type bullet, similar to the German H-Mantle Bullet. The forward end is constructed to expand well, enlarge to a given diameter, and maintain this performance over a reasonable velocity variable. The solid middle, and semi-solid rear end similarly retain their shape, weight, and form so as to penetrate deeply, also within a broad range variable. These bullets cost about twice what other commercial bullets do, but their performance quotient make them worth while for any kind of bear hunting.

A second commercial bullet also comes close to the ideal. That's Winchester's newer 200-grain "Power Point" bullet for the .338 Magnum rifle. Its performance, over the critical ranges of 100 to 400 yards, is comparable.

In 1958, I had the pleasure of field-testing this wonderful bullet, along with a pilot model of the new Winchester .338 Magnum rifle, in Alaska. This was the first test on game of the cartridge in its final, commercial form. On seven different big-game animals, including bull caribou, moose, grizzly bear, and elk (later in Wyoming), that bullet performed ideally and consistently. The paced ranges varied from 100 yards to an outside of 328 yards. Each time the bullet penetrated the full width of the animal's shoulder, lost no weight, expanded on the nose to approximately .70 caliber, and lay just under the hide on the opposite side.

I predict that better bullets for game shooting are in the immediate future for hunters, and that these two examples are but indications of the trend. However, as explained above, production costs of an ideal game bullet are high, and the manufacturers will come forth with the goods, only as soon as the shooters give their assurance that the products will be bought.

Perhaps the most important factor in choosing a bear rifle has been left to the last, and is an apparent contradiction. In short, very few hunters choose a bear rifle, *per se.* Because of the incidental way a bear is often hunted, in con-

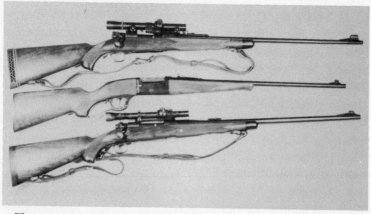

Three popular rifles and calibers which will cover the entire range of bear hunting: top to bottom, .300 H&H Magnum, Weaver scope; Savage Model 99 .300, open sights; and .375 H&H Magnum, Lyman scope.

junction with another species, the actual bear rifle ordinarily
is the rifle which the hunter has along, and has planned to
use on another species. In short, the deer hunter kills his
chance blackie with his deer rifle. The elk or moose hunter,
similarly, happens upon a black or a grizzly, and rolls him
with the outfit meant for wapiti. And, the ram hunter, in
the peaks of divide and water-shed country, spots his silvertip far below, sneaks closer and lets bruin have it with the
outfit really meant for sheep.

Because of the relative scarcity of bears as trophies,
because of their inherent danger to the hunter, and because
of the peculiarities of hunting the species under actual field
conditions, my own experience and observations have made
me conclude that the next higher "notch," in rifles and
ammunition, is necessary rather than the ordnance commonly recommended.

In short, the average and especially the minimum
cartridges commonly used on deer are not quite enough for
black bear, under the real conditions imposed by the hunting field. Likewise, that cartridge ordinarily used for caribou, sheep, goats, moose, and elk (especially the cows and
smaller males often taken for meat), is not quite adequate
for a grizzly. For grizzlies, brown bear, and polars, the most
rifle and cartridge the hunter can handle well is not too
much.

That "handle well" becomes the crux of the whole situation. I am, bluntly, not convinced that *any* inadequate
cartridge should ever be used on bears, simply because the
hunter can shoot it well. My conviction is that each species
of big game demands a certain level of cartridge performance, below which the hunter should never go.

On the opposite side of the fence, I am as thoroughly
convinced that any hunter, after a species of bear and who
currently cannot handle the most effective weapon as well
as a lesser rifle, has a solemn obligation to learn how to
handle the best outfit well, or not go hunting this species.

It's as simple as that.

Here are some recent and modern cartridges which can be recommended for black bear:

> .270 Winchester, using 130- and 150-grain bullets.
> 7X57 Mauser, using 139- 154- and 175-grain bullets.
> .280 Remington, using 125- and 165-grain bullets.
> .30-40 Krag, using 180-grain bullets.
> .300 Savage, using 150- and 180-grain bullets.
> .308 Winchester, using 150- and 180-grain bullets.
> .30-06 Winchester, using 150- and 180-grain bullets.
> .348 Winchester, using 150- and 200-grain bullets.
> .358 Winchester, using 200-grain bullets.

Several semi-obsolete cartridges will duplicate these ballistics. Also, numerous wild-cat cartridges will give comparable power and performance with various hand-loads. All these, of course, may be recommended.

In a broad way, the grizzly, brown, and polar bear are all hunted under much the same conditions as to hunting obstacles, shooting ranges, possible danger to the hunter, and the need for certainty of result. Therefore, cartridges for these three big, tough species may be grouped together. Following are several which are entirely suitable:

> .300 H&H Magnum, with 180- or 200-grain bullets.
> .338 Winchester Magnum, with 200- or 250-grain bullets.
> .375 H&H Magnum, with 270- or 300-grain bullets.
> .300 Weatherby Magnum, with 180- or 220-grain bullets.

My recent experience with the new .338 Winchester Magnum, under all sorts of tough hunting conditions, convinced me that this is the coming cartridge for the really big stuff. With its 200-grain bullet at 3,000 foot-seconds velocity, it has the flatness of range for which the great .300 H&H Magnum has been famed. With the 250-grain bullet at 2700 foot-seconds, the .338 will do nearly everything the world-famous .375 H&H will do.

For these reasons, I believe the new .338 Magnum will come largely to supersede both the .300 H&H and the larger .375 H&H for use on our biggest bears.

For these larger bruins, there are several popular cartridges which may be termed "marginal." Under special, ideal, or even average conditions, they may be depended upon to do the job cleanly.

As examples, the old standby .30-06, with 220-grain bullets, will successfully kill all the above species if both the extremely long and the extremely *close* shots are disregarded. Similarly, the fine .358 Winchester will suffice for all reasonably close shots, if used with 250-grain bullets. Again, such super-intensity 7 mm. magnums as the 7X61 Sharpe & Hart, the 7 mm. Mashburn, and the 7 mm. Weatherby Magnum—all using 160-grain bullets—will perform well on these large species of bears at reasonable "outside" ranges, in open country.

These are not, however, the big-caliber "stoppers." As with other marginal cartridges, they are not for shooting the biggest bears at a matter of yards, in heavy bush where the bullet must plow through, or when otherwise surprising dangerous quarry at extremely close range. In these not-too-unusual encounters, a greater margin of caliber size, bullet weight, and knock-down power often means the saving of one's own skin. Other factors being equal, the larger cartridge will succeed where the "fringe" cartridge would fail—failure here being taken to mean anything less than the complete stopping of the beast in its tracks.

The average hunter will not at first perform well with any of the above cartridges, unless he shoots considerably with lesser cartridges. However, as with any other item of personal equipment, he owes it to the game to make his ordnance adequate. And gaining the ability to handle well any of the above magnums is not too much of a chore, if the hunter goes at it sensibly.

First is the matter of rifle fit. A poor-fitting rifle is always a "kicking" rifle. In order to soak up recoil well, the rifle stock should have these features: A broad butt plate, with rubber recoil pad to spread and dampen the recoil itself; a well-fitting cheek piece and length of stock from butt to trigger which will feel comfortable; a pitch in the stock which will allow the line of sight to come naturally as one throws the rifle to his shoulder; also, a well-checkered fore-arm with ample but not bulky "body," to allow a good hold with the non-trigger hand; and, finally, a mildly curved grip which fits the palm, has similar sharp checkering, and with not too tight a curve—otherwise recoil will cause the trigger guard to bump the second finger, which is an annoyance and sometimes even painful.

Actually, when field shooting, recoil is absorbed at all these various points. The good shooter takes a bit of the push with his left hand (holding it tight, forward), with his face, with the grip, and with the butt plate. Such a distribution takes the severity out of most any magnum rifle, *if the stock fits well*. Otherwise, recoil becomes unpleasant at any or all these points; and the end result is flinching and poor shooting.

No factory stock will do this. The standard factory stock is a good compromise, but can't be made to fit anyone in particular. Hunters range from lanky bean poles with gangling arms and necks like Virginia creepers and fingers like hay rakes to pot-bellied, stubby, short-necked and short-armed little men who are longer around their equators than from their hats to the ground. How can one standard stock fit such diverse proportions and misproportions?

Unless the hunter happens to be that mythical "average" fellow, his least expensive rifle item—if considered in the long run, and over his many hunting years—is a stock tailored to his individual fit. This need not be of extra fancy wood, or too costly. A machine-inletted blank such as Bishop or Fajen makes, fitted by a good stock maker and worked down into a good individual "feel" and finish, will often cost less than some grizzly or polar bear hunters will fork out on booze for their hunt. It's far more apt to get the "shot" where it will do the most good.

In addition to such a well-fitting stock, the rifle should be equipped with a good scope, of $2\frac{1}{2}$ to 4-power, and a sling. Any hunter can see better with a scope sight, and no one can shoot any better than he can see. The sling not only vastly improves the "hold" when shooting from prone or sitting, it takes the drudgery out of rifle carrying.

Lastly, hunters who don't shoot a big-game rifle too much can gradually work up to the maximum power and recoil of a magnum rifle with sensible shooting practice. The best way is with hand-loads, either put up by himself or a custom re-loader. There's a good one in most every fair-sized town.

It's best to begin with reduced charges of powder, with their smaller recoil. The loads, at first, should be comparable in recoil to a cartridge which the shooter is used to. In other words, if a shooter uses a .30-06 and goes to a .338 Magnum, his first practice re-loads should have the recoil of the .30-06, but be loads used in the larger caliber.

Forty or fifty rounds of such ammunition at a bench rest or informal shooting should make the hunter ready for the next step. This batch should be slightly higher in recoil and power.

By a graduated process of going a bit higher each time, the average shooter will arrive at full-powered hunting loads within 100 rounds of shooting. The final practice loads should be exactly the same kind he'll use on the hunt. Further, the final practice should be in sighting in the rifle, with these full-intensity cartridges. By the time he's done, his fear of recoil will usually have been dampened to something of little consequence; and certainly he won't feel it in the presence of his long-awaited bruin.

The big value of all this carefully graduated practice is this: Instead of banging away, missing, and dreading recoil when the guide says, "There he is!", the misery is all previously done. One cartridge *then*, pays for the hundred you've already spent.

CHAPTER 17

Skinning and Saving the Trophy
Bear

The first step in skinning that prize bear is to make certain he's dead. Otherwise, the hunter is apt to become the trophy.

Any downed bear should be approached from above, regardless of the effort it takes to achieve this position. Too, an open space of at least several rods should be maintained between hunter and beast, in case it's only wounded. In his excitement, the hunter, too, should make almighty certain that a live cartridge is in the chamber, and that the safety catch is off, after he has been firing.

There are indications in advance of this, as to whether the animal is dead—the sight picture as the shot was fired, the way the beast went down, and the position in which it may slump. Animals falling and stopping with the feet uphill, with the head folded awkwardly under the body, or sprawled "spread-eagle" with feet extended, are apt to be dead. Beasts lying in a crouched position, with legs well under the body, with eyes in a horizontal plane, or with ears flattened—brother, watch out!

With *any* bear, it's best to consider the downed beast alive until he's known to be dead. So stop, rifle ready, at a few rods and determine this. It can be done by pelting the animal with rocks, hunks of wood, or anything handy. If he's still alive, such a missile plunked into his ribs will usually bring out the fact. At such a range, there is time for a finisher. The trick here is to stay cool, shoot him, and get scared afterward.

Lastly, if the animal appears certain to be dead, gingerly approach to within reach of a sapling, pole, or long stick. With the rifle trained on him, poke the carcass several times. Extreme looseness means he has had it. Any tenseness *may* mean he's still alive. In case of doubt, finish the job with another shot into the neck or heart. With bear hides, only small bullet holes will remain and can easily be sewed up. The tough hide of any species of bear won't tear or rip to a bullet, as will the hide of a deer and other animals.

The next and important step is to get some pictures. Most sportsmen today wear cameras. Those who can afford to hunt bear are also well heeled enough usually to have cameras and some simple skill in their use. The value of such pictures cannot be over-stressed. Years after the happy hunt, these pictures will make one live it all over again. They make good "braggin'" and conversation pieces. They become the envy of hunter friends who couldn't hit the broad side of a barn. And pictures which are well developed will outlast the actual mounted trophy. They're far more portable.

To get a picture of the prized bear is a bit more difficult than the novice would imagine. First, hunting weather is usually not good picture weather—you're just as apt as not to down the bear in rain, snow, or extremely heavy cover. A knowledge of camera settings for any light conditions, and learned in advance, is most useful.

For those hunting on horseback, the best way is to take along a small flash-gun and a few midget bulbs in the saddlebags. These little outfits today are no larger than a half-pound of butter, and make possible good pictures in any kind of light conditions.

The next thing to watch, in the matter of pictures, is

your guide. The average guide is a hard-working, earthy fellow whose job it is to get his novice hunter up to game. Once he accomplishes this, he feels his main job is over. Anything subsequently is sheer work, and the sooner he gets it over with and back to the camp stove, the better all the way around.

Time after time, I've bowled over a prized beast, and before I'd got the empty shell jacked out, the guide, ecstatic that his "dude" had connected, would race to the trophy, knife out, and be into the skinning. Only a similar race by me would prevent *some* sort of butchery showing in any picture I might want to take.

"Hey!" I'd yell, "Wait a minute. I want some pictures."

"Sure, sure." But the minute the camera clicked the first time, or even before, his bowie was whacking things.

To be of most value, trophy pictures should simulate the actual moment in which the beast went down. They should not be gruesome or show any more blood than possible. The destruction by bullets, and wounds, should not show. Pictures should be taken from the side of the beast and from the front end, not from the rear. The genitals of an animal should not show in these pictures. It's an odd thing that many people (who'll view them later) still like to think that animal reproduction is caused by storks, and that what an animal eats does not have to come out. A last thing is to make sure that the distance between camera and trophy is long enough so as not to cause distortion, fore-shortening, or over-exaggeration. Briefly, for 35 mm. cameras and those having 4-inch focal length lenses (most folding cameras), ten feet away from a bear will accomplish this, and include all the bear. Small pictures may, of course, be enlarged to any size, later.

Often to get such snapshots, the animal must be moved into a better position. This should be done with care, so that such a moving does not show from the camera angle. In short, make the finished picture look as natural to the occasion as possible. Where the hunter is to be included in the shot, have him look happy, and not precisely at the lens. If, as the guide snaps the picture, he can have the happy hunter say something like, "We sure knocked the blueberries out of *this* one, didn't we?" the pleasantness of the situation will show in the finished print.

Never in any mug-and-game shot, ask the subject to "Look pleasant now!" Invariably in the effort, he'll look strained and silly.

A dozen different pictures are not too many. It's wise, where possible, to include these on two separate rolls of film, for safety in developing them later. Remember, such moments don't come every day in the week, and the loss cannot be remedied later.

With the pictures done, a few simple measurements should be taken of the whole carcass, for the taxidermist's use later. These include measurements from tail to snout, top of withers to claws of front foot, distance between upright ears, nose tip to occipital protuberance (medulla); inches across the zygomatic arches; and width-and-length measurements of both the front and the rear feet—claw tips to heel, or pad.

Then, and only then, are you ready to peel.

Today's bear hunter is apt to have a guide, whose job it is to do trophy work. This is especially true for grizzly, polar, and brown bear. However, as any good taxidermist will tell you, not all such guides know how to skin and care for a trophy in the field. More, the hunter occasionally runs into a guide whose idea of any work besides riding and eating is a sheer imposition, and who'll haggle off a pelt the quickest way possible, unless deterred.

The hunter who knows how to care for his *own* trophies afield, is the one who'll wind up with the best mounts every time. Not only that, but he can offer valuable help even when a skilled guide is doing the job. He can, in fact, cut the chore in half.

Two tools are necessary for skinning a bear—a whetstone and a suitable knife. The best whetstone is a small one,

1. First cut in skinning a bear is made from anal vent to chin when
animal is turned on its back.

without sharp corners to wear pockets. The knife must be
adequate, but relatively small. The very best type of knife
I've ever found for the job is a two-bladed, folding knife.
It's just like a big pocket knife, with blades just 4 inches
long. One is a thin skinning blade, the other a larger blade.
I have one such knife which has now peeled on seven different grizzly bears, and enough smaller species such as
deer, antelope, yodel dogs, elk, sheep, etc. to corduroy the
road from here to Boise. I carry it at the belt, in a light
leather sheath made for the purpose. It's far more adequate
(due to two sharp edges) than any sheath knife, and many
times safer.

The type of finished mount will determine to some extent
the way a bear is skinned. However, herein we'll detail
the job so that the resulting skinned hide will be suitable
for all types, from a simple head mount to a fully mounted
animal.

First the animal is laid upon its back. Rocks, chunks, and

similar available materials may be laid alongside the carcass, between its sides and the earth, so as to prop it up in this position.

The first cut is one made the entire length of the carcass, from anal vent to chin, and along the middle line of the abdomen. The tail hide should be split on the under side, so that the short tail bone may be removed.

2. Next cut is across from one front paw to opposite paw.

At the head end of the cut, many guides continue all the way to the point of the chin. However, the short hairs at this point allow the necessary sewing, later, to show, in case of full-head mounts and rugs. A better way is to stop this belly-cut just past the center of the throat, at a point even with the rear of the mouth. From that point, a cut is made sideways to the junction of the lips, at the rear end of the mouth. Sewing, later, along this line won't show in the finished mount.

The second basic cut is made across the carcass from one front paw to the opposite one. This cut is made in a straight line. Care should be used that this cut is made along the under side of each leg in the thin-haired portion—not allowed to slip off into the heavy hair at the leg's edge. This line, of course, intersects the belly line over the chest.

A similar cut is made across the animal from one hind foot to the other. This cut is begun at a heel, follows the thin hairs but is *ahead* of the thick hair at the hind-leg's edge an inch or so, and goes to the anal vent from each of the hind feet. The entire cut is an obtuse V-line from one heel to the other.

Care must be exercised so that all these cuts are similar on the right and left sides of the carcass. Otherwise the finished mount won't be symmetrical.

Lastly, at each foot, make an incision all around between the hair and the tough tissue of the foot pad, and at the junction of the two. The foot pads are left with the carcass, but the toes are kept intact with the hide.

The actual skinning may now be started.

With most big-game animals, such as deer, elk, and caribou, the hide peels away in most regions, without any muscular tissue adhering to the skin itself. A bear is different. The hide must almost literally be cut away from the layer of fatty tissue beneath. This takes time and patience, and a very sharp knife.

However, patience in getting most all the fat pared off as the carcass is skinned pays big dividends. It's actually

harder to get the remaining fat off later. And all fat
must be removed, otherwise the hide won't cure properly
and the hair will slip off, ruining the trophy.

With the hide skinned away for perhaps a foot on either
side of the belly line all the way, the next portions to work
upon are the legs and feet. These represent the most difficult portions, and take the most time.

3. Third cut is from heel of hind foot to anal vent, then on to opposite side.

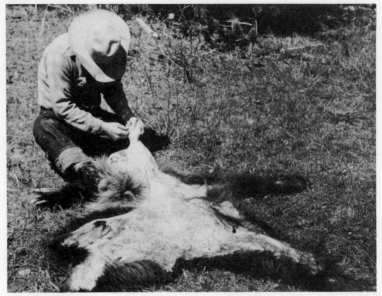

4. The ear cartilages from a bear pelt may either be removed on the spot or after reaching camp.

Briefly, the entire feet must be skinned out all the way down to the last joint of each toe; and with no further cutting than the incision around the foot pad mentioned above. The hide over the foot bones clings with a tough membranous tissue that seems to defy all efforts to remove it. Further, all the cutting of this tissue must be done while the skin of each toe is turned back over itself—quite like trying to turn a garden hose wrong-side out.

It's always interesting to watch a novice "beaver" away on his first bear leg. At first he's enthused, since he's killed the beast. By the time he's down to the wrists, he's sweating and huffing. When he's skinned away to the first toe joints, he usually complains, "Hell, I'll never get this done." And if and when he gets down to those final difficult toe joints, he's apt to explode, "By the powers, I swear I'm going to whack every foot offen this big bastard at the elbows! You just can't *skin* these things!"

He never does, of course, and usually winds up by whittling away on easier parts, letting the guide finish the toe-joints. It is important, though, that the novice hunter *know* how it must be done. Otherwise an unconscientious guide himself might stop short of where he should. When all feet are skinned to this tiny last toe joint on each toe, the final joint is severed at the last knuckle and left intact with the skin and claw, as is each toe pad.

From then, patience, knife sharpening, and more skinning are all that's necessary. The ears are cut away deep against the skull, with the ear cartilages later pared out at camp. The eyelids must never be severed, but are removed by cutting the conjunctiva, which connects the lids with the eyes. Similarly, the lips all the way around are peeled away, after cutting the skin well inside the mouth. Lastly, the snout is cut off well back where the septum joins the skull itself. The extra gristle of the snout is pared away when one has more time back at camp.

At this point, and with the bear skinned all the way down each side, the carcass is rolled over, first one way then the other, and the hide skinned away at the spine all the way along.

With that done, many a bear hunter makes a great mistake—he leaves the skull with the carcass and "high-tails" it for camp before it gets dark. I did this once, after killing a monstrous grizzly in the Cry Lake area of British Columbia. The skull was heavy, useless to the rug I wanted to make of him, and messy. I left it without even making measurements. Recalling that prodigious broad head, and looking again at the mounted rug today, I am positive, the more I study the record bears' skull measurements, that I had one which would have rated high in the Boone & Crockett records. The single lamentable aspect of that fine expedition was the fact that at the time I knew no better, and did not lug in that skull on top of the packboard already creaking with the weight of a huge green hide.

If the hunter suspects he has an out-of-the-ordinary bear, he'd best bring in the skull, clean it up, take temporary measurements, and keep the skull itself until he's certain.

At camp, the meat may be boiled and cut away from the skull. Then, with copious salting, the skull may be transported home, unodorous. Two basic measurements, after the skull has dried for sixty days (required for entering in the records), will give the score. One measurement is across the zygomatic arches, from bony eye orbit to opposite eye orbit. The second is the distance from the base of the skull at the rear (occipital protuberance), over the head between the ears, and to that point of the skull where the bone breaks into the cartilagenous septum separating the nostrils. The sum of these two measurements is the total score.

Record bear heads are constantly giving way to even bigger heads (usually by mere fractions of inches). But to give the hunter an indication of what he *might* have, here are some recent record bear skulls:

The top-ranking black bear scores over 21½ inches.

The top grizzly bear scores nearly 26 inches.

The biggest Alaskan Brown Bear scores almost 31 inches.

The biggest recorded polar bear scores nearly 29 inches.

Once the bear is skinned as above, and the hide and skull taken to camp, certain additional care must be used to get it to the home taxidermist safely. In some of our best hunting camps, supervised by the top outfitters, the outfitter himself will take over from there. He'll either tend the trophies personally, or entrust their care to those of his personnel whom he knows from experience can do the job.

As one example, Don DeHart, the Alaska outfitter, personally works on and examines every trophy brought in, to make certain that no specimen is lost. He even has a connection with some of the country's finest taxidermists; and will, if the hunter wishes, forward trophies directly to them without the hunter having any further bother. Such an arrangement is usually satisfactory all around, but is not always available.

Where the time lag is days, or even weeks, before the

hunter can get his trophy to the home taxidermist, there are certain hazards which must be thwarted. Heat, blowflies, predatory birds and animals, and moisture are the elements which will spoil a green bear trophy.

The first thing to do after getting the pelt to camp is to pare away all remaining flesh and fat; pare down the nose cartilage, and remove the ear cartilages; then thoroughly salt the entire flesh surfaces of the pelt. Fifteen to twenty

5. Surplus flesh and fat are pared off at camp before hide is salted.

6. A whole bucketful of ordinary table salt is spread over the hide and worked into the flesh-side.

pounds of table salt is not too much for the average grizzly hide. The hide is first spread flat over an even surface or the ground, and literally a bucketful of salt poured over it.

Next, this salt is carefully and evenly spread all over the entire surface. It is pushed and poked with the fingers into all orifices such as ear pockets, eyes, nostril vents, and especially the toe pockets. Too much salt for this, is just right.

In cool weather, the hide, by the time it has reached camp and is salted, has all the animal heat from it. If so, it is then safe to roll the entire hide into a snug ball, and leave for two days, to cure. When rolling up, the legs are first folded over the body part of the hide (flesh side up, of course), then the head is folded in. The entire pelt is next folded down the middle, and lastly, rolled into a tight package, endwise. Care in doing this will keep all the salt and brine inside on the flesh side, once the salt makes the pelt "water." The brine does not leak out, and thinly-salted areas are then evenly spread with the liquid.

The rolled pelt should not be tossed in a heap on the ground. This would tend to retain the outside moisture, and any remaining heat. Instead, the rolled pelt should be placed upon a wooden crate, boards, or even a pile of dry sticks, where air will circulate all the way around it. During rain, cover it with canvas.

Bear hides taken in cool weather will often last a week or more when adequately salted in this way. It is far better, however, to check the hide again the second or at least the third day. The pelt is again unrolled and spread. The "bunches" of salt, caused by the rolling, are evenly spread over the pelt again; and those areas which remain moist and white are carefully spread and filled with more salt. At this stage of the curing, salt will tend to stick to the green hide.

With this done, a good way of completing the job is to

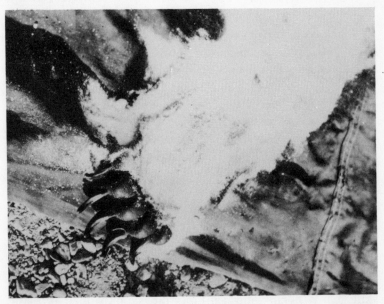

7. All eye sockets, ear pockets, and toe pockets are carefully pushed full of salt so that all flesh areas are salted.

hang the entire hide over a long pole anchored between trees and four feet off the ground, flesh side out. If care is used, not much of the salt will fall off. In this position, the hide will drain off its natural moisture, and, of course, a lot of the salt. The air, however, will tend to dry the green hide, especially the pockets caused by folding. The drying pole should never be placed in direct sunlight, but in open shade. Direct rays of the sun will burn a green hide.

A day of this will usually drain off all moisture. Opening it up also will allow one to see if blowflies are working any areas. The next step is to salt the entire flesh side once more with another layer of salt, spread it evenly onto every part of the flesh area, and roll it up once more. The bundle is then tied with heavy cord or rope and will last until the taxidermist gets it, if kept as cool as possible all during transit.

Clean burlap bags are fine to tie the rolled hide into, for shipping or hauling. So are wooden crates or big cardboard cartons.

Black bears are usually taken in regions where more blowflies and predator birds are found, and likely in warmer weather. Blowflies need warmth and moisture to hatch their eggs. The above procedure will save a black bear trophy even in very warm weather. However, blowflies will lay their eggs, not only in available pockets in the hide, but in the outside hair as well. In addition to the above, I've found that a sprinkling of black pepper all over the areas where blowflies do lay their eggs, will prevent their hatching into maggots. The hide during all preliminary curing should, of course, be guarded against the pecking of predatory birds.

Polar bear hides, being taken in extreme cold, are handled differently. Usually the outfitter, or Eskimo guide, will officiate in this and do a fine job, since these hardy people kill many polars and sell the hides "outside," in many instances for the making of streamer trout-flies.

A polar bear must be skinned soon after it's killed, to avoid freezing. This is usually done in the guide's own house or shack the following evening, if not on the spot.

With the hide off and fleshed, the next step is cleaning it of all blood. Blood remaining in the creamy-white hair turns brown and spoils the look of the finished trophy. The hide is washed of blood in a simple way. A hole is chopped through the ice offshore, over the ocean. A rope is tide to the snout and the entire pelt is swished up and down into the salt water below. Once rinsed as clean as possible, the hide is then rolled in the fresh snow, which immediately freezes, and is rubbed off, taking along with it most of the remaining blood.

Lastly, the clean hide is taken a half-mile away from the Eskimo village, and placed on a high wooden rack to freeze and dry. Eskimos burn either oil or seal fat. Both give off soot which would ruin a fine bear hide—hence the distance between the village and the racks. These racks, made of driftwood, are used from year to year, and left standing for the purpose.

With the green hide entirely frost dried, it may be shipped or taken home as above.

The Eskimo women do all the work of fleshing these hides. At villages like Point Hope, many an Eskimo hunter's wife will clean up a polar bear hide for five to ten dollars. At Kotzebue, one certain Eskimo woman does the job, including packing the dried hide in a metal garbage can for air shipment outside, for around fifteen dollars. The hunter must, of course, pay for the container.

Briefly, the lucky polar bear hunter does very little in the way of field care for his fresh bear hide. Outfitters or guides will arrange everything for him, at small cost. He *should*, however, know exactly what is being done, or neglected, to a prized trophy which has cost him so much.

Occasionally in bear hunting, as indeed with any kind of big-game hunting, the sportsman pays for an expensive hunt, makes a good stalk, and bowls over what both he and his guide estimated to be a perfect specimen, only to find upon racing up that it is defective.

This is especially true of bears. The beast may be slightly longer out of spring hibernation than normal, when the hunter gets to him, and his hide may be starting to rub. Again, shaggy areas of hide seem always, with bear, to be on the side opposite from where the hunter looks and shoots, and cannot be spotted by the guide. Or, as with my friend John Phillips, one grizzly at which he shot was broadside; but the big rubbed patch, which couldn't be seen, was on the very top of his back, and was only discovered later.

In cases where the hunter finds, unhappily, that his bear rug is almost worthless as a trophy, after he's shot the one beast he may ever get to see, he should not be too discouraged.

One of the finest brown-bear trophies I've ever seen was made from a bear whose body pelage was ruined and worthless. The fellow simply had a head mount made of the head and neck, which were not rubbed. With that great head, in snarling posture, looking at one from its place on the lodge wall, the total effect is far better than if the beast was on the floor as a rug. Too, it takes up less trophy space. The blunt fact is, a look at that trophy so impressed me that I had my last Alaska bear finished up as a head mount.

Even in such instances, and where even the neck or head skin may be damaged, the hunter should not despair. If he'll save sufficient *extra* hide, a good taxidermist can often substitute areas of good hide for bad. I know of one damaged grizzly bear hide which a local taxidermist worked over—making completely new ears from body hair and hide, and forms—whose new ears couldn't be told from the original.

Again, in the case of the brownie above, the hunter also saved both great paws, which were not damaged.

He had them made into rustic-table ornaments. They were most attractive and quite awe-inspiring.

The main function of a fine bear trophy, whether full mount, rug, wall piece, or head mount, is not as many non-bear hunters suspect, to clutter up the home wall or floor. Neither is it for the sole purpose of creating envy among one's less rugged friends.

Instead, a fine trophy becomes an increasingly valuable bargain. It allows the hunter many exciting experiences for the original price of one. With time, the hardships of any hunt diminish. The pleasant memories increase. And an even more priceless hunt may, with each viewing of the trophy, be lived over again.

CHAPTER 18

Conclusion

In summary, it may be said that the North American bear, all species, has reached a singular status in two important ways. First, over the many decades bruin has grudgingly won his way from a position of being man's enemy, to a role high up on the list of sporting game animals.

Secondly, and in this position, the American bear enjoys the unique distinction of being hunted entirely for sport, not for meat. Unlike the deer, elk, moose, caribou, mountain sheep, and allied species whose flesh is highly palatable and are therefore pursued at least in part for the table, the bear is hunted for the overall thrill of the chase.

This change in hunting objective, from meat to sport, has, of course, also applied to the other game species. The tendency today is far more toward the sport of hunting than the economic gain. But with the more edible species, the transition has been slower in arriving; and it places the American bruin in the noble position of having arrived at the goal first, and from the humblest sporting position.

Neither our current bear population, nor any annual replenishment, represents a sporting "crop" which either may, or can, be saved for future generations to enjoy. Rather, as with any other game species, it is a highly fluid, completely perishable crop. And as such a crop, it may be conserved only to the extent of some form of harvest.

Such a harvest may be perennial, or permitted to dwindle to extinction. It may remain a harvest of surplus by the hunter, or it may be allowed to become a harvest by the forces of nature.

The only way in which man may preserve this species for future generations lies in the wisdom with which he sets the stage for such a perpetuation. Specifically, this means in the broad, basic areas of wise hunting regulations, the protection of cubs, prohibiting the killing of bears simply as predators and for the sole primal joys of seeing an "enemy" drop, and the establishment and intelligent placement of natural sanctuaries in key regions for each species, to be used as reservoirs from which a surplus may over-flow for sporting purposes.

In a fundamental way, the eventual extinction of the bear species, or its perpetuation, rests within the courage, thinking, and convictions of our generation; and in the degree of foresight and wisdom we are able to instill in the next.

The sincere hope of this author, compounded of thrilling experience and gratitude for it, and perhaps a touch of altruism, is that the many generations yet to come may be permitted the privilege of having their collective and individual blood jump to the primal thrill aroused by three simple words, than which there is nothing more exciting in the whole outdoors:

"There's a bear!"